SMALL BOAT ON THE MOSELLE

Some other books by Roger Pilkington

SMALL BOAT THROUGH BELGIUM
SMALL BOAT THROUGH HOLLAND
SMALL BOAT TO THE SKAGERRAK
SMALL BOAT THROUGH SWEDEN
SMALL BOAT TO ALSACE
SMALL BOAT TO BAVARIA
SMALL BOAT THROUGH GERMANY
SMALL BOAT THROUGH FRANCE
SMALL BOAT IN SOUTHERN FRANCE
SMALL BOAT ON THE MEUSE
SMALL BOAT ON THE THAMES
SMALL BOAT TO LUXEMBOURG
WORLD WITHOUT END
HEAVEN'S ALIVE

For Younger Readers

Adventures in Boats

THE MISSING PANEL
THE DAHLIA'S CARGO
DON JOHN'S DUCATS
NEPOMUK OF THE RIVER
THE EISENBART MYSTERY
THE BOY FROM STINK ALLEY

Non-fiction

THE GREAT SOUTH SEA

SMALL BOAT
ON THE MOSELLE

BY

ROGER PILKINGTON

Illustrated by David Knight

MACMILLAN
London · Melbourne · Toronto
ST MARTIN'S PRESS
New York
1968

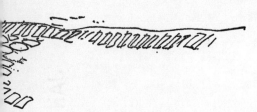

© Roger Pilkington 1968

MACMILLAN & CO LTD
Little Essex Street London WC2
and also at Bombay Calcutta and Madras
Macmillan South Africa (Publishers) Pty Ltd Johannesburg
The Macmillan Company of Australia Pty Ltd Melbourne
The Macmillan Company of Canada Ltd Toronto
St Martin's Press Inc New York

Library of Congress catalog card no. 68-13634

Printed in Great Britain by
ROBERT MACLEHOSE AND CO. LTD
The University Press, Glasgow

Hail, thou river whose vine-planted hillsides yield a perfumed wine, thou emerald stream whose banks are lush with grass. Like the ocean thou carriest the big ships, and like a river hast a sloping bed in which thy waters run onward. Thy clear deeps are as those of lakes, and yet thy quivering current is as that of the brooks.

Mosella, Decimus Magnus Ausonius

MAPS

FOREWORD

'WHAT is a ship but a prison?' It was Robert Burton who asked this poser in his *Anatomy of Melancholy*. It was really a stupid question, for even in his day a boat was a possible release from becoming a professional and pathological melancholic like himself. Burton was in any case not the sort of man I would like to have aboard the *Thames Commodore*, for the only thing that could bring him to laugh was to stand on an Oxford bridge and listen to the boatmen blowing off steam at each other. I think this was impertinent of him, because the bargees did not habitually push their way into Tom Quad to laugh at the fellows of Christ Church boring away in Greek.

But with the question asked, it is reasonable to answer and point out that a ship is the very opposite of a prison. Far from being shut in, one escapes from all those things which on land are not easily avoided — telephone, market trends and traffic jams, cars mounting the pavement, prison, steam-baked bread, committee minutes, detergent canvassers and greenfly. More than that, it is perhaps the only means of discovering that hidden away beneath the flyovers and undisturbed by ring-roads and runways an astonishingly beautiful Europe still exists, a world known for the most part to bargemasters and lock-keepers but mercifully undiscovered by 'bulk tourism', as that industry so ingenuously terms itself. And this, curiously enough, applies even to such a peaceful valley as that of the Moselle, almost devoid as it is of any industry other than coopering and pressing, bottling and storing its own precious wine. From the road the valley is pleasant, and from the water it is a rapture. From the deck of the *Thames Commodore* it is seventh heaven — which is about as far as Roget's *Thesaurus* will take us.

Already I find that I have mentioned the *Thames Commodore* twice, without introducing her formally. There will certainly be

vii

readers curious to know about her birth or anatomy, and these will find at the end of the book a short description and a plan of her insides drawn by my son-in-law and her own second officer, John Silvester Horne. Others will know her already from her earlier voyages — on the Thames and to Luxembourg. I will only say that she is a comfortable ship and what I believe naval men would call well-found. She has never been fatal or perfidious, perhaps because she was not built during an eclipse and rigged with curses dark like the one Milton was so disdainful about. It would have needed an eclipse of unusual magnitude for her to be built in it, for her construction occupied more than a year.

Perhaps one can best describe her as shipshape — sharp at the front, that is, and flat behind. But she is also a ship of reliability and sense and good looks — and with those and a reasonable turn of knots any man should be content. They are characteristics with which one may fall in love, as my wife and I and many others have done when the *Thames Commodore* has carried them over the sea, or through tunnels, or along the winding canals of France toward the Moselle.

Small Boat on the Moselle — yes, but not on the whole length of that splendid river. Its upper reaches feed the channel of the French Canal de L'Est, Branche Sud, and only between Toul and Nancy does the stream become navigable for those green and box-like fishing-punts in which so many Frenchmen sit timelessly, half-asleep in the sun or whistling a song to the fish that may not come and will not be greatly missed if they prefer to stay unhooked.

At Pompey, downstream of Toul, the Moselle first opens its heart to barges. It is a modest navigation here, modelled in the carefree and confident engineering days of the years immediately ahead of the Franco-Prussian war. Then comes a short stretch completed by the victorious Prussians, and at Metz the river becomes the Camifemo — the Canal des Mines de Fer de la Moselle — a practical rather than a beautiful waterway laid out in the 1930s to bring French coal to the Wendels and the other great ironmasters of Lorraine and to carry away their products. Below Thionville lock the Camifemo in turn gives way to the International Moselle Waterway of the 1960s, a highway for

Europa-ships of 1350 tons and more, a river navigation which cuts across the broad plain below Thionville to leave France behind and form the frontier between Germany and Luxembourg, all the way from Schengen to the River Sûre.

The purpose of this last paragraph of potted geography is to show that the Moselle is a versatile river which appears in many guises. When first the *Thames Commodore* entered it at the lock of Frouard below Toul, I had in mind that a book might be written about it. I did not guess that the Moselle would be a river so seductive that we would navigate most of its length five times within two years and that I would be unable to rest until I had walked its heights from France to the Rhine. Indeed it proved to be a stream so rich in discovery and allure that I had sketched its character no further than from the scalp to the neck before, at the lower extremity of the Luxembourg reaches, the book already had as many pages as my Macmillan friends would wish and any reader could devour.

So there it was, and *Small Boat to Luxembourg* covers La Moselle of the French, and also de Musel as the Luxembourgers call it. This present volume tells of die Mosel, the German reaches, the same wine-enamoured and curling course which normally comes to mind when one speaks of 'the Moselle'. More precisely, it takes up the tale just at the point where the Sûre flows in from Echternach to limit the territory of the Grand Duchy. It is time for somebody to climb on the *Thames Commodore's* saloon top to haul down the red lion on blue stripes of Luxembourg and replace it by the black-yellow-red of Germany.

All down the Moselle, from Thionville lock in Lorraine to the confluence with the Rhine, the shores of the waterway are marked off with distance-plaques. Every hundred metres a one-tenth sign stands on the bank, and at each whole kilometre the number is given, counting from the confluence and reaching 269 below the Thionville railway bridge. This is useful for the boatman who may wish to identify his exact position on the thirty-eight sheets of river chart, but it can also help to identify places for those who visit the river by car or on foot. Knowing that land travellers and occasional boating enthusiasts sometimes take a *Small Boat* book with them as an informal guide-book, I have given the kilometre marks in brackets where there is something of special interest to be seen, and added an 'L' or 'R' to identify the bank, for the Moselle is not over-provided with bridges. If the towns and villages are pinpointed to a decimal of a kilometre the feature I have taken is the church, which is usually at the centre.

With these figures cropping up in the text I hope that those who follow the story of this voyage from a chair or in bed at night will also gain something from appreciating how very slowly the *Thames Commodore* appears to be moving on her way down river from Wasserbillig (km. 206 L). I hope, too, that they will stay aboard all the way to the foot of the fortress of Ehrenbreitstein (km. 0). If they do, they will cover the valley at an average speed of about one kilometre to a page. But in the brief time taken to read one page the *Thames Commodore* would not be able to run a whole kilometre. If actually under way she might manage half that distance, but on the Moselle she is more likely to be found at anchor off some straggling village of vintners, or lying at a jetty while her friends are swimming, enjoying the sunshine, or foraging in the hills for raspberries and strawberries and blackberries to round off the supper menu. Wherever she is, she will certainly not be in a hurry. The giant French pushers *Nancy* and *Metz* and *Besançon* may drive their five-hundred-feet-long floating coke-heaps up to Lorraine in two days solid chugging from Koblenz. The *Thames Commodore* is actually capable of overhauling them, but she is more likely to take two weeks over the same stretch of river. No hungry coke-ovens wait open-mouthed for her arrival, and so she may treat the Moselle with more courtesy.

And now it is time to flick off the lines and push out into the stream, give a final reassuring wave to the customs officer at the ferry landing immediately above the imaginary line of the frontier, and head for the gap where the cliffs draw in close on either hand as the river cuts between Wasserliesch on the starboard hand and Igel to port.

ROGER PILKINGTON

Highgate, 1968

I

*Fortunatus on the river — the drapers of Igel — the
Liescherberg chapel — ships of the Saar — the sunken
bells — St Matthew afloat — Konz and the Charterhouse
— the lady of Monaise — the wine canal to Cologne —
Trier lock*

WHEN the *Thames Commodore* slid past the mouth of the
River Sûre to head for Igel, she was conscious of being the
first ship ever to reach those waters from Britain. Two days down
river from Metz she was making history of a minor variety, but
long before her voyage there had been others who extolled the
beauties of that splendid river, the Moselle. The first water tourist
and river enthusiast to leave an account of an actual voyage down
the river was Venantius Honorius Clementianus Fortunatus,
Bishop of Poitiers and a personal friend of Gregory of Tours,
who in the sixth century took ship at Metz and descended like

ourselves to the Rhine. He was in the company of the young Mero-
vingian King Childebert and his mother Brunehaut (Brunhilde)
of the lovely bronze skin, widow of the King Sigbert who had
been murdered when Childebert was only five years of age.

On an earlier visit to Metz Fortunatus had his boat stolen by
one of the palace cooks, as he related in his poem *De coco qui ipsi
navem tulit*. Vilicus, Bishop of Metz, came to his aid with a skiff,
but this boat was too light for him and his companions, and soon
the water was over his ankles. Fortunatus did not omit to make
a proper comment.

'*Obsequium*,' *dixi*, '*remove, modo nolo lavari*.' 'Thank you, but
depart. I do not want a bath.'

When he told Sigbert of his sad adventures the king laughed,
but he told his knights to find the bishop a new craft, and eventually he was waterborne again.

On the occasion of his later voyage down to the Rhine
Fortunatus arrived at Metz on horseback, as he tells in *De navigio
suo*, and there he at once took to his rowboat. Now and again his
craft was caught in the rapids, and he was in danger of taking in
water, but soon he was in calmer waters, enjoying every moment
of his journey just as we were to do fourteen centuries later. Even
then the river was one of vineyards, and downstream of Trier the
bishop gazed in admiration at the rocky heights on either hand,
their shaly slopes green with the dressed vines in full leaf, and
the vintners hanging from the rocks to gather the bunches. Somewhere down-river he managed to buy some, for he held the grapes
in his hand as he sped down the stream in the wake of the royal
watermen.

And what a happy voyage it was. All along the Moselle
Childebert and the dowager queen were served with dishes of the
fresh fish in which the river abounded. The musicians played
until the rock-faces echoed with the sound of their brass, and the
mellower tones of the flutes seemed to be repeated by other
instruments hidden in the woods. It was merely to delight the
people that the king had ordered music and singing to accompany
him down the river, and as the royal craft sped along the stream
the songs of those in the boats were taken up and swelled by those

ashore. The Dark Ages! There is something Pepysian about the scene, and one can only regret that none of the Merovingian music has survived.

Regrettably the *Thames Commodore* forged down the river to no other sound than the regular hum of a pair of very efficient Perkins diesels. But she and her friends revelled in the loveliness of the Moselle as much as Fortunatus had done, and they too looked forward to an evening dish of Moselle fry. We were, I repeat, bound for Igel, and as that village is a mere two miles below the frontier at Wasserbillig the *Thames Commodore* will shortly be there, and while there is still time I must make haste to introduce the Moselle properly and place her squarely in time and space.

Mosella, the Little Meuse — thus the river was christened in Roman times, and the name has remained. And curiously there is a relationship between those two great streams which goes back to a divorce which recently took place. Recently, that is, to a geologist; but a long, long time ago to ordinary mortals.

The Moselle was in fact a partner of the Meuse, the two uniting not far from Toul and each contributing half the combined flow which sawed a winding gorge deep in the limestone and purple slate of the Ardennes. But one day the Moselle in its exuberance of flooding brought down an immense amount of shingle, blocked its own path, and deciding that it would prefer to join the Rhine it doubled back sharply and found an obliging course of an unoffending little river, the Meurthe, a stream which wound gently across Lorraine to wriggle between the Hunsrück and Eifel hills and reach the Rhine at the point where Koblenz has since been built and sacked, built and burned, built and washed out, built and bombed, and finally rebuilt once again. The Moselle being the larger of the two is the one which wears the trousers and supplies the name, the Meurthe being unknown except to a few score of French anglers.

That, then, is the biography of the river as a geologist would see it. But geologists are sometimes tedious, and perhaps we can leave them to their investigations and take the Moselle as she is. For the river has not changed much in human times, except that

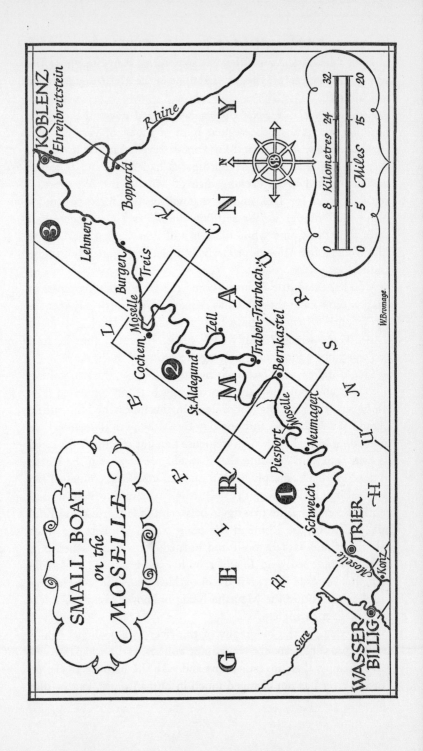

SMALL BOAT
on the
MOSELLE

W.Bromage.

she was rejuvenated and made infinitely more beautiful when the engineers of the International Moselle Company set about adjusting her figure, opening up her wide reaches so that in 1964 Europaships of 1350 tons could at last chug in powerful state up a Class V international waterway, where previously there had been only a smaller and insignificant stream unable to bear shipping.

A river without ships is like a bird without feathers. From the Roman era to the Middle Ages the Moselle was alive with craft, and if once again the bargemen have returned in mightier vessels than ever, with a Mercedes on deck, and a playpen with sunawning and swing and inflatable swimming-pool, they have brought back to it a life which was already present when Ausonius first sang the praises of the stream, sixteen centuries before the *Thames Commodore* dropped anchor off the railway station at Igel (km. 202·7 L) and began to manoeuvre her rump cautiously towards the little jetty.

The first time we descended the river, to land at Igel was impossible. The only jetty was used by the busy little steel boat in which the ferryman rowed the villagers of Igel across to Wasserliesch, and the inhabitants of Wasserliesch over to Igel. Otherwise there was only shallow water, spotted with rocks and stones. But already on our second visit times had changed, and the ferry lay hauled up on the bank, sorely in need of painting. The landing-stage was barricaded with barbed wire, but the *Thames Commodore* always carries stout gloves and wire-snips for such unnecessary obstructions, and soon we had made fast and were ashore. The young Igelers led by a girl of twelve crowded round to watch us.

Why, I asked, was the ferry not running? Because there was no ferryman, the girl said. 'Nobody wants to be a ferryman.' So the Igelers were now cut off, with no crossing nearer than the motor ferry at Wasserbillig in Luxembourg or the bridge at Trier, six miles down river. And that, as she said, was a long way round if you just wanted to go over to the shops, or to see friends. There was a real problem of communication.

'I would be your ferryman if I lived here,' I said.

The job of a ferryman has always seemed to me one of the most peaceful and sociable and useful employments of all. Except for a few drunken reprobates who have taken up the work as a last resort I have always found them the kindliest men. The very way they walk seems to breathe sheer relaxation. R. L. Stevenson once wrote that he could see no reason why a bargee should ever die. A ferryman would, I believe, have an even greater theoretical expectation of life than a bargemaster. That not a man could be found in either Igel or Wasserliesch who was prepared to take a boat across the Moselle was, I thought, a sad state of affairs. Perhaps ferrying was an occupation no longer considered smart.

Igel is a pleasant name for a village, for it means 'hedgehog'. The village is only a small one, cramped on the shore and bounded by a railway embankment on the river side, and without even a footpath along the bank, for the old towpath with its nostalgic memories of the days of the *Moselhalfen* sitting the plodding horses which slowly hauled the cargoes from the Rhine to Wasserbillig, or Thionville, or the free state of Metz, is on the opposite shore. The pretty church stands tightly cramped on a rock as though expecting another hideous persecution under the Romans, and as it is thus raised above the level of the dwelling of ordinary mortals it is not overtopped by the memorial to the drapers. For that remarkable stone column is large enough to tower above the signals on the railway embankment and to look down upon its village neighbours with undisguised disdain. It is more than seventy feet in height.

It is said that when Edward VII was driving in his carriage along Oxford Street he was struck by the magnificence of a building near its western end. He asked his attendant what it might be.

'Selfridges, your Majesty,' was the reply. 'It is a draper's store.'

The king was impressed. 'I wish I were a draper,' he said. 'Then I could afford a proper place to live in.'

I suspect that the Secundini may have been the Selfridges of third-century Trier. The family had their residence at Igel on the Roman highway from Reims to Trier, and the imposing memorial of grey and red sandstone which two of the sons raised to their parents must have been the envy of many less wealthy merchants.

Its particular interest for ourselves, seventeen centuries further down the line, is the great detail in the scenes of everyday life which are shown in relief. Some have weathered away, but there are plenty left to tell us how the drapers traded, and how they conducted their business. One main relief shows us the father, chairman and managing director of the firm and a former volunteer in the imperial forces, taking leave of his two sons as he sets out upon his journey into the land of the dead. If the monument was not broken down in the early Christian centuries, this seems to have been because this relief was so magnificent that it was mistakenly thought to have shown Constantine, the first Christian emperor, and his mother St Helena.

There are gods and goddesses, of course, both Roman and Greek, but more interesting is the kitchen scene, with the chef receiving from servants and tenants the mutton and poultry, game, Moselle fish and fruits. Another picture shows us the family at dinner, doing justice to the *haute cuisine* which they could afford to keep. Then there are the warehouse scenes, with assistants examining and grading cloth, and baling it for storage. A four-wheeled cart brings another load of bales to the merchant's house, and other wains carry away the consignments despatched to meet special orders.

But there still remains one relief, at the base of the huge memorial and on its upstream side, which no boatman should miss, for here we see a Roman barge of the third century, a direct if distant ancestor of the Europa-ships which now send the waves of their wash to slop on the stones of the Igel shore, a ship moving upstream exactly as described by Ausonius in his idyll *Mosella*.

'Thou providest a double mode of navigation for the ships; on the one hand where thy current aids the shipping and the oars beat lightly upon thy wavelets; on the other the upstream mode, the bargemen stretching taut over their shoulders the lines fixed to the masts as they doggedly bank-haul their vessels against the current.' And there it is, carved in relief at Igel, with the men towing along the shore a boat laden with bales of cloth. They are hauling in the ingenious three-legged fashion the Romans developed with one hand holding the taut line which passes over

B

the shoulder, and the other grasping a stout staff which forms a
third leg. The Roman hauler always had two of his three legs on
the ground while he moved the other. It was a steady means of
haulage, and one which could cope with the sudden pulls and
jerks of a swirling current tugging at the boat.

Across the river from Igel the land rises step-wise behind
Wasserliesch (km. 203·2 R) to slope off into the heights of the
wooded Liescherberg. On the top of this hill stands one of the
many little chapels which lie scattered about the edges of the
Moselle valley, nearly every one of which was placed in its particular and often unlikely position for some quite individual
reason. The Liescher Kapelle originated in one of those familiar
do-this-for-me-and-I'll-build-you-a-church vows which reflect so
badly on the human tendency to try to indulge in horse-trading
with the deity — or, in this instance, with Mary.

It seems that some poor man of Wasserliesch became so
burdened with troubles that he made just such a vow, announcing
to the object of his prayers that he would build a chapel in her
honour at the summit of the Liescherberg if she would oblige.
The man was eventually restored to health and wealth and
prosperity, but although he did not actually forget his promise he
kept on postponing the matter of the chapel until eventually he
died without having even begun it.

Some time afterwards a girl from the village called on the
brother of the dead man, saying that the deceased had appeared
to her in the night and told her to seek out his brother and ask
him immediately to begin to build a Marienkapelle on the hilltop,
a thing he had pledged himself to do but had in fact left undone
to his death.

When told, the brother was somewhat sceptical. The man had
been dead for months, and it was not very likely that he should
be knocking people up in the middle of the night to talk about
building propositions. Yet the girl went on to describe her visitor
in such accurate detail that he was soon convinced, and he agreed
to carry out the work.

All the same, for some time he in turn did nothing. And then
one night his dead brother paid him a personal visit in a dream

and made the same request. He then began to sell his brother's possessions to pay for the work, and he engaged a builder. When the materials arrived they were carried up to the tree-line, for this, he thought, was a much more sensible place for the building. Overnight, the beams and boards and stones all vanished, and it was some time before they were discovered again at the very top of the hill, but their mysterious removal was taken as a hint that the man should do as he had been told and not try to improve on the siting. Thus the chapel came to be built where it still stands, and the dead man could have peace at last, safe in the reflection that a reliable brother was an asset worth having.

Below Wasserliesch the remains of a dynamited bridge stand forlornly and rather dangerously in the middle of the river, a reminder of the importance to military strategists of this corner of land where the Saar and Moselle meet. The Romans themselves had a bridge over the Saar to carry their road from Metz to Trier, a distant forerunner of the latest bridge, completed since the Second World War left only the blasted ruins of another. As for the river which flows under its span, one inevitably thinks of the Saar as a sluggish stream of coal heaps and slurry, and grim towns where miners walk about with lamps on their helmets. And, of course, this is a true picture of part of the Saar valley, but the rest is a country of forests and vineyards, and wine-happy villages.

Like the Moselle, the Saar was first made navigable at its upper end. It is approached by the Canal des Houillières de la Sarre — the Saar Collieries Canal — which leads off from the summit pound of the Canal de la Marne au Rhin near Sarrebourg on the back slope of the Vosges. The canal eventually transforms itself into the Saar river, with locks built to the usual French dimensions. But — and this is the curiosity — it leads into German territory and ends there. Beyond the mining area the Saar is not navigable, even though its strikingly beautiful valley once resounded, like the Moselle, to the cries of the drovers urging their horses along the towpath.

So the German barges of Saarbrücken can only reach home by passing through France, and if they were to be regarded as foreigners their position would be intolerable. But, by one of those wise little pieces of statesmanship which are so sensible that they do not make headline news, German bargees of the Saar and their ships count as French in that they can pick up a cargo anywhere in France and take it wherever they wish. In return, French barges are free to carry to and from the German Saar wharves as though they were Saarlanders. This concession to the Saar boats is worth more than one might think. Belgian, Dutch and German non-Saar barges ply into France, but if they carry a cargo to a French destination they are taking a risk of having to return home empty. All empty barges within an area are notified to a regional freightage bureau which offers them the next available cargoes strictly in turn. A bargemaster is free to refuse a loading — perhaps because the material does not suit him, or the destination is not to his liking; but foreign ships may only take a cargo for a foreign destination, or one nearer their own frontier with France.

The Saar carries enough coal in suspension to stain the Moselle where the two rivers mix. This fusion takes place immediately below Konz, a town mainly on the Saar, which shows clearly enough in its name that, like Contz further up the Moselle and Koblenz further down, the Romans knew it as a confluence. The first time we came in sight of Konz my own geography was not too precise and I was a little surprised to see the large river on the starboard hand (km. 201), with the word 'SAAR' spelt out on the remnants of a bridge to warn shippers that they had taken the wrong turning. But the *Thames Commodore* always likes to see what can be discovered up such side alleys as she can find, so she immediately turned her nose into the stream and chugged cautiously up it until she had made perhaps half a mile and was opposite a row of pretty riverside cottages which had survived from the days of the drovers. Anchoring well out from the shore she let her quarter slide over to touch against the small landing-stage of a Konzer who owned a little motor-boat, and who was so delighted to have such an unexpected visitor that he invited my wife and myself to visit his flat later that evening and try the excellent wines he had brought home from the Saar vineyards.

Though no longer navigable along its lower reaches, the Saar used nevertheless to carry considerable shipping. Roman craft

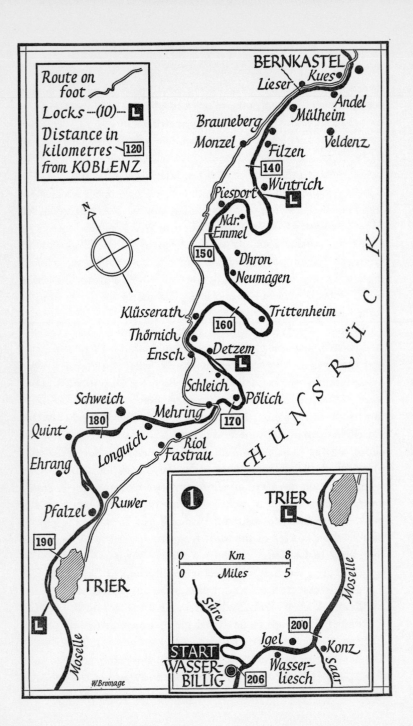

plied upon it, and in the Middle Ages the drovers rode the tow-horses up its bank as they did along the Upper Moselle. Even now we found the towpath still in existence, with faded and rusting notices about how one was not to obstruct the haulage-way, but no ships used the river. It flowed on deserted, waiting for the day when it in turn might become a Class V waterway carrying Europa-ships into the heart of the industrial Saar basin.

Because long ago it was an active river of shippers and fishers the Saar had its cult of St Nicholas, always a favourite in the Moselle country. The worthy Bishop of Myra may be known to children in Britain mainly in the form of Santa Claus, but in Germany he long ago gave his name to the waterman, who in medieval times was generally known as 'Nick'. Far up the Rhine St Nicholas is believed to live in a glass palace on the bottom of Lake Constance.

Nicholas of Myra is said to have appeared to take over the steersman's post on a storm-tossed vessel bound for Myra itself — and that was during his lifetime. Later, when his remains were being removed to the Italian port of Bari, the ship in which they were travelling came safely through many dangers. Thus it inevitably came about that Nicholas was regarded as a sort of Christian form of Neptune, and those who had to do with the water chose him as their patron saint. Fishermen and bargees would place his statue to watch over particular navigational dangers, as for instance on the German shore opposite Ehnen in the Luxembourg reaches of the Moselle. Another such statue stood on the bank of the Saar downstream of Saarburg. It was put there to protect the devotees of the saint from the hazards of a deep near the village of Leuken.

It so happened that the Elector-Archbishop of Trier had had three bells cast at Leuken for the cathedral, three bells named Balthasar, Caspar and Melchior, and because they were so christened they were to be raised into position at the Epiphany. Cargoes were often carried for the Elector by a certain successful shipper of Saarburg, and this same man now contracted to load the bells and float them down to Trier in plenty of time for the occasion. He was a bumptious and haughty individual, however, and for some time past he had stopped giving the customary greeting to St Nicholas and no longer doffed his cap as the other bargemen did. This, of course, was a stupid piece of arrogance.

'Take off your cap!' the lads of Leuken would shout at him in warning as he sailed proudly past the statue. 'Take off your cap!'

The older men shook their heads. 'Leave him alone,' they said. 'St Nicholas can look after himself. He'll teach that fellow to take off his cap like the rest of us.'

With Epiphany as the chosen date, the bells had, of course, to be shipped in mid-winter, when even nowadays the ice-floes may drive dangerously down Moselle and Saar alike. The shipper cast off, pushed out with his pole, and almost at once a large floe struck the stern, swinging his vessel round so that it grounded upon a rock at the edge of the deep. The craft tilted, and one by one the great bells slid over to sink in the deepest water of the Saar. The bargeman went overboard too, to be quickly swamped by the ice and drowned.

And there, the Saarlanders say, at Christmas and Epiphany one may still hear the three bells ring in the deep, while at midnight the water itself is turned into wine — though others believe the colour to be caused by coal in suspension, carried down from the French mines. And if anyone should drown in the Saar and his body not be recovered, then the impious shipper of Saarburg is obliged to toll the bells far down in the deep, because no knell can be rung for the victim on land.

There is also the story of St Matthew's involuntary voyage — for all the best people came to the Saar or Moselle at one time or another, at least in the belief of the people. As for St Matthew, it is not related just how he arrived in the Saar valley, a very long way from the Arabian desert where he is more generally supposed to have spent his later years, but, however he came there, the people of the valley seem not to have liked him, for according to the legend they put him in a wine-tub and pushed him out into the river. Perhaps this is in fact a dim recollection of the early Germanic habit of pushing out floating statues and founding new chapels where they came to land; but, however that may be, the story goes on to tell that, although poor St Matthew was somewhat ill at ease in his barrel, he yet enjoyed the beauty of the valley and wished to land at the prosperous little villages past which he bobbed on the current.

'Land me,' he would call. 'Help me to the shore!'

But always the people only shook their heads. They had no wish to have St Matthew running their lives for them, they said.

And so the barrel with its distinguished occupant floated on its way past one hamlet after another until it reached the Moselle. Within an hour or two it was rocking down the reach on which Trier was situated. No doubt St Matthew was cramped and hungry by now, and as he approached the city of the Treviri he found himself bobbing past a washing-stage where a number of women were busy with their laundering. He called to them.

'Look,' cried one of them. 'There goes a saint! Poor man, we must help him.'

And, unlike their neighbours of the Saar, the women of the Moselle left their washing and ran ahead to where a fisherman was at that moment pulling to land with his catch.

'Put out again, and help him,' they cried, pointing to the barrel in which St Matthew could be seen standing.

The fisherman stared, then pushed out from the shore and rowed to intercept the tub. Taking off his cap — for he was more polite and humble than the ill-fated shipper of Saarburg — he put his arms round the waist of the holy man and lifted him safely into the boat. Ashore the saint was at once taken in hospitably by the women of Trier, and even today one may be told in that city that the site of the abbey of St Matthew marks the place where he was safely brought to land after the selfish people of the Saar had refused to have him among them.

The next time I visited Konz I did so because I was walking and I had to cross the Saar. At the point between the two rivers there is a vast wasteland of shingle with just such a collection of old motor-bodies, oil drums, and rubbish as always accumulates at the edge of a busy modern town. There was also a curious private fishpond belonging to a club of 1911, and what appeared to be the founder members were sitting along its grassy banks fishing, and fishing, and fishing. I do not know whether there were any fish to be had, but presumably a balance must eventually be struck in any small enclosed water between the number of club members, the breeding capacity of the fish and the wisdom of their progeny. I did not see any fish caught, but perhaps I was not long enough on the scene to witness what may be a rare event.

Just below Igel a flight of cables crossed the Moselle, the lines suspended between two immense pylons at a height several times as great as that of the bridge arches further upstream and down. I have never discovered why grid engineers have this habit of expecting ships of quite legendary size to wish to pass under their wires, but maybe they have never seriously considered the matter. All they know is that for the height of riverside pylons the sky is the limit.

One of these private Eiffel Towers was set in the shingle desert of the promontory, and as I picked my way over the churned gravel a team of spidermen was at work. Paint does not last for ever, and a time comes when a pylon (if not galvanised) will begin to go rusty. That moment had now arrived, and ten men were busy knocking at the rust-spots with scaling-hammers. They had thick leather safety-belts which could be clipped round the struts, but not a man among them was using them. Perhaps it would have involved a loss of face to do so, and these agile young men would rather lose life by a slip of the foot than sacrifice face. There they were, fifty, one hundred, two hundred feet above the ground — not that the precise height would make much difference if one should fall — standing on the narrow bars set at a sharp incline, one hand clutching a stay while with the other they battered and clattered away, only pausing to wave an arm or leg cheerfully to me as I passed below. I hope they all survived, for they were pleasant lads. Besides, I would not have liked to help clear up the mess if one of them slipped when waving a friendly greeting to myself.

Though the group of riverside cottages at the old quay of Konz is pretty enough, the rest of the town is little more than a traffic junction which has been destroyed again and again on account of its bridges. It is best left quickly behind so that it may proceed with its worthy trade of making bulldozers and diggers and road-rollers. This is a flourishing business, and before a machine is allowed out into the big wide world it must spend a while in the kindergarten and show what it can do. Along the Moselle there is a vast playground for such machines, with patches of road to roll, great pyramids of earth and piles of broken masonry to move and acres of gravel in which to burrow and grab and doze. To and fro they gambol, tossing earth over their heads or rocking back and forth in a muddy swamp before they are ready for the final gleam-ing coat of paint which will so soon afterwards be scratched and spattered with mud.

Below the confluence of the two rivers the Moselle stretches wide and straight and still towards Trier lock. It is a fine reach for sailing, and the little yachts of the Konzers lie at their offshore moorings, the only fleet of such craft all the way to the outskirts of Koblenz. The valley is not wildly beautiful, for the country on either side of the river is scarred and broken with railway tracks and gravel pits and horrid barrack buildings to house NATO troops and teach them once and for all that they cannot expect good taste from an international army. Two buildings alone stand out from this mass of mediocrity, the Charterhouse of Konz on the right bank and Château Monaise on the left.

The Charterhouse used to be at the edge of Trier itself, and only its farm stood on the broad meadows of the river plain below Konz. Then came the War of the Spanish Succession, when the bridge of Konz became the scene of a violent battle between the French under Marshal Créquy and the Germans commanded by General Grana. Three thousand men were killed in the slaughter for the crossing, and the destruction both before and after the engagement took its toll of many buildings in the country around, among them the Charterhouse. Wisely the prior decided not to risk rebuilding so close to the town walls of the city, where each new war could be expected to bring fresh dangers. Instead the whole institution was moved out to Konz and the new buildings were ranged on the lands of its own farm (km. 198·8 R). And there they still stand, a splendid but not pretentious group from the beginning of the eighteenth century, with a fine baroque church standing very erect to look out across the river towards the foothills of the Eifel.

The peace the brothers sought lasted less than one hundred years before the French Revolution broke, and Frederick William II of Prussia installed in the Charterhouse his headquarters until his army poured over the bridge of Konz to be defeated in France. Soon the war was raging in the Moselle valley itself, and reluctantly the community loaded their modest possessions on a flat barge and set off down the river, abandoning the abbey to its fate. The buildings were left in the charge of a single loyal lay brother who had worked in the kitchen, and it was not long before the institution was commandeered as a military hospital to cater for the seemingly endless flow of wounded and dying left in the wake of the great Napoleon's dreams of conquest. The same solitary lay brother uncomplainingly tended the sick, and when fever broke out in the wards he at length contracted it himself and died. Locally he is said still to haunt the place with sounds of clock-winding, sweeping, washing-up and caretaking in general.

If the goods taken by the departing brethren were modest, this was because the contents of their cellar were too bulky to be removed. At that time the institution had more than eighty thousand vines, which under modern conditions would yield fifteen to twenty thousand gallons annually. The cellars on the property were equal to the need for storage, and when the Friars departed they were naturally sorry to leave behind them such a store of good and valuable wine. They walled up the entrances to the cellar, and long before their flight they had covered over the site of the entrance and presumably planted it up. Then when the troubles were over they would return to find a well-matured vintage awaiting them.

But the troubles did not pass. In 1803 the French secularised the institution. The brothers never returned. Instead, by night the men of Konz and Trier might sometimes be found furtively digging in the precincts of the Charterhouse, burrowing and scratching as though in search of gold.

Da liegt der Keller noch mit Wein,
Er liegt vergraben dort;
An hundert Fuder mögen's sein,
O wüssten wir den Ort!

So wrote a local rhymer more than a century ago.

Yet lies the loaded cellar there,
Filled with the buried wine.
A hundred tuns or more, they swear.
O, were the secret mine!

And still, they say, the wine has never been found. Probably it would not now be worth taking one of Konz's new-made excavating machines to the site, for Moselle wine does not improve with over-long keeping. It is best left buried, with the memory of the friars themselves.

As for Château Monaise (km. 198 L), that is a charming little mansion, as French as can be and so foreign to the Moselle that one wonders how it could ever have come to be there, looking out toward the river with its columned front, its steps and balustrade, and the trees of what once must have been a very elegant formal garden laid out in that neat style that the French alone seem able to bring to real perfection. In fact it was built for a wealthy canon of Trier cathedral, who employed a French architect to design a residence suited to his titled dignity. Poor man, he had hardly moved in before the storm of the Revolution broke and he was driven out. There was to be no more *aise* for a cathedral dignitary for many years to come.

The château now belongs to the City of Trier; for, as the Germans so neatly put it, *da spukt es*, and that is apparently the reason why it was never again to become the favourite residence of some newer titled family or business magnate. The spooking referred to is carried on by a white lady, a sad figure of great beauty to whom none may speak.

This lady in white is not a secret appendage of the regretted canon of Trier but a charming and elegant girl, the young wife of a gay and debonair French officer of the Napoleonic armies.

Always in her lifetime she was dressed in white, and she was already known to the shippers and fishermen as the White Lady. Always in white, that is, until after the French march to Moscow. Till then her husband had returned to her after each new campaign, but now the months dragged on, and no news came other than of one disaster after another. Of the officer himself there was none. Then the shippers who were so accustomed to seeing her wave to them from the balcony noticed that she had changed her white bridal dress for a black one. She had still not heard, but she knew in her heart that her beloved must be lying dead, frozen in the silence of the vast Russian wastes of snow and desolation. Soon she withdrew from the gardens and the river front, and never again was she seen. Quickly she sickened, dying of a broken heart in the pretty château of Monaise.

If I have not heard the faithful lay brother wind the Charterhouse clock, perhaps that is because I have never been inside the building. Nor have I seen the shade of that sad young French widow, waiting in hope through one campaign after another and calling to the shippers for news from the world outside. But then I did not look, for my eyes were straining ahead to pierce the early morning mist for the possible shape of an upcoming Europa-ship, or the string of buoys which marked the course of the water-ski competition. For it was indeed early when we first chugged downstream toward Trier, and the blanket of the fresh day lay heavy enough over the river for us to be unable to see both banks at once. With the barrage only two kilometres ahead we were feeling our way as cautiously as a blind man in a strange city street, when a voice hailed us. It was not the lady in white but a gruff and humped angler sitting in a punt. He was in that glum mood which often afflicts fishermen who of their own accord sit half-frozen for hour upon hour in mist and fog, and he called in a surly voice that to navigate in the mist was *verboten*, and if the police should catch us there would be trouble. But this, I decided, was a moment for turning my Nelsonian ear to him, the ear which for some unaccountable reason cannot hear anything said in a foreign tongue.

Though Trier is now on a flourishing Class V waterway, an attempt was once made to link it to the Meuse by an ambitious canal which was to ascend the Sûre, cross the Ardennes and drop down the Ourthe valley to Liège. This canal was actually begun, but it was never finished. More curious, however, is the tale of another canal which linked the city with Cologne, a channel as unusual in its use as it was in its mode of construction.

For long the citizens of Cologne had been endeavouring to build a cathedral in their city, a building which was to outstrip in size all other cathedrals in the world. The master builder happened to be measuring up the plans for the great doorway when an apprentice began to scoff at him and say that the building was so absurdly large that it would never be finished.

The builder did not welcome this unsolicited comment upon his work, so he very properly sacked the apprentice forthwith.

'Nevertheless,' cried the young man in a parting shot, 'nevertheless your building never shall be finished. Before you have built the final tower I shall have dug a canal all the way to Trier.'

This boast was a rash one even for such an inland waterways enthusiast as the apprentice. But the builder of Cologne seems to have accepted it as a challenge, for he worked faster than ever, so swiftly indeed that his former apprentice had to cheat by securing the aid of that wicked individual the devil.

Years went by, and when the cathedral of Cologne was at last nearly complete the builder was surprised to see an enormous worm come crawling through the ground, pushing the earth to either side. This was of course the devil in an unusual disguise which he had assumed in order the better to dig the bed of the canal. At the same moment the apprentice appeared also.

'See, my canal is finished and your cathedral is not,' he exclaimed. And, as though in confirmation, water came pouring down the cut that the worm had just excavated. Riding on one of the leading waves sat a duck, which had swum all the way from Trier.

While the builder was still staring in amazement at this unusual sight the water rose so quickly that it engulfed him and drowned him, with the result that the cathedral was left uncompleted until late in the nineteenth century. The apprentice was delighted to

see him overtaken by such a fate, but no sooner had the builder
sunk from view than the canal-dozing worm turned upon the
young man in turn and strangled him, leaving him to become the
Cologne cathedral ghost. As for the canal, it was put to good use
by the citizens of both places, for the vintners of the Upper
Moselle used it to send wine to their customers in Cologne without
having to bother with cooperage and casks.

Trier lock (km. 195·8) is like any other lock on the great Moselle
Waterway except that there is a little jetty in the headwater which
is the home of the *Günther*, the only fuel boat on the entire river
below Thionville. In the course of our voyaging we came to know
the *Günther* well, and we always felt a curious moral obligation
to fill our diesel tanks from her hose, the same sort of feeling one
has when coming upon a street musician playing away on an
otherwise deserted pavement. The young captain was a Jugoslav,
and his uncle had for years kept open for him an excellent job as
master of a tanker on the Danube, but nothing would persuade
him to set foot again in a Communist country. His grandfather,
a tug-skipper, had been sent to Siberia and had died there. He
would rather stay where he was, in command of a Shell fuel-boat
which ran at a loss of nearly £300 a month. The company, he said,
could easily afford it, and it gave them a foot in the door for the
days when the railway contracts ran out and the Moselle became
a really busy waterway.

We came to know Trier lock intimately because on one of our
earlier visits we stayed there for some time. Trier is the only large
city in the whole length of the German Moselle, and we naturally
expected it to have an excellent quayside. Curiously enough we
found it had none whatsoever, perhaps because the city fathers
were more interested in the past than the present and had never
begun to take shipping very seriously since the Secundini and
their barge-borne cargoes of cloth had passed away. True, there
were two medieval cranes still standing beside what once had been
a wharf, but the brand-new commercial harbour had been placed
at Ehrang (km. 184), five miles below the town and set in a waste
served by a goods siding but without tram, bus, or even a footpath
nearby. After a number of attempts to draw in to land we had

taken the recommendation of Herr Zengerling, the lock-keeper, and had returned to the hospitality of the quayside at the approach on the upstream side. There was only one disadvantage. We were on the wrong side of the river, and there was no bridge, not even a weir gallery over the barrage. Such care had been taken not to spoil the view that the entire works of the barrage were below the surface of the water. Straight across the river we could see the trolley-bus terminus at St Medard. It was a mere three or four hundred yards away, but the nearest means of access involved a journey of several miles on foot.

However, Herr Zengerling had an idea. He opened a metal hatchplate in the ground, and there was a stairway descending straight into a mysterious subterranean gloom. He pressed a switch, and a light came on.

'You will find others, all the way,' he said. 'Press them, and hurry.'

The steps led far down to below the dam, and from the bottom of the flight a passage ran ahead for perhaps two hundred yards under the barrage, aiming across the river. Bundles of cables lined the walls, red and blue, yellow and purple and black, in lines which converged in the funnel of the dark distance. We hurried along, pressing the light switches as we found them, and as we passed under the width of the Moselle we were surprised to find that others were there also. Occasionally we could see through a door standing ajar to a room where a couple of engineers in overalls were drinking coffee, or poring over some mysterious gadget. Once we met a man with a broom, sweeping the sub-aqueous passage as though it were his front doorstep.

'*Morgen.*' He nodded and went on his leisurely way, whistling in time with his brushing.

At the further end another stair climbed to the daylight beside the strainer of the power-station fed by the barrage. Inside the generator hall below the level of the headwater the huge turbines spun like tops, whistling slightly as they did so. For some odd reason the scene reminded me of a set I had once seen in *The Magic Flute*, with the weird and powerfully suggestive symbolism of the temple of Zoroaster. I almost expected the Queen of the

Night to come in through the wings, glittering with tinsel and darting kilovolt glances from her flashing eyes.

The turbines properly paid no attention to us, but hummed and hummed their private monotones. We tiptoed out of the sanctuary and hurried to the trolley terminus under the trees.

II

THE mooring at Trier lock was more convenient in theory than
in practice, for the duty engineer in the power-station was not
pleased to find two strangers walking up his drive with as much
confidence as one might expect only from the great Ober-
electricity-rat himself. Maybe he had some long-standing private
quarrel with our friend the lock-keeper, for he seemed incensed
that he had not been consulted before the subterranean passage
to the turbine hall was opened for the benefit of mere boatmen,
and he turned the two strangers out, sending them back to the
roadway at St Medard and giving them a detour of nearly eight
miles to reach the *Thames Commodore* where she lay snugly at the
lock only two hundred yards across the water. The two ejected
were our friends from aboard, and we had the good fortune to meet
them on their way back through the town. The engineer, they
said, had locked the main gates and also the access to the strainer
gallery by the intake. Being ourselves very disinclined to be
badgered about by high-handed volt-minders, my wife and I took
a leisurely supper, waited until dark, stole up to the power-station
like 'liberation fighters' or thieves, and, quickly scaling the gates,
ran on our stockinged soles for the trapdoor. Soon we were safely
under the river, following the cable tunnel across to the lock.
However, we could not expect our friends always to be prepared
to do a little breaking and entering, so on our next visit to Trier
we determined to try once more to moor somewhere in the centre
of the city.

Trier has no water-front, no quay with rich medieval houses, no bollards grooved by generations of hawsers. The river on the town side is edged by a bank thirty feet high, to contain the floods. There is a faint attempt at riverside gardens, but not a hint that Trier itself is one of the most fascinating cities in Europe. Everything is hidden away from the boatman's view, or else stands so far back from flood danger that one can only recognise the buildings after first visiting them from the landward side.

First comes the twin-towered church of St Matthias, standing well outside the middle of the town (km. 194·6 R). Trier has the distinction of having the remains of the only apostle to be buried north of the Alps, and although nothing is known of his origin except that he was chosen by lot to fill the place of Judas, there is at least a belief that Matthias went as a missionary to Ethiopia, where he was murdered. But the tireless St Helena, mother of the great Emperor Constantine, acquired his remains on her travels, and brought them to her favourite city of Trier. The basilica became a popular place of pilgrimage, but not entirely because of Matthias — who was only a Trier man by posthumous removal. The church is a very ancient foundation, and is the burial place of St Eucharius, one of the men who brought Christianity to the Moselle valley at a very early date. With him is his companion, St Valerius.

The story known to every vintner along the hills of the Upper Moselle is that St Peter himself sent out three of the men he had trained, telling them to go to the Moselle valley. With Eucharius and Valerius was Maternus, who unfortunately died in Alsace, an event which so upset his companions that they posthasted back to Rome to report the matter to Peter. They were told to return to Alsace bearing Peter's staff with them. Then they were to knock with it upon the ground where they had buried Maternus. This they did, and Maternus was restored to life, to complete the journey to Trier.

Arrived at the city of the Treviri, the three men preached in the market, but the heathen priests worked up the people to a fury and incited them to stone the newcomers. The crowd was about to fling the first volley, when all their right arms were paralysed and the stones fell to the ground. Only after Eucharius had prayed for their forgiveness did strength return to their limbs. Many were very rightly surprised, and they let themselves be baptised by Eucharius and his companions in the market.

Soon the men received support from an influential quarter. Albana was a rich widow and a Christian, and when her son died Eucharius restored him to life. In gratitude she presented her mansion to become the first Christian church in Trier. There the growing community met, and there in the course of time Eucharius and Valerius were to be buried. On its site the church of St Matthias was built in the twelfth century, and the heavy plain tombs of the two men are still there, very different from the great reliquary which holds the remains of St Matthias himself.

As for Maternus, he too is certainly remembered in Trier, and not only in the name of a street — for the Maternusstrasse, Albanastrasse and Euchariusstrasse are all beside the church of St Matthias, with the Valeriusstrasse just across the railway line. As soon as the church in Trier was established Maternus left his companions and went further. He became the first Bishop of Cologne in the fourth century (for time passes swiftly in the transition from legend to certainty), and when he died there was jealousy between three sees as to where he should be buried. Cologne, Tongres and Trier all claimed him, and the matter was settled in an ingenious way. His body was simply placed in a boat and pushed out into the Rhine at Cologne to see where it wanted to go.

This would seem to have loaded the odds very heavily against the people of Tongres, but, of course, the boat only had to come to rest in the diocese and not in the cathedral city itself. The prospects for the see of Cologne looked by far the most favourable, but Maternus was carried upriver by eddies, or wind, or sheer saintliness, and first ran aground at Rodenkirchen in the diocese of Trier. The delighted citizens fetched him back to that city, and he is buried in the cathedral.

In fact Trier was a city of great splendour in the early centuries of the Christian era, and second only to Rome itself. Even that would have been an opinion confined to Rome, for the people of Trier had no doubt about which came first.

'I see the imperial buildings rising to such a height that they almost reach the stars in heaven,' Eumenius wrote of Trier in the year 310. Eumenius was an eulogist, a public relations man, and thus given to slight exaggeration, but Trier must certainly have been a magnificent place, and even if it did not contain skyscrapers it had some luxurious institutions. One of these is still to be found as an area of ruin at the upstream edge of the town. When St Matthias is on the starboard beam the first of the bridges is already in sight, but before it is reached one is gliding past the Barbara-thermen (km. 193·3 R), tantalisingly hidden behind the trees.

These Roman baths merely came to be known by the name of the medieval suburb in which they lay, and nowadays there is little left above ground to hint at the richness and splendour of an amusement-place which survived into the era of the Franks before people began to strip it and use it as a stone-quarry. In the heyday of Roman Trier these baths, even more luxurious than the Imperial Baths in the same city, must have been a bustling scene of gaiety, and physical culture, of dining-out and gossip, laughter and plotting and amorous intrigue. Merchants, vintners and ship-masters, aristocrats with their attendants carrying the bathing-wraps and changes of clothing, all came and went at their leisure in the marbled passages and ante-rooms. There were masseurs and manicure attendants, and no doubt it was a good place for a lady to have her hair made up in the newest mode. One could have a warm swim there, too, and then retire to a quiet corner to pick at bunches of sweet grapes while listening to poets and musicians; or, if one was thoroughly tired of culture, there was a skittle alley very much as one might find it today in a riverside pleasure-garden.

The bridge (km. 193·1) which crosses the river just below the site of the Barbara baths is one of the most astonishing sights on all the Moselle. It has eight arches, two of which are occupied by the navigation channel, but the curves and the roadway they support sit somewhat curiously on the massive buttresses, as though they were a job-lot bought second-hand. On the balustrade over the buttress some way to the right of the centre there stands a crucifix, and below it with his feet just above the bulk of the bullnose itself is St Nicholas, ready to wreck any bargee foolish

enough to adopt an insulting demeanour toward his brethren
further upstream, near Saarburg or opposite Ehnen in Luxembourg. Of this Trier statue there is a tale which is also told of both
the others, and perhaps of all Santa Claus statues down the river.

The bridge of Trier has always been a difficult passage, and if
nowadays it holds no terrors for a single barge or for the *Thames
Commodore* the giant French pushers have to treat the narrow
arches with respect. And it is because the bridge was never a
simple passage that long ago the patron of bargees was placed
upon its upstream side, so that he might be invoked in good time
by pious captains. Before the days of motor-vessels, when a barge
was descending the river it had no other motive power than *kalter
Druck*, or 'cold pressure', the phenomenon that on a sloping river
a laden craft would run perhaps half a knot faster than the flow,
because it was actually sliding forward on the friction-free watery
incline. This slight margin provided steerage way, but in floodtime there might be whirls and surges, especially where the water
was bunched up by such stout obstructions as the buttresses of the
Trier bridge.

Once when a barge was approaching the arches on a rough and
swirling river, the bargemaster saw that he was in danger of being
wrecked, and calling to St Nicholas he promised him a candle as
tall as the mast of his ship if he should come through in safety.
Sure enough, he passed the bridge without striking, and as he
swept beside the statue he made a rude gesture and cried 'No,
Nicholas. You shall not have such a reward.' The story of the bells
in the Saar should have been a warning to him that it was unwise
to take such liberties. On his next voyage Nicholas had his revenge
and wrecked him on the buttress. And that was the end of ship and
mariner.

With seven buttresses standing in the water, one would expect
both the statues to be on the fourth or centre one, but they are not.
They are where the centre of the bridge used to be, two arches on
the right bank having long ago been buried under the embankment. The earliest picture of the bridge in its original form is on
a fourth-century coin of Constantine, for the bridge is in fact a
Roman one. Or, more correctly, the buttresses are Roman, the

flat wooden roadway of Roman times having eventually been
replaced by medieval stone arches, which in turn came to be
changed for more modern ones.

Though the upper works are undistinguished, the impression
given by the buttresses is one of tremendous strength. They are
built of sandstone surrounded by enormous blocks of hard basalt,
some of which are more than a yard high and three yards long.
These formidable stones of a dark purplish hue are strapped
together with iron cramps, and they have been able to stand up to
sixteen centuries or more of hard battering by the water of the
Moselle — to say nothing of the impact of an occasional impious
barge. That they have done so is partly due to their shape, for the
Roman engineers were very competent men and understood that
a semi-circular shaping on the downstream side would cause the
least eddying and backwash, whereas the upstream faces would
need to be sharply pointed, not just to deflect the water but to
break and throw off the heavy floes of ice which would drive down-
river in the winter and might pile against flatter buttresses to dam
the stream and break down the bridge.

The bridge has of course been blown up, but curiously not since
the seventeenth century. In 1945 it would have shared the fate of
most German bridges had not a local man who had an affection
for the bridge prevented a stupid waste of effort by treating the
guards with liquor until they were incompetent. At least that is
what the people of Trier maintain, and it may well have been
true, for the last weeks of conflict in Germany were everywhere
marked by a struggle between fanatical commanders who wanted
to wreck everything and the more moderate inhabitants who had
no great wish to foot the bill for repairs.

Below the Roman bridge are the two splendid medieval cranes,
the first (km. 193 R) being a replica built two centuries ago but
the other (km. 192·6 R) a piece of mercantile machinery erected
by a local barge-owner in 1413. They are ingenious, these cranes,
for each has two jibs projecting at opposite sides of a slated cap
which stands on the top of a round body like a small Martello
tower. The works are inside the body, but the principle was that
a load could be lifted from a ship, the whole top could then be

The old port, Trier

swivelled round, and the load could be lowered to a cart in the roadway by the quay. While this was going on, the other jib would be over the ship, ready for the next load.

Somewhere near the upstream crane were found the remains of the piles of a yet earlier bridge which seems to have been a structure of the last decades B.C. No doubt this is the one which Tacitus referred to when describing how Cerialis beat back the Treveri when they rose in rebellion in 70 A.D. and tried to storm the city across the bridge.

With so much to look at it was difficult for us to concentrate on the job of finding a landing, and we ran right through the town before we realized that we had found none. The reason why it was so difficult to come to the shore was that Trier itself lay in the tail-water of the lock, and instead of stretching from bank to bank the shipping channel was no more than a dredged gulley flanked by shallows on either hand. At the further edge of the city we turned and had begun to nose our way inquisitively upstream again, when a helpful police boat which had noticed us cautiously searching and probing with our sounding-pole came speeding up to hail us and direct us to run a little further up and then cut straight over to beside the first of two medieval cranes. There, they said, there was plenty of water. We followed their directions and immediately ran into less than three feet of water. But the *Thames Commodore* has always been good at extricating herself, and as a barge happened to be coming up-river we pushed round the stern to meet the wash at right angles, and then as the very first wave began to lift her she gave a burst of power and bobbed out backwards into the deep again, to saunter downstream once more.

The wall below the upstream crane was once busy with the bank-hauled craft of the Middle Ages, and it was there that shortly before Christmas of 1839 a hissing and wheezing, a puffing of steam and a cloud of thick black from a slender smoke-stack heralded the arrival of the *Ville de Metz*. The Trierers shouted and waved, salvos of cannon greeted the graceful paddle-wheeler as she ran through the arch of the Roman bridge and swung round to draw in at the wall, the first steamer to arrive at Trier. She was a French ship operating from Metz, and she was to be followed a few months later by the stately *Mosella* of a German company, a ship that was to become a great favourite with the people of Trier.

Unable to take the mooring of the *Ville de Metz* we passed beyond the second crane to where a long eyot was drawn out into a breakwater. Between this broad strip of dike and the right bank lay the passenger harbour, a dead piece of water with shallows at the top and four floating jetties along the shore. Two of these belonged to the big white ships of the Cologne–Düsseldorf line, the *Luxemburg*, the *Saarbrücken* and the *Trier*, three enormous vessels which between them kept up a regular service along the whole length of river from Trier to Koblenz. We came to like these ships because they often saved us money, for we could pass the locks free if in company of a barge or passenger-ship, instead of paying ten marks at each step. We had all the steamer time-tables aboard so that we could calculate when to be under way to use their services to pay our way for us. Nevertheless, our gratitude did not extend so far that we would pay the 100 marks (about £9) which they asked for the overnight use of their Trier jetties. Presumably the fee was pitched at this height to make quite sure that no yachts would clutter the stages and be in the way of the ships.

The other two stages belonged to the *Stadt Trier* which ran a daily trip to Nennig, three locks further upstream; and to the ship of the Klosterschänke Pfalzel, an inn a few miles down-river. The *Stadt Trier* was away from its jetty in the daytime, and the Pfalzel boat during the night, but there was an overlap of a couple of hours in the evening when both ships might be in port. Their skippers were generous in offering us the use of their jetties, but it meant moving twice daily and spending two hours or more at anchor in the stream when both the ships were at home. This continual coxing and boxing on the water tended to interfere with our visiting the city, and there was the added trouble that German motor-boats small and large had a way of lying on the *Thames Commodore's* flank. They were very welcome to do so, but the result was that when we moved from one jetty to another or out into the stream we often had these others attached to us so that we moved as a whole raft of shipping. Sometimes the owners had gone ashore, and when they returned they would find their craft in midstream, so we would have to ferry them out. Though delighted to perform these public services we at length found it less exacting to anchor in the middle of the river and row to and fro as we wished.

This port (km. 191·5 R) from which the steamers ply is really at Zurlauben, a gem of a little suburb of shippers and fishermen which forms a row of village houses still intact. It was here and in the Barbara quarter that the members of the guild of fishermen lived, a brotherhood which was very active as late as the end of the eighteenth century. The cluster of pretty dwellings is hidden behind the massive dike, but of all parts of Trier this is certainly the most picturesque. Many of the houses are inns from the days of the medieval port, and each has a little garden across the lane, a bower with tables and chairs and sometimes a charming period summerhouse just tall enough to peep over the bank. In one of these houses was born Georg Schmitt, composer of the *Mosellied* which resounds from the throats of vintners and villagers at every festival down the valley.

It was about 1846 that Schmitt was travelling on the river aboard the *Mosella*. The ship ran twice weekly to Koblenz and back again, connecting at Trier with the *Providence*, one of the famous 'Inexplosibles' built at Nantes and brought by a long and circuitous route to the Moselle. The *Providence* belonged to the French company in Metz, and she ran from Trier to Nancy, so at that time it was possible to travel the entire length of the river by steamer — something which even on the new waterway can no longer be done.

The caterer on board the *Mosella* was a Trier man by the name of Junk — a not uncommon name in the city even now. When he saw Schmitt he went up to him.

'I'm glad you've come,' he said. 'In the cabin I have a poem which you must set to music.' Taking him down below, he poured out a glass of wine for Schmitt. 'Sit down, and get on with it,' he said.

The verses were not by Junk himself, but had been written by Theodor Reck, an evangelical priest who was devoted to the Moselle. Schmitt at once set to work, humming away as he did so. Before he had even finished the glass of golden Moselle (as he told in one of his letters) he had composed the song, and when Junk came below again, Schmitt sang the verses through to him, accompanying himself on a guitar. Junk was delighted, and so were the passengers and crew who were brought in to hear a repeat. The wheezing ship rang to the gay refrain, and by the end of the day's run the song was already established, ready to spread up and down the length of the Moselle and eventually to acquire the status almost of a national anthem.

The reader who has an eye for ecclesiastical detail may have noted the extraordinary juxtaposition of the words evangelical and priest in the last paragraph. Can such things be? In the diocese of Trier, yes. Trier is very conscious of being immensely ancient, no ordinary see. Did not Constantine himself embrace Christianity within its bounds? Is not the cathedral the lodging of the Holy Coat? Did not Europe once tremble at the might of the Archbishop-Elector of Trier? Yes indeed, and for that reason Trier can go its own way and have a few harmless idiosyncrasies. One

of these is to confound outsiders by calling a pastor a *pfarrer*
or priest, and a Catholic priest a *pastor*. Another, which is more
confusing socially, is that men wear their wedding rings on the
wrong hand, and so appear to be bachelors going around with
other people's wives — an illusion which no doubt gives the
modern Treveri a huge amount of amusement when they travel
among men of other and lesser breeds.

From the 'Sarlawen' as the Trierers call Zurlauben, it is only
a short walk through not very interesting streets to the market,
which suddenly opens out as a bustling and colourful centre to
the city. At one side is the site of the old 'Steipe' where kings
and emperors would stay. Sadly it was blown to pieces by a bomb,
and now there is a pleasant space where one can sit and drink wine
or eat cream cakes and wonder at the inscription boldly carved
on the rose-pink wall in letters of gold — ANTE ROMAM TREVIRIS
STETIT ANNIS MILLE TRECENTIS. It is a splendid boast and one which
can hardly be true, but as it is such a large lie it is confidently
believed by many a patriotic native of the city. Trier was founded
— in popular imagination, if not in fact — by a certain Prince
Trebeta, of whom Sebastian Münster related in the fifteenth
century that he was driven out of his Asiatic homeland by Semi-
ramis, who had been busy founding Nineveh. His expulsion must
have been violent, for he never stopped in his headlong flight
until he reached the beautiful and happy valley of the Moselle
where he decided to settle. Wise, strong and no doubt handsome,
he built himself a great palace on the tall sandstone cliff, and
across the water at its foot he established the town which he called
after his name, Treberis. 'This happened in Abraham's time,'
wrote Münster. 'Founded more than 2,000 years before Christ,
the city is 1,300 years older than Rome.'

Merian the famous engraver of prospects of German towns and
cities is even more precise. 'It is the oldest city in all the world,'
he wrote. 'It stood for 1250 years before Rome, and was founded
in the sixteenth year of the Patriarch Abraham — that is, in the
year 1966 after the creation of the world, 310 years after the flood
and 39 after the death of Noah; although perhaps we cannot be
entirely certain of this.' Much truth lies hidden in that last

Trier, Hauptmarkt and St Gangolf's

remark. Trier was certainly a Roman foundation in the land of the Treviri — a people of whom Tacitus wrote that 'They make out that they are Germanic in origin. Indeed they do so with particular pride, hoping that by claiming such distinguished blood relationship they can dispose of any similarity to the flabby Gauls.'

Across from the wine-garden the triangular market is filled with flowers. It is a pleasant scene with plenty of life to it, and the heavy ecclesiastical sound of deep-voiced bells drifting over the house-tops from Trier's innumerable churches and foundations. Among the stalls stands a fine fountain, which has no doubts at all about the excellence of the city in which it stands.

'Happy is that city where prudence holds the sceptre, holy justice guards good men and puts the bad to the sword, where fortitude is supreme in time of adversity, and that which is worthy is governed by a gentle temperance.' So reads the inscription over which the cherubs sit, straining to hold open the mouths of the curious creatures which gape at the public from the top shelf of their splendid fountain in the market. Above them stands St Peter, well posed to look over the tops of the trolley-buses and the gay umbrellas of the flower-stalls. By chance we first arrived at Trier on 29 June, when the flower-sellers scale his pedestal to give Peter a suitable annual posy. He had just been decked out with a sheaf of gladioli which he held in the crook of his stone arm, the inclination of his head giving him very much the appearance of an artiste graciously acknowledging the admiration of the audience.

Between the stalls stands the Trier cross, a very ancient market cross which has wonderfully survived across the centuries to remind the people of a very curious happening, half buried in the darkness of earliest medieval records. On the cross itself an inscription says that, 'Archbishop Heinrich erected me in the year 958 of the Incarnation and the second year of his episcopate, in remembrance of the sign of the cross which came from heaven upon the people.'

In the tenth century Trier was again prosperous, just as it had been before the onslaughts of the Franks. Life was gay and by no means dangerous — or so it seemed. And then one day an elderly man appeared at the gate of the Palace, saying that he had a matter of great import for the Archbishop's ear. The servants tried to turn him away, or at least to learn what his business might be, but he refused to reveal it to any but Archbishop Heinrich himself. Grudgingly admitted to an audience the man told the Bishop of a terrible dream which had come to him in the night just past. He had dreamed that he was standing on the Marcusberg — the steep hill immediately across the river from the Zurlauben

passenger port — when he saw a fearful serpent or monster
creeping down the hillside, breathing enmity toward the city. At
length it flung itself into the river and the waters rose as a flood
to engulf the town and its people. He interpreted his dream not
as a sign of an impending flood but as a warning that an enemy
was about to advance over the Marcusberg, intending to descend
upon the city to destroy it. The army should at once be mustered
and held under arms, ready to meet the threat the moment the
enemy appeared, he said.

The Archbishop was not inclined to listen to such a prophet of
doom, and after telling the man to forget his dream he had him
politely shown out. The dreamer then canvassed the people in the
streets, only to be laughed at or reproved for his pessimism. At
length he despaired of finding any to listen, and like some great
figure of the Old Testament he stood in the market and cried a
triple woe over Trier and its people. Then he knelt in prayer,
crying for forgiveness to be given to the people who refused to
heed the signs, and interceding for the city itself. As he did so, the
legend relates, the sky darkened, a storm cloud drove down upon
the city, and a nameless dread fell upon the people. There was a
terrible hush, a sense of impending disaster, and then from the
storm-dark sky the rain began to fall. Down it came, as it so often
may in the Moselle valley after a week of great heat, but with just
this one difference: the rain was not in ordinary drops. It was a
downpour of tiny crosses which fell upon the cobbles and on the
heads of the people themselves.

Archbishop Heinrich pondered. Perhaps the visionary was right
after all. He ordered the troops to be alerted, and the men of Trier
flocked quickly to the colours. Under the Archbishop himself the
burghers marched out of the town and over the bridge, to follow
the winding road to the top of the Marcusberg. And there in the
distance they could see a column of the dreaded Huns weaving
its way across the plateau, just like the monster in the dream of the
seer.

Before the Huns could reach the edge of the Moselle heights
the men of Trier fell upon them, and after a fierce battle the
invaders were put to flight. At length the victorious forces returned

to the city, and to celebrate these strange events the Archbishop had the cross put up in the market where all men might see it and remember that one should be ready to heed a warning, however strange and improbable it might seem.

At the other end of the main street of Trier there stands one of the most famous of Roman buildings, the immense and powerful Porta Nigra, time-blackened and sturdy, its massive stones still held together with iron cramps. It is sixteen centuries old, a fortified gateway built as a bastion against the menacing Germanic tribes of the untamed country outside and so designed that invaders could be shot down from the sides or trapped and slaughtered from above. Though never completed, it rises three storeys high above its own archway, a formidable memorial to the power of Rome, but the Romans had long vanished when it came to have a stranger tenant than any guard of the watch.

In the year 1026 Archbishop Poppo went on a two-year tour to the Holy Land, accompanied by a scholarly monk who had come from the famous monastery on Mount Sinai and so knew his way around. This man was named Simeon.

Upon their safe return to Trier, Poppo asked Simeon what he would wish to have as a reward for his services. No doubt he expected his companion to ask for a canon's stall or some other appointment in the cathedral, but to his surprise Simeon asked to be allowed to withdraw completely into a life of prayer, removed altogether from the world. He wished to be walled up in a cell in the Porta Nigra, with neither door nor window but only a hole in the roof through which some food might occasionally be dropped to him.

His wish granted, Simeon lived for seven years, immured in the ground-floor chamber of the eastern tower. When he died, Archbishop Poppo decided to convert the Porta Nigra itself into a great church in his honour — a two-decker church, the upper of which was for the inmates of the Simeonstift (or St Simeon's Foundation) next door. It must have presented a most extraordinary appearance, for one Roman tower was later capped with a steeple and the other with a choir and gallery walk. The entire ground floor and the Roman archway were buried in a great ramp of earth, on which was set a broad flight of steps which would have done justice to St Peter's in Rome. When Trier came under Napoleon's sway, the Emperor ordered the demolition of everything non-Roman in the construction of the Porta Nigra, and he had the arches dug out again, but eventually the gallery and the choir were allowed to remain as curious embellishments of the original Roman design.

Just as the Roman gate became a hermit's cell, then a church and finally an ancient monument, many others among Trier's famous buildings have changed their use across the centuries. The Archbishop's Palace built in a riot of rococo in the eighteenth century testifies to the splendour to which the clergy of Trier had risen, yet it only held the Elector for a brief eight years before he moved his residence to a new palace in Koblenz. When the troops of the French Revolution streamed over Trier they converted the palace to a hospital, and later it became a Prussian barracks with stiff-booted troopers stamping up and down the marble stairs and strutting along the elegant garden walks. Then came the Second World War, which reduced it to a ruin and provided the opportunity for the palace to be restored again in all its splendour of pink and cream, with little putti amusing themselves in the nooks and bowers of one of Germany's most delightful public gardens, or impudently blocking their ears with sandstone fingers while the brass band of the fire brigade plays beneath the trees on a Sunday afternoon.

The palace is strangely — and I think mistakenly — built on to one of Trier's other great buildings, the Basilica, in such a way as to obscure about half of one end of it. One can hardly imagine an architect of the baroque having done anything quite so extraordinary, but there it is — even if each building would be better on its own. As for the Basilica, that too has changed its use across the centuries. Once this huge building was actually the judgment hall of the Emperor Constantine. Then it became the residence of the Frankish rulers, and later of the Electors. It was eventually converted into a church, and sharing the fate of the rococo palace in the destruction of 1944 it was finally rebuilt as a great evangelical church in the heart of the oldest cathedral city of Germany.

D

And how curious it is that the brilliant glass mosaics, and the fish-pond font and the great organ itself should blend so admirably with the vast apse of Constantine's builders in thin red brick and semi-circle arches. If it is so moving a place on a Sunday morning, perhaps that is because one is conscious of its immense time-span, of the fact that Constantine himself sat within that great semi-circle where the thin and emaciated modern Christ now hangs from the cross on the communion table, and that its days of splendour as a judgment hall in Augusta Treverorum followed so close upon the time when Rictius Varus, governor under Diocletian, decided that once and for all the province of Gaul would be rid of the pestilential new religion which was so quiet and self-effacing and yet somehow undermined the prestige of the Roman deities, and so of the Emperor and his provincial representatives.

The storm broke in Germany when the Theban legion arrived, a unit which came from Egypt but nevertheless appears to have been composed almost entirely of Christians. Thyrsus was the officer in command of the contingent which was detailed to Augusta Treverorum, and upon which in the year 286 fell the full fury of Rictius Varus. On the field of Mars — where now St Paulinus' Church stands as a memorial to their martyrdom — the young Roman soldiers stood stiffly, waiting their turn to be cut down on the order of the governor. All day the slaughter went on as the men, true to the example of their officer, refused to deny their faith. Next day the butchery spread to the civil officials, the Consul Palmatius and seven councillors being beheaded in public, together with a number of Christian merchants and their families. On the third day the Christians of Trier were slaughtered in such numbers that legend relates that the blood from the bodies flung into the river dyed the stream red as far as the outskirts of Neumagen, more than twenty miles downstream.

It is said that many years later a penitent from Trier went to Rome for pardon, and the Pope sent him back to his native city to bring a parcel of earth. When at last he returned, the Pope took the soil in his hands and squeezed it until there dripped from it the blood of the martyrs of Trier, by which the penitent was absolved. As for Varus, he was condemned to become the municipal ghost of Trier. Sometimes he turns up in literature as a sad shade forced endlessly to roam the city, carrying out good deeds. Yet this is hardly in character. More lifelike are those portrayals which tell of a savage dog with dripping fangs, lurking in the shadows to bite the innocent and defenceless.

Not that cruelty vanished overnight with the renunciation by the Emperors of their ancient pantheon. Constantine saw the cross in the sky and gave the Christians their freedom of worship, but it was his cruelty which in the end brought Trier to its fate. One can walk the deserted and grass-grown amphitheatre of this imperial city and remember that it was there that Constantine sat with his Empress Minervina to watch the fun as Askarich, the handsome captive king of the Franks, walked out bravely into the arena, standing to face wild beasts crazed with hunger by planned starvation. With Askarich was his companion and stalwart brother-in-arms Merogais, and these two princes were followed by score upon score of Frankish victims. The Romans yelled and screamed with delight as the arena became strewn with more and more bodies, raw and torn and twitching. Certainly it was a memorable matinee, but it was also the beginning of the end of Roman might in Trier, for the Franks were to take terrible revenge. Three times within thirty years they fell upon the city, killing and burning, wrecking and pillaging until little but rubble and ashes remained where once the glory of Gaul had stood, proud, supreme, 'reaching almost to the stars.'

The *Thames Commodore* is all the while lying at anchor below the Marcusberg, hinting that we have only covered two pages of the course as drawn on the Moselle chart published jointly by the German and French navigation authorities. A further twenty-six sheets remain to be sailed before we reach the Rhine, and it must surely be time to turn the windlass and pull up the hook. But she must be patient, for one cannot leave Trier without at least a glance at the cathedral. Yet to venture inside the Dom is to be so engulfed in a sea of church history and architecture that with the ship due to sail we shall stay outside. The fact that the building is as usual under repair makes this easier.

Trier and its Dom are inseparable from the Holy Coat, said to be the seamless coat for which the guards diced at the foot of the cross. It was brought from Rome in 326 by Constantine's mother St Helena, along with other relics which she acquired in her tireless travels in search of objects of reverence. She made over the coat to the Bishop of Trier, and it was placed in a vault between the towers of the cathedral. There it remained for more than eight centuries, but in 1196 it was removed to a reliquary within the new high altar.

The coat is mentioned in the early medieval epic of King Orendel, legendary monarch of Trier:

> *er wart gewurkt zware*
> *von eines schönen lambes hare.*
>
> *Wove it was, from the hair of a fine lamb.*

'*Here, nu envar uns nit mere,*' cried the pilgrims in those distant times. 'Lord, never more leave us.' And slowly they would file past the grey woollen garment brought by St Helena. Then again the coat was hidden away and not until 1512 did it make another appearance. More than one hundred thousand pilgrims streamed into the city to see it, and from then on the appearances were a little more frequent. But the Thirty Years War and the French Revolution so threatened its survival that it was hidden in Ehrenbreitstein fortress, in Augsburg, in Bohemia, and wherever it might be safe. At last when Napoleon had come and gone the coat was brought back from exile and this time a quarter of a million pilgrims poured into Trier to view it. In 1933 it was again placed on view as a reminder to the people of some of the values which appeared to be vanishing so rapidly, and after that it had to wait until 1959. Nowadays it is likely to be shown only once during the lifetime of each bishop, but with cars, special trains, coaches, Luxembourg airport and even river boats to bring visitors, their numbers are more likely to run into millions.

Although the Holy Coat is not on view, one may see outside the cathedral another curious object, a slightly tapered shaft of bluish stone lying prostrate beside the main portal. The stone has just the right slope to make it a good slide for small boys, and its hard surface has been worn silk-smooth by generations of young trousers. This stone is the Domstein, and it is actually part of one of the four great pillars which held the roof of the original Roman church, split and shivered when the burning cathedral collapsed during one of the onslaughts of the terrible Franks. Fragments of the others form a rough group in the cloister garden, and around them are buried the centuries of cathedral dignitaries.

The boys who even now will slide down the obliging length of the Domstein may not all be able to sing the traditional song, the *Lied vom Duhmstaan*, but at least they know all about the stone, and just how that massive piece of rock came to be there. A broken column? Certainly not. It was never part of the cathedral at all. Not quite.

When the great cathedral of Trier was being built, the master mason was short of workmen and transport. A resourceful man, he decided to ask the devil for his help, and knowing the fiend to be somewhat averse to church architecture he told him that the city fathers were building an immense drinking-hall, but that the project was unfortunately held up for lack of stone. Satan was delighted to hear of this imaginative piece of town planning, and he volunteered to help. For months he worked away with great energy, cutting and squaring blocks of sandstone along the sides of the valley, and hauling them to the site. Indeed, he worked so hard that the mason reckoned him the most conscientious labourer of all.

As time went by, the building was nearly ready. Occasionally a side-chapel was added or an altar was put in position, but whenever the devil asked what these things might be the builder concocted a suitable tale. The chapels were for private boozing parties, the altar-like slabs were gaming tables, he said. So the devil — a simple fellow, one might think — continued to work, pleased at the prospect of a really flourishing palace of vice.

It occurred to the mason that the fiend could hardly be expected to stand mutely through the consecration service without making a scene, so he summoned him and explained that a particularly large block of stone was needed for some very special purpose which I have forgotten. Perhaps it was to be for the select bar.

Satan was impressed and said he would fix it, so the mason quickly added that he wanted this particular stone to be bluish, of just such rock as one might find far away beyond the Rhine, in the Odenwald.

Off went the devil, and as soon as he was well on his way to the country beyond the Rhine the clergy and people were quickly called together. The bells were rung, and the service of dedication began.

If the clergy were hurrying, so was the devil. Poor fellow, he was in such urgent haste to have the public amenity finished and open that he decided to return by air, bringing the rock with him. As he came gliding down over the Hunsrück forest he could already hear that dreadful sound, the clanging of church bells. Realizing that he had again been tricked he soared up to a great height and threw, aiming the rock to strike the Dom itself — and if he were lucky the clergy too, and the deceitful master-mason for good measure. But he had never been an accurate missile-aimer, and when the vast piece of rock struck it did so immediately beside the main portal with its statues of three of his particular enemies — Eucharius, Valerius and Maternus. And there it has remained ever since.

III

SHIPBUILDING is known to have been an activity in Trier as
far back as the year 289, when the Emperor Maximian had
some ships built at a Trier yard to add to the fleet which was to
sail to Britain to attack the renegade Carausius, and these Roman
craft ranged from ships the length of the *Thames Commodore* —
though with only two-thirds her beam — to eighty-footers. As we
sailed away from the modern city of the *Treviri* we found that the
new Class V waterway had already brought fresh prosperity to an
ancient local trade, for on the right bank below the town a shipyard
was hammering and clattering at the hull of a new Europa-ship
on the stocks. At our next visit a pair of heavy barges were under
construction, and when once again we passed that way there was
a Rhine car-ferry nearly complete. Only a week later we met her on
her trials further down the Moselle, travelling so fast that we
could not hang on her skirts.

To leave Trier must always be unwelcome, but at least the exit
by river is a pleasant one. To port the tall cliffs of red sandstone
tower above the valley, but soon they fall away and one glides
past the pretty waterside village of Pfalzel (km. 187 L), where
indeed a small palace or its remains are to be seen, right along the
shore. For this was once the residence of the Archbishop-Electors
of Trier, and before them of Frankish kings and of the Roman
governor. Palatiolum it was, Pfalzel it is, the home of the Klosterschenke or 'convent-tap' boat which so obligingly lent us its jetty
at Trier.

Of the convent itself there remains the church, and also a strange tale of a nun who played a particularly ingenious trick on the Archbishop. With the assistance of the devil she made a most unusual cope or cloak which she then presented to him. Upon wearing it he was immediately flooded with terrible carnal desires and felt as though he was being dragged off to hell, but being a strong-minded man he promptly took off the garment and handed it to one of his attendants, then to another. Each in turn was seized with the same lecherous longings.

This would never do, the Archbishop thought, and so he had the nun ejected from the convent. But it then appeared that each nun was as bad as her sister, and having begun the clearance in the interest of institutional purity the Archbishop had to carry through his purging until the whole institution had been emptied. And that, says the tale, was how the convent of Pfalzel came to an end; but the English traveller Octavius Rooke, who descended the Moselle by coach more than a century ahead of our own voyage, remarked darkly that 'the garment, however, still exists and is worn by many.'

But Pfalzel is also the scene of the legend of the fair Genoveva, the pure and beautiful wife of the Count Siegfried, who was coveted and hungered after by the wicked bailiff Golo. Continually repulsed he managed like Iago to poison the mind of the husband, but at least Siegfried did not strangle his guiltless wife. Instead, he merely drove her out of the castle to die of hunger or as the prey of wild beasts — which one must assume to have been boars, or conceivably wolves.

So generous by nature was Genoveva that she did not wish her husband to be guilty of her death, so as she left home she took off her ring and flung it into the Moselle, not from anger but merely to release him from his vows — for in those days marriages could be dissolved without further ceremony than that. Then she disappeared into the night, and no doubt Siegfried thought he was well rid of her.

The months passed, and then it happened that Count Siegfried was out hunting. At the end of the day he pitched camp with his retinue somewhere beside the river. In deference to the presence of their lord, two fishermen came to the camp and presented him with a splendid fish which they had just taken in their net. When the creature was cleaned for the pot the cook found in its gut a ring, which proved to be that of Genoveva.

Certain that she had been drowned, the count was overcome by a mixture of satisfaction and remorse, and when at last he fell asleep he dreamed of Genoveva in all her loveliness and beauty — but, alas, she was being pursued by a horrible dragon. He told the dream to Golo, who advised him to forget it. Yet only a few nights later the count had an even more distinct dream, one in which he saw a hind of purest white fleeing through the forest before a relentless huntsman whose only thought was to hound the creature to its death. Waking suddenly with a sense of horror, Siegfried was certain that the albino deer must be Genoveva, and himself the cruel man hunting the defenceless creature to kill it. Calling his men, he ordered everything to be made ready for a hunting party. There was no time to be lost.

The retainers must have been surprised at this irrational demand, but they did as they were told, and at first light the party set off with Count Siegfried in the lead. Sure enough, they had not ridden far from Pfalzel when a white doe was started from cover. The Count spurred his horse in pursuit, and racing after the creature he at last came within range and let fly an arrow. The hind faltered, then seemed to summon a final burst of energy, for it bounded ahead into a thicket and there fell, exhausted. It collapsed at the feet of Genoveva herself, who was huddled in the entrance of a rough cave, crouched on a bed of branches and moss, her little child clutched to her bosom.

Siegfried flung himself on the ground and begged her forgiveness, which she freely gave. The doe which had kept her alive with its milk lay dying, but now Genoveva was taken back in triumph to her castle. As for the baby boy, the inheritance of the Count's own features dismissed any doubts about his parentage, and he was later to become the Count Palatine of the next generation. Golo very rightly came to a well-merited end, and his head was exhibited on the castle battlements as a warning to any who might feel inclined to bear false witness against another. And although the villain has been forgotten, the cave is still to be seen on the Hochburg hill behind Pfalzel.

Hardly are the walls of the old Electoral residence of Pfalzel astern than the river bends away to the left. On the right bank a stream running swift from the hills pours a reddish brown flood into the Moselle, and it evidently also carries something which delights the Moselle fish, for at the confluence we found a host of anglers, not sitting sleepily on the shore but wading out knee-deep and actually hooking fish as we passed them. They were not big fish, but for a good Moselle fry one only needs small ones, perhaps a dozen or more to the pound. No doubt they would end up that same evening fried deep, and bread-crumbed, and washed down with a good glass or two not of Moselle but of Ruwer, for the modest stream which here joins the main river is the Ruwer itself (km. 185·6 R), the name of which is spread round the world and known to any who may be curious enough to read the classification markings on bottles of exported wine. 'Mosel-Saar-Ruwer' it runs, even if the wine is certain to be Moselle — for I doubt if the vintners on the slopes of the Ruwer produce more wine than their private customers can consume; and as for the Saar wines, the mere name would weigh too much against them in countries which think of the Saar in terms of coal. But the Ruwer wine is certainly good in its own right, even if that right is limited.

The village at the confluence is also called Ruwer, and it is so bound up in its own private stream that it does not bother to offer a frontage to the Moselle, or put out a jetty for any possible visitor by water. The only time I went there was when I left Trier to follow the Moselhöhenweg.

The Moselhöhenweg (or Moselle heights trail) is as its name suggests a foot-trail which follows the hill crests all the way from Trier to Koblenz. It leaves Trier in a district known as Tabaks-mühle and heads first for Ruwer by one of the most horrid city exits a path could have, for it passes by railway sidings, cement dumps, a sewage works and some down-at-heel allotments, so that one might think oneself in an outer London suburb. The trail is badly marked, which is not altogether surprising, for it leads straight through an encampment of the sort of families about whom no questions are asked — or, if asked, are answered with a flash of a knife. There are dirty hens, mangy dogs, large second-hand cars and flashy caravans. There are children too, in decidedly unplanned quantity, dark-eyed and Mediterranean and with attractive features under the dirt; and men leaning on whatever is handy, as such men do. I always find the best defence is to stare them out of countenance, advancing straight towards them. No man stared out of countenance will do more than shift his feet, look away, and perhaps spit.

I have never seen such a murderous-looking collection of men as inhabit the land beyond the Tabaksmühle of Trier, and I was glad to leave them behind and have the smell of mere sewage instead. But at Ruwer the path turned away from the Moselle, and a little way up the side-street I stopped and bought an ice, for it was a very hot afternoon. I asked the two women in the shop which way the footpath went, towards Fastrau.

Fastrau? A footpath? If I meant the motor-road . . .

I said I did not mean the motor-road. I meant the trail, which was marked with a capital M, for Moselhöhenweg.

They had never heard of a footpath. There was a road down the main valley, and another up the Ruwer, and of course there was the railway track. That was all. As for these mysterious Ms I was talking about, they had lived there all their lives and there were no such signs in Ruwer, the two women assured me.

From experiences in the Black Forest I was not surprised at the answer, but I pointed out of their doorway and indicated an M in white paint on the house opposite.

'M! Yes, an M! Well, fancy that. It must be something new,' said one of the women. 'I haven't seen it there before.'

I pointed out that the paint was already beginning to peel a little. Obviously it was some years old.

The other woman nodded. Come to think of it, she had seen the M on the wall since a while back, perhaps years as I said. 'But I never knew what it was,' she said. 'I thought it must be something to do with the government.'

I did not bother them further, but decided to follow such rare signs as there were and trust to my map — which turned out to be very far from accurate. But I had soon climbed right up to the highland of the forest and plodded ahead through the woods of pine or beech, continually coming to lumber-roadways or trails which my map ignored. After an hour or more I dropped into a dell, and there I met a gnome. At least he looked like a gnome, though he had exchanged his red-bobbled cap for a battered pork pie. Certainly he had the familiar reddish face and nervous features and thick glasses which all the better gnomes have. He was about five feet in height, or rather less, and he was standing at the edge of a rusty-looking swamp. Beside him were a brief-case and five wine-bottles. He started as I trod on a dry stick, then smiled in a shy way.

I then noticed that close by where he stood a small jet of water was issuing from a little copper pipe. I had long been waiting to find a spring, as I was extremely thirsty, so I crouched down, filled my hands and took a draught.

It would not be fair to the Sauerbrunnen to say that the water tasted like London water after the plumbers have been in. It was decidedly more chemical than that. But it was also deliciously cool, and so fizzy that the warmth of my hands made it bubble and simmer.

'*Kohlensäure*,' said the gnome, watching me savour the peculiar tang of the spring water. 'Carbonic acid gas, And iron, and I do not know what other minerals. It is good for the circulation, the liver, the digestion, the metabolism. Very, very good indeed. People come from far and near to drink of the source.'

I said the water tasted quite pleasant, at least when one was as thirsty as I was. And I took several more gulps.

'I come along to fill my bottles,' said the gnome, pointing to them. 'Five bottles, enough for two days. Every second day I come and fill them, summer and winter alike, in the heat or in rain, or in snow and ice. The water makes me healthy, you see. *Es macht gesund.*'

I asked the gnome where he lived, and he told me he came up from Schweich with his bottles. Every second day, summer and winter alike he brought them up, filled them, and returned home.

Glancing at my map I saw that Schweich was some five miles away, across the Moselle.

'I don't think it's the water which is so beneficial,' I said. 'Anybody would be healthy if they trailed ten miles through the woods every second day, carrying a load of empty bottles up the hill and about fourteen pounds of mineral water and glass down again.'

He considered. 'Perhaps you are right,' he said, rather to my surprise. 'Of course, the exercise must be good for the heart, the liver, the circulation, the metabolism.' He looked at the spring with a very serious air. 'Yes, yes. No doubt the walking is good for me. But do you not think it may also be true that if I did not continually have the water of the Sauerbrunnen to give me health the exercise would kill me?'

I was hardly familiar enough with the geriatrics of gnomes to answer this one. But I could see that in one way he was right, for in the Sauerbrunnen he had something to live for, this little ancient of days in the macintosh and squashed hat. One day he was fetching the water, the next he was drinking the bottles empty so that he could trail up through the woods again, true to the time-table by which his life was regulated. To tramp up for a refill might not be much to look forward to, but I could see it was quite enough for him. He was contented, happy in a quiet kind of way. And as for his heart, liver, circulation and metabolism, perhaps they would have won prizes anywhere.

Saying farewell to the gnome I left him to fill his bottles and struck downwards through the forest. Every trail seemed to fade out into a thicket, and soon I was lost. But trying to direct myself by the direction of the shadows I at last broke out of the woods above a little vintners' village, which turned out indeed to be Fastrau, and following a track through the vines I came upon the smiling hamlet of Riol, standing well back from the Mosel shore (km. 174 R). All the land falling gently from the woods toward the river seemed to be decked with orchards, for Riol is one of the homes of the fruit from which the Trierers make their *Viez*.

De Viez dat is ä liewen Trank,
Hen ess mir liewer als de Wein.

There spoke a proper Trierer, a man who found Viez a lovely

drink and preferred it to wine. And the Pfalzelers seem to appreciate it too, for in that village it is said that

Eine Poorz Viez und ein Viertelchen Käs
Machen keinen Pfalzeler bös.

I first met Viez when two American friends who were on board our ship decided to take a car to see the Igel memorial and the valley of the Saar. When the driver took his leave he thrust into my hands two bottles without labels. Each contained a litre of some clear liquid. I sniffed at the corks.

'It is Viez,' said the driver. 'You will like it. You cannot come to Trier without drinking Viez. All true Trierers drink Viez.'

'Is it a wine?'

'No, it's Viez.' And with that he waved himself away.

Viez is a coarse and somewhat strong cider, and in Trier it is served in a particular species of white earthenware mug called a Poorz. So the lines above can now be translated something like this:

'A mug of cider and a hunk of cheese
Will never make a Pfalzeler sour.'

A Poorz of Viez, these homely earthy words have a truly Moselle sound about them, and yet they have travelled a long way down the scale of the centuries. Perhaps Ausonius himself may sometimes have sampled a mug of the drink on his visits to Trier — for in Poorz lies the Latin *portio* and in Viez the *vice vini* or wine substitute. But however that may be, the modern Treviri are so addicted to this drink — and that within a few miles of some of the best vineyards in the world — that others along the valley refer to them as 'Viezbrüder.'

As I picked my way between the rows of apple trees at Riol the fruit lay heavy on them, but not yet ripe for the presses. Wasps were busy everywhere, but in the village itself only a few hens were shuffling their feathers in the dust and a group of children were playing a kind of hopscotch. A dog lay in the shade, panting, but otherwise the place seemed deserted. Riol was waiting until the apple harvest, when the presses would again run with the golden juice and the village would resound with bustle and laughter, the creak of wains and the throb of tractors.

Riol is not spectacular. It is just an orchard hamlet with an air of old age about it, for indeed it is of long standing. Long ago it was Rigolodunum, and above the village there probably lies the site of the battle in which, according to Tacitus, the Treviri were annihilated in 70 A.D. Valentinus was their commander, and his forces were gathered behind earth ramparts at the edge of the Hunsrück plateau overlooking the Moselle. They waited, uneasy — and unwisely. At length the dreaded Roman column could be seen marching along the valley, a long thread of blocks of precision, the arms flashing in the sunlight. Below Riol they halted, turned from the valley and marched straight up the sloping ground towards the earthen ramparts the Treviri had raised. Volleys of stones and sticks met them, arrows and spears were hurled at them, but the disciplined troops did not halt. In mechanical tempo they marched up and over the banks of the fortification to strike down those early people of the Moselle, or to make them captive and drag them down to the valley, to slavery. Escape was impossible, for just when flight seemed to be the only solution the Roman horsemen appeared behind the positions, riding down from the Hunsrück heights. The Treviri were to pass from history, only Valentinus being accorded the calculated ignominy of execution in Rome itself.

Beyond Riol the Moselle trail plunges into fir-woods so steeply ranged on a northern slope that they rarely see the sun. The forest was refreshingly cool after the baking of the mid-afternoon, and a tang of resin hung in the air, mixed with a musty smell of fungus. As the path traversed the hillside I came to a clearing, from which far down to the left I could see a Europa-ship pushing powerfully up the river, throwing off to either side a broad wave, which trailed away into a pattern of symmetrical sloping ribs like a child's drawing of a Christmas tree. The sun awning was stretched over the captain's quarters, and I could just make out the jet of water where one of the hands was playing the hose over the steel deck to keep it cool. Astern of the ship the village of Mehring was clumped along the further shore at the foot of an immense expanse of vineyards. Striking down through the wood and over lush meadows of damp grass I came to the river bank, and judging that I was far enough distant from any villagers who had not binoculars I quickly stripped all my clothes and plunged into the Moselle to freshen myself before crossing the bridge to find a hotel for the night.

But before entering Mehring we must retrace our steps. The Moselhöhenweg has cut off a wide bend of river below Ruwer, so we shall have to return aboard ship and make our way down the valley, this time by water.

At Ruwer the Moselle swings through nearly a quarter of a circle to flow due north across a plain of its own past making, a wasteland not unlike the gravel-pitted expanse by Konz. The city of Trier was quick to realize that it was to have an outlet to Rotterdam and thence to all the world, and so in this flat land it excavated a mighty inland port (km. 184) with warehousing and dock-side railway, silos and harbour offices, and everything except the humblest inn or the simplest means of transport to the world outside. It is a fine harbour, but only for those who are content to stay aboard ship and have no contact with landlubbers, for the nearest place — apart from a NATO barracks dropped in the same dismal desert — is Ehrang, so long a walk across a dusty and bulldozed landscape that it is better left unvisited.

Yet the *Thames Commodore* always likes to push her nose into inland ports, just to see who is there. Like launderettes and public libraries, inland ports are excellent centres of gossip, and she can be certain that sooner or later she will discover an old friend lying at a quayside to load or discharge. And so it proved in the great new inland port of Trier-Ehrang, for she had hardly swung into the entrance than she saw lying against a length of the smooth cream-coloured quay the *Wilhelm Droste*. She drew cautiously alongside, so that I might lean across to knock on the cabin door and call to Kapitän Booz to show a leg. This he eventually did, somewhat sleepy and still in his pyjamas, because his ship had only made port late the night before.

The *Wilhelm Droste* was as bright and colourful as usual. Her anchor-buoys hung by the winch were picked out in triangles of red and blue and yellow. All along the 300 feet of her smooth

torso the paint gleamed and the brass shone in the morning sun.
It was four years since I had shaken the skipper by the hand, for
our encounters had usually been fleeting ones on the Rhine, or by
Remich bridge in Luxembourg, or in Alsace. On those occasions
there had only been time for the briefest exchanges as the two
craft sped by in opposite directions.

'*Wo geht es hin?*'

Rheinfelden, then Besançon in the Jura, we would hail back.
'*Und sie?*'

'Rotterdam. *Auf wiedersehen,*' his hailer would shout.

'*Gute Fahrt!*'

These encounters were typical of the social visits bargemen
might pay to each other, the whole being transacted in the few
seconds that the distance between the ships was not too great.

Sometimes a lock might offer the chance of ten minutes of chat, but that was unusual — particularly on the Moselle, where craft were always ranged head to tail.

As Captain Booz now for the first time could greet the *Thames Commodore* at close quarters I reminded him of a remark he had once made, one which I have often quoted to waterway societies in Britain and had even relayed to one of the Ministers of Transport particularly obsessed with the notion that commercial carrying by canal was a thing of the past, a waste of time and energy. The captain remembered the occasion as well as we did ourselves, and he had every reason to do so, for the old *Commodore* had been the first ship to make a social call upon his own vessel.

Four years before this encounter in the new port of Trier we happened to be lying in the little harbour of Bodenwerder on the Weser, when one day the *Wilhelm Droste* crept cautiously in, stern first, her bulk filling the entire entrance. She was decked out overall with fir branches and ribbons, for this was to be her maiden voyage and she was bound for the Rhine, taking on or discharging stone at various points on the route to match her draught or her freeboard to each of the waterways in turn through which she was to pass. She had been built on the Weser, right there at Boden-werder, and they had had to take her forty kilometres up river to find a place wide enough for her to turn and head downstream toward her future as a busy Europa-ship.

Captain Booz welcomed us aboard and was delighted to show us proudly over his fine new vessel. Stepping carefully in our stockinged feet so as not to put a particle of dust upon the floor we admired the push-button cooker, the oil-fired central heating, the bathroom and saloon, in fact all the fitments of what might have been a large modern flat.

Then the captain walked round the harbour with us, and taking off his shoes he came down the old *Commodore's* companionway to see how life went on in a really small craft. It happened to be one of those years when Britain nearly but not quite succeeded in entering the Common Market, and at the time we were lying in Bodenwerder it was assumed to be a foregone conclusion that she would be admitted.

'So, now that Britain is joining the Common Market I shall bring the *Wilhelm Droste* to Birmingham,' said Captain Booz. 'That will be the day!'

It would indeed, I thought. The *Wilhelm Droste* was more than four times the length of the locks on the Grand Union Canal, one of Britain's 'large' waterways. She was twice as broad too. I had to tell Captain Booz that the idea was a good one, but not practicable. When I told him the dimensions of the waterways of Britain he thought I was being comic.

Now, four years after our first meeting, Britain was still not in the Common Market, the Grand Union Canal to Birmingham was still just as it had been in the days of the horse-drawn barges of the early nineteenth century — except that the barges on it were even fewer than before. I never thought the chances of Captain Booz pulling in at a Birmingham quayside were very great, but now they looked even more slender.

'Well, if I shan't see you in Birmingham we'll meet again,' I said. '*Auf Wiedersehen. Gute Fahrt.*'

And meet again we did, that same year, in a waterside inn at Emmerich, where we had landed to clear the customs. Captain Booz had decided to stick to the Rhine and its connections and leave the British Waterways to narrow-boats of smaller capacity.

From its northward course the river swings east again at Quint (km. 181·5 L), a village with a very un-Germanic name which in fact is no more than an abbreviation of *ad quintum lapidem*, the fifth milestone from Trier along the valley road of the Romans. Issel (km. 179·5 L, *Insula* of the Roman era) lies ahead, a village with the chapel of St George so close down by the water that its weather-vane and mellow walls bob and writhe inverted on the wash of passing ships. To port the heights of the Meulenwald lie a mile or two back from the river, but to starboard the abrupt cliff of the Angelberg lowers over the valley. In its face was once secured the end of the cable for the Schweich ferry, and though this has long ceased to ply across the water it has at least left its beautiful tower on the bank opposite (km. 178·2 L), a neat and serious-looking hexagon with a handsome pointed hat and the ferryman's lodgings attached.

It was a wise Elector of Trier, the Archbishop Clemens Wenzeslaus, who built the tower and installed the ferry, and it was at this crossing that the ferryman is said once to have had a remarkable passenger. He had taken aboard a friar in a heavy cloak and cowl, and the boat was already pushed out into the river, when it sank almost to the gunwales, as though a pair of laden wains were aboard and not just the sole passenger who had called to the ferryman with the familiar Moselle cry of '*Hol iwer!*'

'I would dearly like to know what you are carrying under your habit,' the ferryman said goodnaturedly as he manoeuvred the steering oar.

The friar opened his cloak just enough for the ferryman to see inside.

'God forgive me,' cried the ferryman, for so fearful a thing he had never seen in all his life. White-hot from the blast-furnaces of hell a man stood there within the cloak, firmly held in the grasp of the friar, who was uncharred and unharmed. 'God forgive me!' And he plied his oar to slant the craft so that the current would strike on the port side and push the float quickly over the river to the Schweich bank.

For the ferryman knew very well who that glowing figure must be. Complete in the trappings of an official of third century Rome it was none other than Rictius Varus, the same who had slaughtered the Christians until the happy river was stained dark all the way to Neumagen.

It seems that the Bishop of Trier had been returning home late when the city ghost tried to frighten him as a black shadow of horror across his path. The good Bishop Matthias von Eyss was not a man to be easily scared even by the most evil of spirits, and he was certainly not one to be trifled with in such a way. He thought the matter over during the night, and the very next morning he summoned a devoted friar and ordered him to catch the evil spirit and deport it.

Festbannen was a practice often used by priests in the Moselle towns; it was not exactly exorcism but more a sort of compulsory rooting to the spot. The Bishop had this in mind for Rictius Varus, and he told the friar to convey the shade of the Roman governor

to the Meulenwald forest behind Schweich and fix him there so
that he might never escape. That was how the good man (who in
some versions of the tale was the worthy Bishop Matthias himself)
came to board the ferry with his heavy load. All such wicked
spirits were heavy, either because of the sheer weight of their evil,
or else because in some cases the priests enclosed them in a full
suit of leaden clothes so that they could not run away — as was
done with the town ghost of Remich, further upstream.

If that is what the Schweichers know for certain about their
ferry, and how Rictius Varus came to cross it into perpetual
banishment, they will add that in the depths of the Meulenwald
one may yet hear the Roman official roaming by night through the
forest, chased by the terrors of hell — but only within the limits
of the territory assigned to him by the friar. As for the ferry, it no
longer exists. A bridge has taken its place, and the tower of
Clemens Wenzeslaus has become not a ruin but a small shop to
cater for the needs of the campers along the bank. Beside it is a
landing-stage, and on this we drew in for the night so that on the
following day we might visit Schweich.

Of all places on the Moselle, Schweich is probably the dullest.
Somehow it was largely destroyed during the Second World War,
but there is no evidence that it was ever more beautiful than it is
now. Indeed I was surprised at its lack of charm, for I had already
met the gnome from Schweich, and I believed these little people
to like more attractive places. But here at least on the left bank
the fruit-trees give way to vines, the rows rising steeply to the
wooded hill-tops. And very ancient this industry of the local
vintners must be, for when King Pepin gave the rights over
Schweich to the abbey at Prüm he laid down in the charter that
the village had to deliver five *Fuder* of wine annually to the abbot.
A *Fuder* varies somewhat from place to place, but is rather more
than 200 gallons. So a tithing of the wine was expected to yield
one thousand gallons — and that was in 762.

The Meulenwald in which Rictius Varus was confined is the
most excellent place for evil spirits, goblins, kobolds and other
denizens of the dark forest, but on its slope behind Schweich
there also sprang forth the 'Holy Spring' which was such an

attraction in the seventeenth century. From far and near the
people came, some by wagon from Cologne and the Rhineland,
others by way of the prosperous Schweich ferry, and still more by
ship. Healthy and sick, blind and crippled or just out for a few
days of adventure outside the walls of a convent or monastery, the
lay and clerical alike streamed towards the spring. Shipmasters
did good business, and so did the innkeepers and caterers, the
stallkeepers and candle-sellers and all those who knew a com-
mercially useful place of pilgrimage when they saw one. A whole
village of booths sprang up as a semi-permanent fair, and the
visitors were relieved of any money they had to spare. It was like
the pool of Siloam, a contemporary ecclesiastic wrote. The water
issued 'thick as a walnut' from two brass pipes, but so great were
the crowds that any who wished to drink its healing virtue had
to queue for a quarter of an hour. Any man determined to fill a
barrel to take home with him had to wait until late at night, else
the impatient crowd might press and trample him to death.
'Never was there such deception and foolishness,' he wrote.

Schweich on the left bank, Longuich on the right (km. 176 R),
the river broadens and deepens as it runs towards the foot of Riol.
Longuich (Longus vicus) has a bridge of its own, and it had added
a landing-stage only a few days before our arrival. Gay with
wreaths and flags, it invited us to pull in and visit the Wine
Festival, which we did. It was one of those simple village affairs
with a brass band and Bratwurst, the vintages of last year on tap,
a shooting gallery, a row of swing-boats and all the boys and girls
brushed and combed and in their Sunday best — for it was in
fact a Sunday. It was all very happy, very orderly, and a notice
above the swing-boats said that rides were not permitted to drunks
or those suffering from nervous diseases. But as there will be more
time for wine festivals further down the river we had better leave
Longuich before the Klosterschenke boat arrives and wants to
use the landing-stage.

Ahead the Moselle appears as a mountain lake, for on the bend
beyond Riol the hills to either side close in so tightly that they
almost nip it off. In fact they cut its width by nearly half, and to
starboard the steep slopes of the Hunsrück are darkly wooded

with pines, while oak and beech flourish on the cliff-tops, and walnuts are dotted among the little fields at the edge of Mehring (km. 171·8 L), and the little town itself has a reminder that the bridge is a new fangled method of crossing the water, for here again a handsome ferry tower built by the same Elector Clemens Wenzeslaus stands four-square beyond the roadway which sweeps along the water's edge on the new promenade of the International Moselle Company.

Mehring, Pölich (km. 168·5 L) and Schleich (km. 166·5 L) lie as close neighbours along the left bank of the wriggling course of the river. Each is concerned only with wine-growing, and is grouped as tightly as possibly on the narrow flat land at the foot of the shaly slopes. Opposite them there is no village all the way from Riol to Detzem, for either the cliffs leave room only for the track of the little Moselle valley railway, or the Pölichers have managed to perch some precarious vineyards upon them where the slope is such that a man can just manage to scramble up it.

These villages cannot have changed much over the centuries. Hoeing, tying, gathering the grapes and pressing, the work of the vintner has only altered inasmuch as there are now synthetic sprays, and tractors with cable and pump attachments. Horses no longer pull the wains laden with barrels, but wine and love and paying taxes — if now to the Bundesrepublik instead of the abbeys of Prüm, or Himmerode, or St Maximin's in Trier — are still the annual round. Only the plague has gone, longer ago than the horse, and the executions which were such a feature of the medieval scene are no longer an entertainment. Instead, the vintner's family can watch Wild Western gunmen shoot people down on the television.

How justice was administered in Schleich is set out with admirable detail in one of its documents. The abbot had the right to put any accused man of the village in the stocks for three days and nights, and then for a similar period in the tower if none could be found to go bail for him. So six days passed, and on the seventh the executioner was summoned to put the man on the rack and stretch him until everything that was to be known had been revealed. If he should plead guilty, he was then delivered to the bailiffs of the town, who were to sentence him according to his deserts. It is pleasant to think that this was so, but much depended on the notion of what one really deserved, and in medieval times one was fortunate to escape with a mere chopping off of hands with an axe.

Probably the victim would be sentenced to death — not so much from a desire for revenge, but for the pragmatic reason that public example was considered an excellent thing and thus became a main plank of justice until comparatively modern times — and he would then be handed over to the executioner. The four sheriffs of the town conducted him out through the town gate, each of them armed as if for battle in case the poor man had friends who might try to snatch him from the authorities.

Thus the victim would be led away along the river towpath to where the wheel and gallows were erected, and there he would be effectively hanged, and his body would afterwards be placed on the wheel for the benefit of the crows. The cost of all these proceedings was to be paid out of the man's own estate, or failing that by his accuser. In the last resort it fell on the community; but not upon the sheriffs, who were rewarded by the abbot with an annual grant of wine to the extent of fifty gallons apiece, which they were to select to their own taste from the abbatial stock in the town. When they had decided upon the wine the court messenger was to climb upon the barrel, sit astride it, push his staff in through the bung-hole and stir the wine right down to the lees, so that each of the sheriffs would have as good or bad wine as his fellows, for everything where justice was concerned was done with the strictest impartiality and regard for the public good. For similar reasons, no doubt, the sheriffs were accorded free angling rights throughout the river. So the task of conducting men to their execution was not such a bad one after all.

Malefactors at Mehring were hoisted to the gallows on the Calvary Hill behind the town, where an old *Bildstock* or votive cross known as the Spinnerkreuz still recalls a curious event on the occasion of one of these public entertainments. A certain man of the town, named Spinner, was in the crowd which had gathered to watch the stringing-up ceremony, and the criminal had already been pulled up the ladder and the noose was even then being tied around his neck when Spinner remarked in a not very sympathetic voice that he would very much like to know what it felt like to be up there, ready to take the jump into a slow strangling death. His words were loud enough to be heard, and the victim did not miss them.

'Stop,' he cried, as the executioner tied the knot. 'Stop! I have an accomplice, and he should not go free.'

He pointed at the imprudently outspoken Spinner, who was at once seized by the sheriffs and taken away for examination, together with the condemned man.

Spinner swore by heaven and earth that he knew nothing of the matter, but his protestations did not impress his judges. They had the word of his confederate, who had nothing to gain by peaching on him. It did not take them long to declare Spinner guilty and sentence him to be hanged along with his fellow criminal.

So when the sheriffs returned to the waiting crowd on the Calvary Hill they now had two men to be hanged. As he was the minor criminal in the affair Spinner was to be hanged first, and he was dragged up the ladder, still protesting. The hangman placed the noose around his neck, and he was just about to be launched upon his slow transfer to another world, when once again his companion called out.

'Stop! Stop! He is innocent of the crime. I heard him say that he wondered what it felt like to be trussed for hanging, and I only wished to give him the opportunity. Now he knows.'

So in the nick of time Spinner was rescued. In gratitude he had the cross placed on the hill at the spot where he had stood under the gallows. And one may assume that if ever he went again to watch an execution he kept his mouth prudently shut.

IV

ANYWHERE but on the Moselle Mehring would rank as a
reasonably pretty village, but on this particular river it cannot
compete against other entrants in the beauty competition. It is
mostly new, and it has no very definite character. This is not its
own fault, for it must once have been a pleasant town not only
of vine-dressers but of shipping. Forest timber was once loaded
here for the Rhineland cities, and there was a hostelry for the
Halfen and their horses, where they might stop at the end of a day
of hard hauling on the tow-rope. There was an active band of
fishermen, and the town cows grazed contentedly on the wet riverside meadow which went by the pleasant nickname of Kühstanti-
nopel. But at last there came the fate which overtook most Moselle
villages, their houses packed tightly on the limited space available
between the foot of the hill and the edge of the river. The place
caught fire, and was burned from end to end. That was in 1840,
during the fair of St Medard, and the homeless either left the
town or built on the meadow. So things continued for a few years,
but in the 1850s the majority of the inhabitants threw in their hand
and took ship down the Moselle — not to some neighbouring
township, but bound for America.

So Mehring is not old architecturally. And if I found it somewhat unwelcoming when I arrived there after my swim in the
river this was perhaps my own fault. However that may be, I
walked round the town and entered every hotel and Gasthaus
without finding one where they were not sitting in half-darkness

watching football on the television — and this at supper-time in the middle of July. No doubt this is a foolish objection on my part, and perhaps I was brainwashed at Rugby into thinking soccer a silly game, but I would have liked it no better if it had been cricket. I like to see what I am eating, World Cup or no, and to have my meal without a commentator working himself up into paroxysms of excitement, or fury, or despair. But I am willing to admit that the emptiness of Mehring's streets and the fullness of its inns showed that I was very much in a minority of one. Indeed the staff in the hotel were themselves so preoccupied with watching the screen in the corner of the room that one course of my meal went by default.

My other irritation was, I think, more reasonable. I came down at eight o'clock for breakfast and found the whole house locked and silent. I could neither enter the lounge, nor the kitchen, nor even walk out through the front door. I had the run of my top-floor bedroom and its balcony, but otherwise it was a choice of sitting in the toilet or on a stone staircase. By making considerable noise I eventually roused a member of the household, but it was nearly nine o'clock before breakfast arrived. And nine in the morning is an hour by which most Germans seem already to have done half a day's work.

Mehring's vineyards have been hoed and raked, shaled and dunged for a long time indeed. Some of the slopes used to have Roman names, and more than one thousand years ago a register listed over fifty vintners. How many there are now I do not know, but the puff-puff-puff of their faithful diesel tractors on the hillside tracks showed that they were busy long before I could at last have my breakfast and leave the hotel. They were very anxious to help me find the path, but in this area it seemed to have no markings, and I was obliged to climb up through the vineyards and then make my way across the bare upland fields. Soon, however, the scenery improved, and the trail led through dark pinewoods, where the uppermost cones were creaking and cracking in the sunlight. One of the vintners had told me to watch for a little chapel and to leave it on my left. Sure enough I found it, a shrine perhaps eight feet square with a pewter candle-stand, two benches and a madonna. Inside a long legend in rhyme told how it had been built in 1860 by one Peter Lentes, burgher of Klüsserath down on the river, out of thankfulness for his threefold rescue. On three separate occasions he was *scheintot* or apparently dead, and on the last of these he had even been laid out for some hours in his coffin when by a great effort he silently implored help and was seen to move.

This experience of being nearly buried in error on three occasions would be enough to make any man erect a chapel. More curious was the fact that a century afterwards his little shrine, set miles from anywhere in the wilderness of the Eifel woods, should evidently be frequented. There were several vases of flowers, all of them fresh within a few days, phloxes and marigolds, clarkia and hydrangea, chrysanthemum, sweet william and ferns. How they came there I do not know, but somebody not only brought flowers but swept the floor and dusted the seats.

It is towards the end of the haul over the top from Mehring that the Moselle trail from Trier first begins to be really beautiful. It leads steeply downwards through tall beechwoods and suddenly bursts out at the top of the vineyards to look right down upon the bed of the river where Piesport faces across to Niederemmel. 'Weinort Piesport' is written across the bridge in letters large enough to be read a mile or more away, and yet for all its fame and its self-advertisement Piesport is the tiniest of places — perhaps because the soil of the sunlit slope is so valuable for vines that no space can be spared for anything but the most essential houses and the church. In fact many of the vintners live across the river, and always there are tractors coming and going over the Piesport and Niederemmel bridges, carrying tanks of spray, loads of poles, and sunburned wine-maidens with bunches of raffia to tie the shoots.

This land opposite is a broad piece of farming country round which the river turns a splendid bend. There are some vines, but there are orchards too, and fields of barley and wheat. And as one sits on the hill opposite and looks down upon the promontory so far below one realizes that the village to the right is none other than Neumagen. It is a common enough name in any land —

Nijmegen, Neumagen, Newmarket. But this particular Neumagen is the Noviomagus where Ausonius lived, and where he wrote the poem in praise of his beloved *Mosella*. And for that reason alone we must approach it by water.

The first lock below Trier is at Detzem, and at Pölich the barrage is already in sight — but only just, for such care has been taken to improve rather than spoil the Moselle scenery with the navigation works that very little is to be seen other than the pair of red or green lights signalling to downcoming vessels the state of the lock, and the line of piles against which they may lie to wait.

All along the Moselle valley one comes across stables for tow-horses, or the old cranes of Trier, or references to emigrants leaving by ship, and once there were even the services of fine old steamers such as the *Mosella* and the *Ville de Metz*. Indeed the river was a route for cargo and passengers from as far back as there are any records at all, yet in the late nineteenth century things changed. Shipping on the Moselle became virtually extinct — killed by the Prussian railways aided by the Moselle's own habit of alternating between droughts and floods, both of which made it impossible to undertake regular or planned voyages with sizeable ships. Instead of tow-trains of barges it was steam trains of steel trucks which carried the goods through the valley, trains hauled by splendid German locomotives with all the works on the outside, powerful puffers which left a heavy pall of brown-coal smoke to drift across the valley.

But after the Second World War the French began to push for the creation of an economically sound water link between the Ruhr and their own iron industry in Lorraine. 'Economically sound' meant that the waterway must have the certainty of water enough for laden Europa-ships under all conditions, and a minimal chance of flooding to a degree where navigation would have to be suspended. After long negotiations the International Moselle Agreement was concluded in 1956 between France, Germany and Luxembourg, by which a waterway was to be constructed all the way from Koblenz to Thionville, where it would connect with the already existing port basins and the Camifemo (*The Canal des Mines de Fer de la Moselle*).

The distance from Thionville to Koblenz is 270 kilometres, and along this course the river falls some 300 feet. Locks would be needed at intervals, but changing the river from a free-flowing stream into a series of pounds was not so simple. Villages might be close to the water. There was the fishery to be considered, street drainage in riparian towns, the water-table in the meadows, the production of electricity at the barrages. Besides, the Moselle was a valley of vintners, and vintners have a way of keeping their wine in cellars. Any considerable rise in the ground water would flood them, and so special steps had sometimes to be taken to isolate them, and to protect the foundations of buildings. Miles of roads and lanes had to be raised or shifted altogether, and villages close to the water protected with walls or banks. And all these works had to be carried out with an eye to the view down the valley and the natural beauty of an age-old river course, for the Moselle was one of the most alluring river valleys in Europe, and long before the Grand Tour days it was a favourite with visitors. If Ausonius and Venantius Fortunatus had written verses in praise of its beauty, that romance and charm was in no way diminished by the passage of time. There was no industry in the valley other than that of vintners and coopers, fruit farmers and woodmen, and innkeepers.

Difficult though this assignment was — quite apart from the mistrust and opposition of a somewhat conservative valley population — in less than eight years the whole waterway was complete. Rocks had been dynamited or chiselled away to the tune of one million lorry-loads, and more than twice the quantity of soil and sand and gravel had been removed by dredging. When the *Thames Commodore* made her first run down the river it had been open for nearly a year, and if in places the banks still looked bare they would not do so for long. Planting would continue over the next few years while the ships forged past on their way from the Rhine to Lorraine and back again, and indeed a year later the bareness of new-broken stone had disappeared. Already the Moselle wore her new clothes with ease and dignity.

The works eventually cost about eighty million pounds, of which Luxembourg was asked to pay only a very small share (about one quarter of one per cent) and the rest was shared by France and Germany on a two-to-one basis. Much of this sum was needed for the fourteen barrages and ship-locks, of which ten were on the German reaches. At each barrage there was also a small pen for cruisers and yachts, and a waterchute for canoeists. Ladders and stairs were provided for the fish and eels, so that the barrages would not prevent migration. As for the channel itself, this was from 130 to 260 feet broad with a minimum depth of nine feet all the way, and in spite of its immense loops, through the necks of which the railway ploughed so easily, the river itself was not short-circuited by cuts or tunnels, partly because the rock was not very suitable for drilling a canal through the hills, but also because there was a feeling on the part of the engineers that to take the Moselle or its water away from its own self-fashioned bed might well ruin the aspect of the valley.

Because such care was taken to keep as much as possible of the works below water the Moselle weirs themselves are not visible from upstream, and from below they appear only as a broad thin line of waterfall which may be increased to a thundering torrent in time of flood. And as there is no superstructure there is no bridge, and the public have no chance to view a ship using the lock except at Detzem (km. 166) where the end of the pen is crossed by a roadway running to a large island in midstream. This bridge is a favourite halt for the week-end visitors, and the *Thames Commodore* was always sure of an audience gathered to wave her on her way as she slipped out of the lower gates to pass the village.

Detzem itself (km. 165·5 R) is almost beside the lock, and just as Quint was the fifth Roman milestone so this village is *ad decimum*, the tenth. But not on the same road. Whereas Quint is on the old Roman trail which ran across the Eifel to Andernach, Detzem is on the valley track from Trier to Neumagen and Bingen. It is a village with a fine pointed spire of slate to its whitewashed church, which stands very stalwart on the rising ground at the top of the river bank. Behind the houses lie a few small fields, and beyond them vines, vines and more vines extend all the way to the top of the Alsberg.

We once stopped at Detzem on our way up the river. It was only

nine o'clock when we set out into the village, and the sky was not
yet fully dark. Walking up the alley past the church we found
ourselves in a main street with richly tanged manure-heaps in
front of the houses of the vintners. There was not a street-light
to be seen, nor even a glow in any window through the length of
the village. When one walks at night through a French hamlet one
can be sure of setting up a succession of howling dogs, the noise
running like a fuse from house to house until every inhabitant is
almost as wide awake as the dogs, but at Detzem the creatures
were either better fed or more placid by nature, or maybe they
tended to share the kindly and philosophical outlook of their
masters the vintners. Not a dog stirred, nor a cat, and I doubt if
there were any owls. The village slept on, unaware of our visita-
tion, dreaming only of what the weather would be on the following
day, the feast of St Lawrence.

> *Ist hell der Sankt Laurentius tag,*
> *viel Trauben er versprechen mag.*
> *Wie Sankt Laurentius sich verhält*
> *ist der ganze Herbst bestellt.*

> *If Lawrence day is bright and fine*
> *The year will bring a vintage wine.*
> *For as St Lawrence's indeed*
> *So all the autumn is decreed.*

St Laurentius (or Lawrence) is not the only patron of the vineyards, but he is one of the particular favourites of the vintners of
the Moselle. A courageous deacon of the early church, he was the
missionary link between the Pope, who was hidden in the Roman
catacombs, and the outside world. In the autumn of 258, under
the Valerian persecution, guards found their way into the galleries,
discovered the Pope and his four companions celebrating the
Eucharist, and slew them on the spot. The next day Laurentius
was tracked down as he went about his missionary task.

The Romans seem to have genuinely believed the Christians to
have vast riches and treasures hidden, probably in the catacombs,
and there was a rumour that Laurentius himself was keeper of the

hoard. No doubt this was because he was known to be continually distributing alms to the poor and needy. Taken before the judge he was first interrogated about the alleged treasures, and he at once said that he would produce them if given three days in which to collect them together.

At the end of the allotted time Laurentius appeared before the Roman judge with a crowd of beggars, broken-down old people, the sick and crippled.

'These are the treasures of the Christian Church,' he declared. 'These are its riches.'

It is said that Laurentius was slowly roasted to death on a grid-iron, and in that the Mosellaner sees his connection with the vine. For 'as St Lawrence roasted on the grid, so must the grape be heated by the glow of the shale.' And, of course, his day, 10 August, falls during the critical period of ripening, when every hour of heat and sunshine is vital to the success of the vintage. But the grape is of southern origin, and probably the story of his martyrdom spread up from the Mediterranean in the wake of the vines themselves.

Detzem and Thörnich to the right, Ensch and Klüsserath to the left, where the Moselle begins to swing through half a circle, the vintner villages cluster in such quick succession that they are almost continuous. Some have room enough to form a huddle of brownish houses, others are so confined by the river in front and the vines behind that the houses can only be strung along the shore in a single or double line. '*Lang wie Klüssert*,' they say on the Moselle. As long as Klüsserath (km. 162 L) with its magnificent south-facing hillside so green with vines that one can smell them in midstream, the aroma seasoned with the sulphur of the spraying.

Soft and gentle as the valley, so these villages lie mellowed along its shores, their houses blending so perfectly with the background of shale-covered slopes and bluffs of cream-brown rock that one can almost pass them by without noticing their presence. There may be a ferry to carry the vintners and their tractors to the further shore, but otherwise the villages have little contact with the world beyond the slope at their back, and none have any claim to fame until Trittenheim (km. 156 L), which lies beyond

F

the smooth rounded promontory of the Laurentiusberg, on which stands the chapel of St Lawrence, very white and capped with bluish-purple slate, set all alone among the vines.

This little chapel is one of the famous landmarks of the Moselle (km. 158·3 L). Originally it was merely a chapel in honour of the vineyard saint, but it became the parish church of Trittenheim when the terrible plague years of the mid-seventeenth century drove the people further and further back from the river and up the hillside. Those years are recalled by the plague-crosses still to be seen on the walls of the houses near the church and post office in Trittenheim, little thank-offering calvaries put up by those who were spared. There was the Black Death too, which took such fearful toll among the people that there were only seven couples left to erect seven crosses for their own deliverance.

At last the pestilences subsided, and such of the villagers as remained began to find the climb to St Lawrence's longer and longer — as indeed it was, for they themselves had removed back to the shore of the Moselle and freed the hillside for the vines. So a new church was built in Trittenheim itself, and for nearly two centuries St Laurentius stood half-forgotten until a couple rebuilt it in memory of their two boys killed in the First World War. But because of the sharp bend in the river this church and indeed the whole of Trittenheim is hidden from view until one has swung to port through half a circle to run down toward the bridge, at either end of which stands another of the plain but beautiful towers which once served to hold the ferry cable for the crossing.

The first time the *Thames Commodore* drew in at the jetty just above the bridge was on just such a hot summer's evening in August as would have delighted any vintner. One of the duties of friends invited for a voyage aboard the *Thames Commodore* is to set out immediately to beg some ice for the evening wine, for though the ship has in fact a refrigerator, at this time it was electric and we did not use it except when making long runs, because the consumption of current was too great. However, we had already discovered that the efficiency of the salesmen sent out by refrigerator makers was such that nearly every house in Europe had a deep-freeze containing trays of ice which were never used until the unexpected arrival of the *Thames Commodore's* runner, who appeared with an ice-bucket and asked if he might have some. People were always delighted to help us by providing ice, though sometimes the freezing trays were so tightly held in their own icebergs of a year's standing that it took some time to extract them.

Trittenheim was our first ice-call on the German Moselle, and I was at first surprised when our usually successful ice-hunters returned to report that there was no ice in Trittenheim. They had tried the inns, the wine-cellars, the postmistress, and had asked everyone they met on their way. The Trittenheimers had scratched their heads and suggested some possible ice-provider, but not one of the recommended houses turned out to have a refrigerator.

It then occurred to me that vintners did not need refrigerators. Every house had its own cellar for the tuns and bottles, and there *im kühlen Keller* vegetables or any other goods could be stowed which had to be kept cool for a while. In an exclusively wine-growing community such as Trittenheim, ice would be a great rarity. I was wondering whether we should not have to do without, when a broad and jolly-faced vintner walked out to the end of the jetty. He had with him his wife and a small boy, and having seen the Red Ensign on the stern they had decided to examine the ship more closely.

I asked the vintner about ice. He thought hard, and said that there was indeed a house with a refrigerator, so my wife and I set off with him and his family to find it. We soon discovered that the good lady had such a machine, but she had never filled the ice trays with water. What would be the point? Who wanted ice anyway, except in fancy drinks — and surely nobody would want vermouth or spirits when there was good Moselle wine to be had at a right temperature and straight from the cellar.

We apologised for the inane request. The business made us feel like Americans wanting iced water before their coffee.

'But you shall have ice,' said the vintner. 'I live not so very far out of Trittenheim, and we have ice in our freezer, I know.'

So off we went, heading out of Trittenheim in a downstream direction. The vintner talked such idiomatic English with a slight

Irish accent that we wondered how he could have come by it. He then explained that he had been a prisoner at Ludlow, where he had worked on the estate of an M.P. landowner for whom he had a great admiration. He had learned all his English there, and no doubt the Irish flavour had been picked up from one of his fellow-workers.

He had thoroughly enjoyed his time in England, not least because he had acquired a girl-friend who was a nurse at a London hospital. London was a long way from Ludlow, but he managed to visit her none the less. The guards at the camp were usually Home Guard men, he explained, kindly souls who were not particularly military by nature and who understood the natural inclinations of ordinary men. Particularly, he said, if they could get a good pair of boots as part of the bargain. By one of those curious freaks of supply and demand the Germans at Ludlow were well provided with excellent boots, and a pair of these quickly induced the guard to wink, turn his back, and leave the gate open.

In this way our vintner friend could make the evening journey up to London, take his nurse out for a spree, and leaving the city in the small hours he could find a lift back to Ludlow. There was always a lorry going that way, and the drivers were very decent men, he said. If he told them he was a prisoner playing truant to take his girl-friend out for the night they would never think of giving him away. The English, he thought, were reasonable.

But one night he stayed very late, so that that he missed the last chance of transport to deliver him at Ludlow before eight o'clock, and when he arrived at the camp he found the genial guard had been replaced by a younger, efficient, somewhat national-socialist individual. His night out cost him twenty-eight days confinement.

'But who would care? For an evening with a girl like her it was worth it!'

At length we reached the vintner's establishment, a large house which hinted at the money which could run in the sap of the vines. It was guarded by some extremely fierce and efficient dogs, as uncompromising as the replacement guard at Ludlow. They were driven into an inner compound, and then we were admitted to the house itself. We were led at once to the cellar, where our host brought out a rubber pipe, dropped the end through the spigot-hole of the furthest barrel in the row, sucked at it, and siphoned off three glasses of his best wine, a special vintage which he prized so highly that he did not sell it at all. The barrel was preserved for his own family and for special occasions.

'Such as the visit of the *Thames Commodore* to Trittenheim.' he said. '*Prosit!*'

And a very fine wine it was, as good as the best of the famous vintages further downstream. We savoured it, 'chewing it' as they say in the valley, and began to appreciate the need for guard dogs.

'A splendid vintage,' we said.

'As good a wine as you will find along the Moselle,' said the vintner, rolling it over his tongue. 'But then you know, the Moselle valley is unique. Its people have learned something no others have. You don't believe it? Ah, but they have. The Moselle — that is the only part of the world which has learned to compress all that is good in two thousand years of civilisation into slim green bottles.'

On the meadow below the bridge of Trittenheim there is a fine bronze of a seated figure in simple medieval monkish clothing, holding a book. This man is Johannes von der Heiden, who was born in Trittenheim as the son of a vintner and became one of the most learned men of the fifteenth century. He had the advantage of a stepfather who had no patience with his longing for learning, and thus it was that the boy would slip out after dark and learn reading and writing and Latin at the hands of the village priest. As soon as he was old enough to do so he left home and took himself to the university, but when he was only twenty-one he was overcome by homesickness and decided at last to set out from Heidelberg for his own village in the Moselle valley. On his way across the Hunsrück forest he was overtaken by a violent storm, and he had to take refuge in the abbey of Sponheim. He stayed, and within a year he had become abbot.

When he took office the abbey was encumbered with debt, the morale low, but Trithemius — to give him the name by which he

was to be known all over Europe, a name which identified him
with the vine-growing village of his birth — set about reforming
it with all the energy of a brilliant young man. In particular he
developed it as a seat of learning, and while his monks copied
manuscripts he himself wrote on a wide range of subjects — the
classics, Thomian theology, science and humanism. Soon the
library of Sponheim contained two thousand volumes, and its
fame spread so far that scholars and the nobility came from far to
see it, and to converse with Trithemius himself. Others came too.
The sons of peasants flocked thither for instruction in elementary
learning, and his own stepbrother came to study under the abbot
before returning to the valley to become the parish priest at
Klüsserath.

So Sponheim rose to fame and brilliance. The Pope and the
Emperor corresponded regularly with the abbot, and so did the
Electors of Brandenburg and the Palatinate. Still Trithemius
remained humble, dedicated to his work as a scholar, but envy
began to gnaw at some of his brotherhood. No Emperors and
Electors wrote to them, no princes rode across the forest wilds to
to see them. And besides, there was that business of Mary of
Burgundy, the dead wife of the Emperor.

The story is that on a night of new moon a cloaked figure
appeared at the abbey, his face carefully hidden in the folds of his
garment. He demanded to see Abbot Johannes, and was admitted.
Trithemius at once recognised the man as the Emperor Maximilian, and asked him what service he might perform.

The Emperor said he would like to have the spirit of his former
wife raised. The abbot appeared thoughtful, then taking the
Emperor by the hand he led him out into the court and pointed
up to the stars, identifying the constellations and in particular two
which were like staves.

'You see there, my lord, the two ways of government,' he said.
'The one is the rod by which evil princes beat down their subjects
without mercy so that those little stars which you see below the
rod flow as drops of blood and tears. In the garden of eternity,
where the seeds of time will ripen, that staff will stand as a dead
and withered stem. But the other will flourish and grow as a great

tree under the warmth and light of the summer's day, for it is the
staff of righteousness, a rod of pure gold upon which those who
lean trustfully will be supported, a staff which is of benefit to them
as well as to their subjects. You, my Lord, must choose with
which of the two you will rule.'

Maximilian may have been surprised by what must have seemed
an irrelevant reply to his request, but soon another star was singled
out for attention. It was just rising.

'That one, my Lord, is the bright and beautiful and tearless
face of your young and glorified wife,' said the Abbot. 'See how
she smiles upon you, having left her pain and tears behind her to
blossom as pale roses on her empty grave. Look how she beckons
to you from heaven to join her there in the fullness of time, in
the garden of God.'

The Emperor gazed, lost in thought.

'Then choose your staff of government,' Trithemius went on.
'Perform deeds of mercy as a monument to the wife you loved.
A ruler must act. We priests have indeed a magic power given to
us, and it is that of wiping away tears of sorrow and giving you
the strength to walk in the paths of righteousness.'

So, with the Abbot's blessing, Maximilian departed into the
night which lay star-spangled and clear over the forest of the
Hunsrück.

That is the legend, and it is probably true in substance. And
something of the Emperor's nocturnal request must have been
overheard, for it gave the Abbot's envious subordinates the chance
for which they had waited. Quickly the rumour was spread that
the Abbot was a sorcerer, that with the aid of the devil he had
actually conjured up the shade of the beautiful Mary of Burgundy.
For Trithemius it was the end of his work at Sponheim. Knowing
well that such allegations would take hold on the mind of the
people he sorrowfully decided to leave the abbey and retire to
Würzburg, where he died.

A great figure from the late Middle Ages, Trithemius now sits
on the riverside lawn of his home village, looking across the water
as though wondering whether the little train of the Moselbahn
will be on time at the tiny station below the bridge. He is perhaps

remembered most for his dictum, '*Wissen ist lieben*' — to know is to love, but in Trittenheim itself the schoolchildren are more likely to learn first of all the words he wrote in a letter to the Abbot of St Matthias at Trier, saying that to him no kingdom, no province, no town was more glorious than his own homeland, the land of the Moselle, once the proud queen and chief of all the peoples of Europe.

Some of Trittenheim's vineyards lie behind the town, on the smooth back of the Laurentiusberg and on past the chapel to where the slope falls steeply to the road and river. These vineyards face south-west, but so tightly is the Moselle bent upon itself that the slopes across the river from the landing-stage also face south-west. Looking out over the water from on deck we faced the seat of the famous Trittenheimer Altärchen, and sure enough a little altar was there on the face of such of the slope as was too rocky and steep for vine or vintner to take a hold. Downstream beyond the bridge the terraces of Trittenheimer Apotheke were stacked tightly above each other to the tree-line at the very top of the hills, and from the earliest hours of morning the tractors were chugging across the bridge on their way to spray the rows, or came bumping back again to fetch another tankful of chemical.

Trittenheim lies at the beginning of the Middle Moselle, the area of the most famous vintages, and the sweep of its vineyards extends green and smooth on the right bank all the way to the very edge of Neumagen. Only a single building lies at the foot of the hillside where it begins to drop towards that little town. It is a chapel, and beside it stands a tall tree as though to mark it upon the landscape. A series of Stations of the Cross is ranged along the edge of the vines from Neumagen to this place, which is connected with the earliest history of the river, for tradition says that the original Martyr's Chapel built at that spot on the river bank (km. 154·1 R) was put there to mark the point to which the river was stained with blood all the way from Trier when Rictius Varus slaughtered the men of the Theban legion and the other Christians of the city.

Neumagen itself (km. 152·5 R) is only a few minutes away. On our first descent of the river the shore was so encumbered with rocks and heaps of dredging that we could not attempt to draw in. Next time the town had bought a floating jetty, but it still had to be painted. At our third passing the jetty had its undercoat but still sprawled obstinately on the foreshore. Determined to see Neumagen we sounded our way out from the shipping channel and dropped anchor in what we thought was a suitable place, but the current teamed up with a strong valley wind to drive us down the stream yard by yard, pulling the anchor through the shale. However the local agent of the passenger vessels came to the shore and hailed us, offering us the free use of their private landing-stage. No ship was due for three hours, he said. Until then the *Thames Commodore* was welcome to be the guest of the Cologne–Düsseldorf Line.

If Trittenheim is wine and Trithemius, Neumagen is wine and Ausonius, who stands pensively between the shrubs in a tiny piece of parkland below the Peterskapelle, a little chapel which now serves as a war memorial, an ancient building with only a pietà to express the sorrow of the villagers. Ausonius stands with a wreath round his head, a lyre in his hand, and a slightly puzzled expression as though he cannot quite remember the tune. And indeed in real life the poet must often have strolled along the river bank at Neumagen, even if he did not carry a lyre.

Decimus Magnus Ausonius, the son of a doctor, was born at Bordeaux about 310 A.D., and after studying there and at Toulouse he became head of the department of Grammar and Elocution at the University of Bordeaux — to put the matter in modern terms. Among his pupils was one who became a particular friend, the same Paulinus who later became the bishop in honour of whom the magnificent Paulinus church was built in Trier by that master-craftsman of baroque, Balthasar Neumann, on the traditional site of the martyrdom of the Trier Christians. The original church may well have existed during the lifetime of Ausonius himself, or not long afterward.

Ausonius was sufficiently well known in literary and academic circles for the Emperor Valentinian to offer him in 367 the post of private tutor to his son and heir Gratian, who was then only six years old. Thus it was that he came to Trier, to the Moselle valley he was to love and praise, a landscape he would so gladly have shared with Lucana Sabina, the wife he had wedded in Bordeaux and who died when only twenty-eight. To the end of his life he lamented her death, and he never married again.

In 383 Gratian was murdered in Lyon, and Theodosius took his place. He regarded Ausonius highly, but Ausonius did not wish to remain for ever at the court on the Moselle. He withdrew to a family seat on the banks of his beloved Garonne, relinquished the offices with which he had been rewarded, and settled down to a short retirement before he died at about the age of eighty-two.

His poem *Mosella* was written in his Trier days, and its attraction lies less in its value as poetry than in the happy picture it gives of a river which in many ways has not greatly changed in the sixteen centuries since he wrote of its charms.

'Where in the blueness the river reflects the shade of the hills, the water itself seems to have leaves, and its surface is as though planted with vines. What colours tint the wavelets as Hesperus stretches out the evening shades! The hill-sides swim suspended on the swell, the vine trembles, inverted, and the grape harvest heaves in the crystal of the water. In illusion the bargeman may count the rows of green vines as he ploughs down the middle of the stream where the outline of the hills mingles with the water, and the river throws back the limit of the shadows.' This is as much the Moselle of today as of sixteen hundred years ago, and no poet has ever better given the true character of the river than did Ausonius of Bordeaux.

'Thou, with calm waters gliding onward, dost not feel the ruffling of the wind or the check of hidden reefs; nor art thou compelled by foaming shoals to rush in swirling rapids. No islets break thy stream. . . .' Here perhaps Ausonius was more poetic than accurate, for the Moselle was never a safe navigation until the canalisation of 1964, and its rocks and shoals took their toll of many ships at one time or another. Certainly there must have been occasions when even the stolid bargemen of Gaul were overset. But the poet was certainly accurate when he described the two modes of navigation, the downstream craft driving along with oars, and the upcoming vessels bank-hauled by ropes held over the shoulders of the towmen and attached to the mast exactly as shown in the relief on the Igel monument. For the shippers of the Moselle had already discovered that a tow-line attached at a height would not foul the bankside bushes and reedbeds, and that if the point of attachment were some way back from the bow the boat could be steered much more easily.

It was in or about 370 that Ausonius came over the Hunsrück forest on the road from Bingen, accompanying the Roman forces on their triumphal return from a decisive battle against the Alemanni. From the hilltop behind Niederemmel he looked down upon the magnificent stretch of river and the fortified town where Constantine had built his summer residence surrounded by vines. The sight moved him greatly, recalling as it did by its vineyard slopes and sunlit reaches his native Garonne — which in fact is a less imposing river than the Moselle, even if larger.

'At last I saw at the outer confines of the lands of the Belgae Noviomagus, splendid citadel of the heavenly Constantine. . . . Like the prospect and charm of Bordeaux, my beautiful homeland, the whole scene smiled alluringly upon me.'

The heavenly Constantine. Indeed it was at Neumagen that — according to Eusebius — the Emperor was marching over the Layenberg hill, along the road leading out of Noviomagus towards Augusta Treverorum that just as the sun was sinking he beheld a cross formed of rays of light, hovering in the sky and bearing the inscription *In hoc signo vinces*. Constantine and his companions were perplexed, for none could be found to interpret the portent. Then at night the Emperor dreamed that he saw Christ with just such a cross in his arms, and the vision told him that he was to carry a similar symbol instead of his Imperial standard, so that by its power he would vanquish his enemies.

On reaching Trier Constantine had the jewellers and metal-smiths brought to him, and ordered a cross to be made. It was in the form of a silver lance with a crossbar, the whole overlaid with plates of gold. Above the cross was a golden crown, richly jewelled, and beneath it the letters XP (or CHR) as the monogram of Christ. Constantine's own standard waved from the arms of the cross, and the staff of the lance carried portraits of himself and his sons.

The prophecy that the Emperor would be victorious under the sign of the cross was fulfilled in 312 at the battle of the Milvian Bridge in Rome, and in gratitude the Emperor issued his famous edict at Milan in the following year, guaranteeing freedom of worship to the Christians and forbidding all further persecution. There are of course other places which claim to be the original site of the vision, but Neumagen is sufficiently sure of itself to have the letters IHSV (*In hoc signo vinces*) above the cross of the Electorate of Trier and the rampant lion of the Berleburgs in the town arms proudly displayed above the door of the town hall.

V

CONSTANTINE apart, Neumagen has twice erupted into the grand political scene. First it was in the seventeenth century, when the Thirty Years War had at last ground to a halt, and the delegates to the conference of the Peace of Westphalia were gathered in Münster, where their portraits are still to be seen in the hall in which the signing took place. The negotiations dragged on for some years until deadlock was reached, as it so often does in international dealings which concern a large number of differing national interests.

It happened that the Sayn-Wittgenstein family had by marriage come into possession of Neumagen, and the lord of the manor for the time being was a delegate to the Peace Conference. No gentleman from the Moselle would in those days have dreamed of travelling into the flat and wine-barren land of Westphalia without taking his own supplies with him, and Sayn-Wittgenstein had arrived with a quantity of his own best Neumagen vintages. If I remember correctly the deputy mayor of Neumagen who explained all this to us as he led us around the town said that it was a matter of a train of wagons carrying ten *Fuder* — altogether some two thousand gallons of wine.

By the time the conference became so hopelessly bogged down that no solution seemed possible, the lord of Neumagen had consumed all but one of the barrels. He accordingly summoned the delegates to confer with him, and had them served with the wine, which was the most superior of all his varieties — perhaps some such draught as Neumagener Rosengärtchen hochfeine Spät-Auslese Eiswein, prepared only from the finest grapes left on the vines until overtaken by the first hard frosts of late autumn. So wonderful was the savour of the wine that enmities were forgotten, frayed tempers soothed, and the deliberations for the Peace of Westphalia were concluded there and then in a spirit of the greatest cordiality.

It was because of this achievement that in 1959 Neumagen decided to try the same procedure again. The Summit Conference was sitting in Geneva, when one morning the Foreign Ministers of the United States, Britain, France and Russia each received a package containing a quantity of bottles of wine together with a letter.

Neumagen, Germany's oldest wine-locality.   *3 June 1959.*
To Messrs. the Foreign Ministers at the Foreign Ministers' Conference, Geneva.

Most respected Sirs!

The chronicler relates that in the year 1648 a tun of Neumagen wine played a considerable part in bringing to a successful conclusion The Treaty of Westphalia, which brought order to Europe for a long period of time. This prompts us to send you herewith sample bottles of Neumagen wines from the following slopes:

Neumagener Laudamusberg,
Neumagener Engelgrube,
Neumagener Rosengärtchen,

in the hope that it may also be granted to the wines of our own time to lighten the negotiations concerned with such difficult problems of the high politics of Europe. We promise that, if the Summit Conference should indeed succeed in establishing for a long period the peace so earnestly desired by all peace-loving men throughout the world, we shall be ready to put at the disposal of each of yourselves, as Foreign Ministers of the four nations who bear responsibility for the world's peace, a tun of the best Neumagen vintage from whichever of the slopes you may decide after tasting these samples.

We are convinced that the pure Moselle wines of Neumagen will be to your liking, and we confidently believe in your desire and ability to conclude a lasting peace.

For the Council and Community of Neumagen, EVERZ (*Mayor*).

For the Vintners, SCHUH.

In reply, three letters were received at the town hall of Neumagen. One was from the personal private secretary of the British Foreign Secretary:

at the United Kingdom Delegation, to the
Foreign Ministers' Conference, Geneva.

Foreign Office, S.W.1.
June 19, 1959

Dear Herr Everz u. Herr Schuh,

I have been asked by Mr Selwyn Lloyd to thank you for the three bottles of wine from Neumagen which reached him yesterday, together with a copy of your letter of June 3 addressed to the four Foreign Ministers. Mr Lloyd will sample the three vintages with much interest. Nothing would give him greater pleasure than that he and his three colleagues should, by the ultimate success of their deliberations here, prove themselves as worthy of the generosity of Neumagen as the plenipotentiaries who signed the Peace of Westphalia in 1648.

A letter from Mr William M. Gibson said it was really a very kind thought to send the bottles of such excellent wine to the Secretary of State. They had arrived just as Mr Herter was leaving to fly to Washington, but they would be carefully preserved until his return. Meanwhile, Mr Herter sent his sincere thanks to the members of the vintners' association.

The third note was addressed to the Mayor of Neumagen and said that the writer felt it his duty to inform him that M. Couve de Murville was very impressed with the idea of sending him some bottles of wine, the quality of which he had described as praiseworthy. He sent his heartiest thanks to the Mayor and all the vintners of Neumagen.

'But there was no answer from the Russians,' said the Deputy Mayor. 'They never even said thank you.'

'Russians don't write letters,' I said. 'I have often written to Russian officials about canals, or boats, or books. I have never yet had a reply. I expect they liked the wine just as much as the others.'

'Perhaps we should have sent them spirits.'

'You wouldn't have heard for spirits either,' I said. 'For all you know they liked your idea; but to say so is not in their way of thinking.'

'Hm,' said our guide. 'You may be right. In any case, the conference did not succeed.'

'No,' I said. 'And to me that is incomprehensible. For two hundred gallons of your best vintage I would have been prepared to compromise on almost anything.'

Neumagen is the place where, in the nineteenth century, many of the most famous Roman sculptures of the Moselle valley were found. They came there under peculiar circumstances. Noviomagus was very sensibly established by the Romans in the angle between the Moselle and its tributary, the Dhron, facing across the larger river to almost sheer cliffs which rendered attack from that quarter impossible. It was a place of shipment for local produce and a posting-station on the Roman road from Trier to Bingen. But in the third century the German tribes began to raid the countryside, and the Roman authorities decided to encircle the place with a defensive wall. For the foundations they quickly raided all the mausoleums and memorials of the wealthy families in the surrounding country, taking the masonry and embedding it in the base of the fourteen-towered rampart. Much has of course been lost, and perhaps some of these monuments had been broken down by the Germani or other raiders before the Romans decided to strip them, but so much was indeed removed to Neumagen and buried there that by great patience it has been possible to piece together thirteen complete tombstones, a number of altars, and a few family vaults.

Many of the carvings are famous, and they are reproduced in casts on the walls of the houses where they were found. There is the fine lady sitting at her toilet, her lady's maids around her, one holding the mirror so that she may contemplate her hair-do, others with the oil-flask and the ewer of water. On another memorial the wealthy landowner sits in his counting-house while the tenants pay their rent in cash and the accounts clerk notes the details in the credit column. There is the tutorial scene, too, with the private tutor instructing the sons of the merchant, school-book in hand, the older sons seated and listening intently to their lesson while their younger brother finds it difficult to concentrate upon such abstract thinking when he knows that so close at hand there is the river, with bathing and fishing, and racing in rowing-boats.

Perhaps most famous of all are the pieces of the great monument to a local barge-contractor and wine-shipper. The carvings show two Moselle ships of the third century, foreshortened in order to compress their length into the space of the memorial, but showing in great detail how the wine was stowed and shipped. The oars-men, almost life-sized, sit in a row on either side of the barrels, and they are shown in intriguing detail. As with any more modern gang of men, there is the one who is dapper and neat and well-shaven in contrast to the young man who prefers to grow his hair and leave his beard unkempt as a sign of what others might interpret as laziness but what he himself is convinced is a certain modernity and independence. And at the stern sit the steersmen, one of whom has long been known as the *fröhlicher Steuermann*, the 'Happy Helmsman'. He likes wine, one can see.

The ships bear animal heads, Viking fashion, but fore and aft, and the bow is pointed with a snout at the waterline and an eye as well. The ships are moving downstream, the rowers facing the direction in which they are going, rowing after the fashion of Mediterranean fishermen today.

The Romans certainly used such transport-ships to carry their arms and troops on the Moselle. In operations against the Batavii of the Rhine delta and the tough Frisians of the northern marches, the supply route was by water and in part down the Moselle. But it comes as a surprise to find that cargo-craft were in use, and even more that the wine was carried in modern-looking cask-shaped barrels and not mere amphora jars.

G

Neumagen, cast of the Roman wine-ship

Until quite recent times the wine of Neumagen was sold ex-cellar, barrel included. To move a cask of anything up to one ton weight was not easy, and until pumps came on the scene it was the task of a special guild of *Schröter*, or barrel-pushers, to convey the barrels along the roadway and down to the waiting ships. A

close look at the arrangement on board the Neumagen wine-ships
of Roman days suggests that the same system was then already
in use, for the sculptor has provided enough detail to show that
even then the casks were designed for shoving, just like those still
used by some of the Moselle vintners — that is to say, the thin
hoops of iron which hold the staves in place are covered over with
withies, the ends of which are carefully shaped and bound with
willow. The object of this was to prevent the thin iron bands
being damaged when the barrels were moved, for there was always
the risk that such a metal hoop could be scored and might give
way, so that the barrel would burst and the wine be spilled.

Before the system was changed to selling the wine in bottles,
the *Schröter* received one Thaler and a gallon of wine for each
barrel they moved, in return for which they stood the entire loss
if any damage occurred between the cellar and the barge or
railway wagon to which they conveyed the cask. It is no wonder
that they invariably started work by reciting the Lord's Prayer
with bowed heads.

To lift a barrel, an inclined barrel-loader would be placed
between the cellar and the pavement, much like those still used
by brewers' lorries when supplying inns. Two men hauled on
ropes hooked to the rear edge of the cask, and a third walked
backwards up the ladder, shoving with his back. In this way the
barrel was brought up to a wagon, and when loading it on a barge
the cask was slid down the same ladder into the vessel.

Old prints show that from medieval times onwards the barrels
were loaded lengthwise in the ships, just as they are in railway
wagons. This prevented rolling when the boat or train accelerated
or slowed. But the Neumagen wine-ships show them laden cross-
wise, and no doubt a larger cargo could be carried in a comparatively small craft if they were placed in this way, a lower layer of
barrels on special stands or cradles, and an upper layer resting
between them.

It may seem strange that in one of the Roman wine-craft the
foreman has his ear pressed against one of the barrels as though
listening. Probably the Roman bargemen were no different from
their later counterparts and took the opportunity to auger a tiny

hole and insert a straw for their own enjoyment. A twig would later be driven in to stop the hole, and broken off flush, so the theft would only be detected if the barrel had eventually to be taken apart for repair. Modern wooden barrels have sometimes been found bristling inside with plugs where the transport men have helped themselves to the contents, and the Gauls employed by the Roman contractors were doubtless up to all the tricks of the trade. Certainly the Happy Helmsman of Neumagen looks as though he has put away several mugs of Moselle wine and is now listening contentedly to the gurgling and slopping in the partly emptied cask. And even though the original is in the Landes-museum at Trier, the Happy Helmsman can be seen in a cast just behind the chapel, and also in a modern copy in concrete which stands at the entrance to one of the wine establishments close by the terminus of the cheerful little Moselbahn. There he is visible to all who pass by on the water, if they know where to look for him.

Besides having specialists in wine-transport, the Romans certainly knew something of the enemies of the vine, and several authors mentioned remedies which must have been difficult to come by. Bear's blood, rubbing the stems with a beaver skin, it was all in the usual vein of Roman recipes, and no doubt just as effective. Like his medieval successor, the Roman or Gallic vintner only gathered what was left after the bugs and lice and viruses, the sparrows and starlings, grasshoppers and caterpillars and even the deer, wild boar and wolf had satisfied their almost insatiable appetites on the grapes. In the nineteenth century new diseases were added, which left the vintner only two choices — to tackle pests seriously, or to see his livelihood wiped out.

The increased trade between the continents brought chocolate and coffee, tea and tobacco and cotton in quantity to the European market. But it also brought pests, and four of them came to attack the European vineyards — returning the compliment paid by those which had emigrated to America to ravage the forests. One of the worst was the *Oidium*, which reached England on American vines in 1845, crossed to Bordeaux, and ruined scores of thousands of vineyards in western Europe. It can be kept within check by

sulphur dusting, but cannot easily be exterminated. Perhaps worse
— and more notorious — was *Peronospora*, which arrived in
Provence in 1878 from America, wiped out the vines, and spread
to the German vineyards. This fungus can be kept under control,
but six, seven, or even nine successive sprayings are necessary
each year to keep it down. Often as we voyaged down the river in
the early morning we would hold back to allow the ferries to cross
the stream and deposit on the further shore another pack of vineyard tractors equipped with spraying gear, ready to carry on the
incessant fight against *Peronospora*.

If *Peronospora* causes the greatest expense of time and labour
and materials to the vintner, the vine-louse *Phylloxera* runs it a
close second, for this quickly-multiplying insect has withstood all
attempts to exterminate it. Sitting out the winter in a wingless
form on the roots of the vine, the creature crawls up in the spring
and lays two kinds of eggs — large ones producing females and
small ones which hatch to males. The sexes mate on the bark, and
the females lay large winter eggs from which parthenogenetic
females arise to form galls filled with eggs, which in turn give rise
to the wingless forms to survive the next winter. This is a complex
arrangement, and the only way of dealing with *Phylloxera* for
certain has been to graft the vines on root stocks which are immune
to them. Unfortunately, this is costly, and the vines bear less fruit
— but by no means so little as if the insect were allowed to have
its own way.

Neumagen, Dhron and Niederemmel lie as a trio of wine
villages in the loop of river. Dhron (km. 151·2 R) retires from the
river bank and clusters round the stream of its own name, the
Rhodanus parvulus of Venantius Fortunatus; Niederemmel (km.
147 R) also prefers to keep its distance, lest perhaps the winter
river should drown it. It is famous not just for its wines, but for
that astounding piece of Roman craftsmanship in glass which is
to be seen in the Landesmuseum at Trier, the Niederemmel
beaker, in which the main goblet is surrounded by a lattice of
delicate circles and bows attached only at points to the layer
beneath, a wonder of ingenuity which could not be surpassed by
the most ingenious of glassworkers today. Otherwise the village

is only notable for a remarkable schism which for long divided its Catholic community.

After the Revolution the whole of Germany up to the Rhine was seized by the French, and the authorities insisted on the clergy all taking the oath to the Constitution. Originally this was in fact an anti-church oath, but once Napoleon had made his peace with Rome it was little more than a formality. Nevertheless, the parish priest of Niederemmel refused to take the oath — partly on conscientious grounds, but perhaps also because a Frenchman had been installed as Bishop of Trier. He refused to recognise the Bishop, and being ordered to leave French-controlled territory he removed to the diocese of Limburg, just across the Rhine. Many of the Niederemmelers supported him in this action, even to the extent of giving up house and home to accompany him. It was sixty years before the last of them was persuaded to return home again, but Pfarrer Feyen never came. He eventually died on the further shore of the Rhine, unrepentant and still exercising a profound influence on his flock at Niederemmel, whom he supported in any resistance to the Bishop and the (in his opinion) 'unlawful' village incumbent.

Across from Niederemmel at the foot of one of the steepest vineyard ranges lies an even better known wine name in the village of Piesport (km. 148 L) — for, after Bernkasteler, Piesporter wine is the most likely Moselle wine to appear on the wine-list of a British hotel or restaurant. It has done so for centuries, for already in the Middle Ages the English were demanding shipments of Piesporter, the most discerning greatly preferring it to 'Hock' — which was the nearest the Englishman could come to pronouncing the name of Hochheim near the junction of Rhine and Main.

Piesport is a charming village, very small, quite unspoiled, a single street cramped so tightly between the foot of the vines and the river bank that it has not even room for its own cemetery. Land in Piesport is too valuable for burying, so the dead have to cross the river to the Niederemmel shore, which faces away from the midday sun.

'Weinort Piesport' proclaims the lettering which stretches across the wide span of the bridge (km. 147·9) which joins Piesport to Niederemmel. Curiously enough there is another bridge within half a mile (at km. 147), and this is an example of the same bullish self-will which led the Niederemmelers to maintain their schism for half a century against all reason.

The Piesport bridge was built by the Piesporters. Admittedly it ran straight across the river to Niederemmel, but what of that? To the Niederemmelers it was a foreign bridge, a work of others. Well, if the Piesporters and Trittenheimers could afford to build their own bridges, so could the Niederemmelers. Even if the times were not easy they would do so at once.

Times were indeed far from easy. The mark was shaky, inflation was rampant, the currency as yet unreformed. But the Niederemmelers were not to be put off. Whereas the citizens of Metz had once paid for their bridge over the river with best suits of all who died, so the whole of the Niederemmel bridge was to be financed by a toll of the local wine. How many gallons were needed I do not know, but Niederemmel has plenty of acres of vines. Besides, wine is not always cheap. Piesport's best has in some cases realised two or three pounds a litre — and that in Piesport itself, direct from the vintner.

Piesport's pleasant church stands up very straight and pointed like so many along the Moselle, and it is dedicated to St Martin, another favourite patron of the vine. St Martin of Tours spent some time at the Imperial court in Trier, and perhaps that is how he came to be known down the Moselle valley; but he is also said in France to have improved the culture of the vine in the Loire valley. Another connection with the vine is that he refused to sit at table or drink wine with the Emperor Maximus, whose hands were red with the blood of the innocent. Perhaps more practical is the fact that Martinmas (November 11) is at exactly the right season to become the traditional harvest home festival of the vintner.

It may have been the same high use-value of their precious land that led the Piesporters originally to build their church at the very top of the slope, far above the upper vine-line, but more likely it was a desire of the early Christian missionaries in the valley to seal their victory over a local pagan hill-top site by planting the church upon it. Patiently the Piesporters would toil up the hundreds of feet from their dwellings every time they attended church, but inevitably the attendance itself began to decline. By the seventeenth century their churchgoing — or at least the climb up to St Martin's-on-the-Hill — was confined to christenings and feast days. The church building decayed, and late in the eighteenth century it was pulled down, the villagers managing to carry its stones down to the village to build instead the new church of St Martin which stands so handsomely below the bridge.

When walking the Moselle trail I broke out of the edge of the wood immediately above Piesport. It was a day of great heat, so I did not drop down the winding descent into the village, for I had happened upon a little *Strausswirtschaft*, very rightly called the 'Schöne Aussicht', the Lovely View. A *Strausswirtschaft* is an establishment which is allowed to operate for a certain period every year without a licence, selling only its own wines. One can probably come by better and cheaper wine in such a place than one can find in any other, and at the Schöne Aussicht the lady of the house made me a lunch in the form of a *Strammer Max* to go with her vintage. It was the strammest Max I had ever had, being an open sandwich ten inches in diameter and consisting of six slices of ham sitting on buttered bread and topped with a fried egg and gherkins. I do not know who the Tough Max was after whom this speciality is named, but perhaps he was a chucker-out — for the same sort of dish in Holland is called an *uitsmijter* — and after such a lunch on the balcony at the top of the hot shale slope of vines I was ready to throw anyone out myself. Or, which was rather more strenuous, to trek onward over the hills toward Kues.

The next day was to be the fourteenth of July, when all over France people go delirious with patriotic fervour, sitting motionless at the tables of open-air cafés with their glasses of wine and wondering why everyone else is so morose. But this particular fourteenth also happened to be the occasion when one of Britain's new technical universities was installing its first chancellor, and the lot had fallen upon my brother. As this was something of a family event I felt impelled to send a telegram. In mid-afternoon the trail dropped down to a little village named Monzel, a place of vintners and farmers hidden away from the river near the outlet of a sort of suspended valley (km. 138·5 L). Sure enough there was a post office.

'A telegram?' The woman was so astonished that anyone should seriously wish to dabble in that improbable kind of communication that she made quite certain she had not misheard before hunting for the block of forms. 'A telegram,' she repeated. And then, 'Where to?'

'England,' I said.

At this the good lady went out into the street and called to a friend to come in and see what was happening. Nobody had ever sent a telegram abroad — which I could well believe — and here was a Herr who wanted to send one to England. England! For the will of God what was she to do?

Her friend was large and comforting, and thought it an excitement, a challenge to the telecommunications of Monzel.

'But it is impossible. England! To think of it!'

'It must be possible,' her friend said soothingly. She was sure that communications across the sea could be made. The people in the *Fernmeldeamt* at Bernkastel would know how to do it. The simplest course was to ring them, give them the message by phone, and leave them to transmit it.

I took the form and began to write the address. It consisted of only two words, and the postmistress begged me to go no further until we were quite certain that the Bernkastel men were equal to the task of getting a message sent there. I was careful to write in capitals, and when I had finished she took the paper and began to read it into the phone.

The first word was 'University'. 'Like *Universität*,' I said, 'only with an *ypsilon*.' This was transmitted to Bernkastel, who said they understood. The postmistress then started on the name of the town.

'Low-oog-ha-bow-row-oog-ha! Is that right?'

'Not quite,' I said. 'But it doesn't matter if you spell it out. In England they pronounce it Laffbre.' I wrote it down: *Laffbre, Liex.*

The postmistress passed on the information. It seemed to confuse the Bernkastel telegraph office, particularly when she said the Herr swore it was Laffbre and yet spelled it with a Low-oog-ha.

By now the Monzel post office was filled to its small capacity. One woman volunteered that she had a cousin who knew somebody whose nephew had married in England. This seemed reassuring. Bernkastel reported that they had Low-oog-ha identified. All was well. I began to write the message, but I had not completed the first word before the postmistress began to wring her hands in despair.

'It is too much. No, no, it cannot be done,' she exclaimed. 'A whole telegram in such a tongue! *Nein, nein, nein!*'

However, she was prepared to accept the message in German, and no doubt it eventually reached Laffbre in a somewhat altered form — for I doubt if the Loughborough post office was necessarily faultless in its transcription of German words, not just portmanteau-words but real travelling-trunk-words of twenty letters and more — such as *Universitätskanzlerbruder* and *Moselhöhenwegwanderung*. I wrote the telegram in this style because I imagined the Germans charged so much a word. So they did — but with a limit on the number of letters.

With the telegram sent I was free to continue, the villagers pouring out of the post office as I walked off down the street to follow the Moselhöhenweg to Lieser. As usual there was not one single example of the 'Capital M on a dark background' which was supposed to mark every turning and fork. It seemed that the local rambling societies had thrown in their hands, for in the woodlands beyond Piesport I had often been obliged to beat down nettles with my stick, a sure sign that nobody had walked that way for some time. I was already sixty kilometres from Trier, and apart from the gnome by the spring I had met nobody at all on the trail, other than vinedressers about their business. The map proved to be very inaccurate also, but the workers in the vineyards always knew which was the way, and now I again relied upon their directions. And so I climbed through the vines, bittersweet with the curiously unreal smells of new agricultural chemicals, and out to the top of the long knife-edge of the Brauneberg, a vineyard comb looking far down to the river, and to the village of the same name on the other shore (km. 136·5 R), a very beautiful and steep slope justly famous for its wines. A large Belgian ship was chugging down the river, carrying steel bars from Lorraine. She looked like a toy — except that one cannot buy a toy barge, as I know after trying for years to do so — and from her stem a pattern of herring-bone waves ran out to break upon the shores and surge back across their neighbours, forming a mass of little rhomboids set in rows down either half of the stream.

Beyond the river and 300 feet below me, the fields and orchards lay still in the windless afternoon, the villages a little back from the shore and nestling among their trees — Filzen (km. 137·8 R), Brauneberg itself (km. 136·5 R) sundered by the stream from the rich south-facing slope at my feet, Mülheim (km. 135 R) with the mellow buildings of its one-time convent. Then vines once more, lying over the rising ground which sloped gently towards Veldenz a mile further inland. Mülheim proclaimed its identity to the boatman in man-high letters on the floodwall, its name clearly legible from the hilltop, but Veldenz tucked itself away at the foot of the Hunsrück woods, shut within the valley of its own stream.

Both these villages have their tales of ladies long ago. There is a poem about Mülheim — and I think it is of this village and not of Mülheim in the Ruhr — verses which relate the foolish parental behaviour of the miserly father of three daughters who one after the other fell in love and wished to marry. The eldest daughter was merely forbidden to wed, and languishing in heartbroken obedience she sobbed her soul away and died within a few weeks.

Yet the father did not learn. When his second daughter happily announced her wish to marry, she too was ordered to put the thought from her mind. Yet it was her mind which gave way under the strain, and the poor girl lived the rest of her life in a madhouse. Then came the third and youngest, and in due time she too told her father that she intended to marry a young squire of the neighbourhood. A third time the father pronounced the ban rather than part with a dowry, but this spirited young girl did not die of a broken heart. Nor did she become insane. Very sensibly she at once fled from home and married her beloved. For this she was promptly disinherited, but I doubt if she really minded. The father seems to have been the type of man who would have made her life at home unbearable.

At Veldenz the heroine is the lovely Irmina who had sadly to be parted from her beloved when he went off to the Middle East to cleave the Saracens to the navel. As he spurred his horse down the valley Irmina wept and wept, but as soon as her mother judged that the time was opportune she bade Irmina to stop crying, take stock of her own undoubted beauty, and realise that there were plenty more fish in the sea. There would be no lack of suitors, she would see to that.

But Irmina still wept and wept. She would ever belong only to her true love, the one who had pledged himself to her with the ring she always wore night and day and which somehow seemed to whisper to her of his undying devotion.

Irmina began to waste away, as such girls will, and her mother decided that to cure her the attachment must be broken. She reasoned and reasoned that Irmina's fiancé must surely by now be dead — cleft to the navel, no doubt, by a Saracen scimitar. Better forget him, dry the eyes, and start again. If she would be a sensible girl Irmina would throw away her ring, and by so doing she would be simply absolved from any further bond to the dead warrior.

Curiously enough, Irmina let herself be talked round, and at her mother's suggestion she dropped the ring down the well. It disappeared into the depths, but it seems that neither mother nor daughter had noticed that the bucket was at the bottom. So the ring was eventually brought up in a pail of water, and returned by the serving-maid.

The mother decided next time to bury it in the garden, but once again she had not reckoned with all the probabilities of nature. When the ring was buried a bean was inadvertently interred beneath it, and the shoot passed through the lover's token and brought it back to the light of day and right up the side of the house to shine outside Irmina's own window.

Irmina, it is said, was much frightened at the sight, or perhaps merely at the size of the bean plant. Yet to have her ring back delighted her, and once again she lost herself in thinking only of her departed lover. This infuriated her scheming mother, who already had the succession arranged. She now demanded that Irmina rid herself for ever of the silly token. Together they would put it in the fire, and there it would melt.

Her daughter reacted firmly. It would be a sin to destroy a pledge given in love, she said. Whether her young knight were still alive or long since dead, she felt herself wedded to him in her heart, and she could never marry another.

The mother's patience broke. She snatched at Irmina's hand and there was a struggle. Irmina was no match for her mother in strength, and she felt her ring being pulled off. Yet the old woman had not yet managed to fling it in the fire when the door burst open and the hero was there just in time, safe and sound, ready to clasp his faithful Irmina to his breast and make her his bride. And that he did, immediately with the original ring, thereby acquiring at one and the same time a most happy and adoring wife and a decidedly unpleasant mother-in-law.

Tales of young women apart, this stretch of river below the Brauneberg has a strange history. When the same young King Childebert who sailed down the river with Venantius Fortunatus from Metz to the Rhine heard that the See of Verdun (on the Meuse) was unfortunate in having no land in a vine-growing district, he quickly presented the bishop with two Moselle vine-yard properties at Mülheim. It was evidently a highly prized part of the valley, for in the tenth century the Church of St Paulinus in Trier already had four claims staked among the vineyards at Kesten (km. 139 L) at the foot of the same rise on which Monzel stands. The colonial territory of Verdun was later confirmed by Barbarossa, although it was an area within the sphere of influence of the diocese of Trier, which owned the left shore and had the rights of the ferry on the main road which here crossed the river to Mülheim.

This territory around Mülheim and Veldenz is curious in having for long been a protestant enclave entirely surrounded by the catholic domains of Kurtrier (Electoral Trier, that is). Not just the two villages themselves but several of their neighbours from

Burgen to Andel (km. 132 R) once formed a diminutive principality, for one of the family which originally held and protected
the Moselle vineyard properties of the Bishops of Verdun introduced the Reformation, and later these protestant lands became a
little dukedom in their own right. Protestants from Trier sought
refuge there, and the tiny state developed a character all of its own.
Its ruler, Georg Hans of Pfalz-Veldenz, travelled widely, and on
one of his journeys he brought home from Scandinavia a daughter
of Gustavus Vasa as his wife. A wise and tolerant man, he insisted
upon freedom of worship for catholic and protestant alike in his
domains. Dutch fugitives from the terror of the Duke of Alva took
refuge in Veldenz territory, and the little principality began to
establish itself as a place of manufacture and trading.

Alone of the men of the Moselle, Georg Hans of Pfalz-Veldenz
had an ambitious scheme to provide a fine system of waterways.
Four centuries before the International Moselle Company built
the locks along the river he was planning to canalise both the Saar
and the Moselle. It may be that he was prompted to such thoughts
by the immigrants from Holland, or perhaps it was the idea of
Anna Maria his Swedish wife, who came from a land where canal-
building had already been attempted; or maybe on his northern
travels he had seen for himself the immense benefits which came
from waterborne trade. Whatever started the idea in his mind, he
also longed to link the Moselle with the Meuse and Scheldt and
so turn Mülheim into a port with access to the sea.

His plans were the joke of the courts in Europe, and his attempts
to win support for his system of waterways were haughtily
rejected. Forced to attempt the impossible with the wealth of so
tiny a dukedom he quickly fell into debt and died in disappoint-
ment — like so many other far-sighted waterway planners since
his day. Then came the Thirty Years War, and although through
its Swedish link and its protestantism Veldenz was on the winning
side, its industrious villages were occupied, pillaged, destroyed.
After lingering on, the poverty-stricken land of Veldenz was seized
by Louis XIV, who ingeniously took advantage of the defunct
connection with Verdun to claim it for France. The protestants
were hunted down, their rulers driven out. The War of the Spanish

Succession finished the work the Roi Soleil had begun, and Veldenz went up in flames. The tiny state was finally extinguished.

When Childebert gave vineyard territory on the Moselle to the Bishop of Verdun, the episcopal vintners no doubt found themselves in good company, for churches and abbeys and monastic institutions were among the first of the vineyard owners. Even now one may see their arms carved over the arches of vintners' establishments up and down the river, and the mere names of many of the fine wine-growing slopes reflect the interest of the medieval church in things viticultural. Abtsberg and Domprost, Maxberg (St Maximin's of Trier, that is), Nonnenberg and Prälat, Paulinusberg and Klostergarten, the labels on vintage bottles speak of the far spread of ecclesiastical ownings. But by no means all the names are connected with church ownership. Very often they reflect the pious nature of the wine-growers in the villages, who would perhaps name a particular slope 'Ölberg' (Mount of Olives) or 'Himmelreich' (Kingdom of Heaven), or 'Paradies'. And where they had put up shrines, these would sometimes figure in the name by which the slope came eventually to be known — as is the case with Altärchen at Trittenheim. Or the villagers might directly christen a slope in honour of one of the Saints, especially the patrons of the wine-grower. Laurentiusberg and Martinslay (*Lay* meaning a cliff), Petersberg and Hubertslay are only a few of the positions thus dedicated.

Then there are names more obviously descriptive of the hillsides themselves and the colour of the shale or stone, names such as Schwarzlay, Grauberg, and the Brauneberg itself. Or they may hint at the way a site lies open to the sun, as with Reil's Heisser Stein (Hot Stone), and names such as Sonneberg and Feuerberg. A few may derive directly from the Latin of the Roman occupation, but more common are those which tell of the flora and fauna as in Vogelsberg and Nussberg, or Falkenlay and Geierslay — these two latter cliffs being haunts of birds of prey. So, when one sees the label of a Moselle wine, one can often close the eyes and dream of the slope from which it has been won. Down in the bottom is the river, blue and peaceful, with a passenger vessel laden with holiday-makers, a ferry carrying the tractors to work, the strong and rosy-cheeked girls sitting perched on side-seats over the wheels, perhaps a Swiss Europa-ship bound for the port of Trier, even the *Thames Commodore* herself, happily thrusting down the stream on her slow journey towards the Rhine. To either side the land rises steeply to the slopes, north-facing and thickly wooded or southerly and with the face turned to the clear sunlight. Wehlener Sonnenuhr brings the vision of that great range of even slope, emerald in its dress of leaves of the Riesling vine and with the sundial set in its face to tell the vine-dressers how long they have laboured in the vineyard; and of course a sundial is only effective in a situation which can count upon lengthy sunshine. Piesporter Goldtröpfchen — a lovely name this, redolent of the rich clear gold of the wine from that incomparable hillside across from Nieder-emmel. Graacher Himmelreich — and could any slope be more like the vintner's vision of the Kingdom of Heaven?

But it is time to move on, down river. From the summit of the sharp-ridged Brauneberg the Moselle trail zigzags down through thickets, dropping quickly not to the Moselle itself, but to the River Lieser (km. 134·9 L) which here rushes impetuous and heavy with reddish mud to throw itself into the larger stream, its mouth crossed by an ancient pack-horse bridge, built for the *Halfen* so that they might cross the tributary without slackening their pull on the tow-rope. When I arrived, the land was churned and furrowed by the machines which brought up the materials for two new bridges, one over the Lieser and the other to cross the Moselle to Mülheim. I felt an irrational sadness that the ferry which long ago had belonged to the Archbishop of Trier should soon be stilled, so I paid my few pfennigs to cross upon it, just for the ride. Then I set out again along the towpath which once the plodding horses of the *Halfen* had stamped firm.

Ausonius wrote of the Lesura, the quick-flowing tributary. Otherwise the village of Lieser itself (km. 133·8 L) is notable only for a rather ugly château behind the railway embankment. But Lieser, too, has its wines of local renown, and the vineyards extend to where the road cuts away from the river to pass on the landward side of the harbour of Kues. On foot I wandered along the pro-montory and stripped to bathe in water still reddish from the contribution of the Lieser river. For decorum I stood on a sub-merged shoal, a training wall of the old river, while the Bernkastel trip boat came and went. Then I dressed, made myself tidy enough to stand a chance of acquiring a bed for the night, and set off round the inner end of the harbour toward the little town of Kues, once the home of the Krifftz family.

The *Thames Commodore* had a great respect for the Krifftzes, for about the year 1400 one of them was so enterprising and successful a barge-owner that he excavated for his own considerable fleet the original harbour of Kues, across the river from Bernkastel. Five and a half centuries later this same port had been recut and enlarged to make a basin one-third of a mile in length, a handy refuge for Europa-ships in time of ice or flood, and a harbour which had the one good and deepwater quayside along all the German reaches of the river (km. 130·7 L).

Three long blasts and two short ones, and she swung round the end of the mole to pull in at the quay, ready to lie in comfort at one of the most enchanting points of all the splendid Moselle, exactly half-way from Thionville to the Rhine.

H

VI

*Nicholas of Kues — the Cardinal's hospital — Bernkastel
and the Archbishop's doctor — the Moselle vineyards —
the vintner's pests and enemies — Maurus's burial — Franz
the ferryman — burning of Burg Landshut — the Bernkastel wine festival — Weinstrasse and procession*

IN the year 1438 two theologians from the Moselle valley
attended the Council of Basle. They came from the adjacent
villages of Lieser and Kues, and an epigram about them has
survived.

> *Nicolaus de Cusa et Johannes de Lesura
> Pervertunt injuria in jura.*

That this piece of after-dinner humour is in Latin hints that it
had its origin in clerical circles — probably in the byways of the
Council of Basle itself. Nicholas of Kues and John of Lieser, the
two men who could turn wrong into right — this was indeed an
unkind assessment of their characters. Although John of Lieser
never became well known, Nicholas of Kues was famed throughout
Europe, and if the *Thames Commodore* came to have a proper
respect for him this was not just because of his ecumenical
endeavours, or his scientific thought so far ahead of his time, but
because he was of a water family. His father was the same enterprising medieval barge-owner who built Kues harbour.

Kryfftz, Crypfs or Kreves — however we might care to spell
the name, in medieval times it meant crayfish, or *Krebs* as it would
now be written. The learned man had many friends and many
enemies. To the former he was Cardinal Cusanus, but his detrac-
tors preferred to use the crab or crayfish designation. For indeed
the family arms were simply a pictogram, a crayfish proper, which
Nicholas later embellished with a cardinal's hat and hat-strings.

Cusanus was born in one of the most delightful houses to be seen on the Moselle. Below the steep pitch of the roof a row of gothic machicolations runs round the front, and at one side the building projects upwards solely in order to display the arms of the cardinal himself, with crayfishes large as lobsters and so pinkish red that they seem to invite one to dinner. At the back the house has a roundish turret known as the Pulverturm, because the French — the perpetual villains of the valley — stored gunpowder in it, but at the side where the village street of Kues leads away from the quay frontage two families of swallows have built their nests beside a corbel over the first-floor level and far above the curious little triangular niche which holds a shrine of the virgin. On the corbel itself a line is inscribed, with the brief statement, *Mosel* 1784, a reminder that the placid river of summer can carry down more water from the winter rains in Lorraine and the Vosges than it can easily dispose of. The winter after we were there, the water was almost up to the table top in the parlour of this same pretty building and of the others along the waterfront.

The house stands right beside the harbour, and on each of her five runs along the Moselle the *Thames Commodore* would dock at the quay immediately opposite. One day I was standing looking across to the house when an elderly woman on a seat under the trees spoke to me.

'You like the house?'

'Yes,' I said. 'It's most curious, too.'

'Then come inside,' she said. 'I live there.'

And so I went into the home where Cusanus was born to the wife of the medieval shipmaster. There was nothing there in the way of relics of the great man himself, for these were collected elsewhere, but on one of the upstairs walls were two framed photographs which intrigued me. The first was taken in 1870, and showed the French army retreating across the river on a pontoon bridge. They did not use the stone-arched road bridge for the excellent reason that it had not yet been built. Between Bernkastel and Kues there was only a bridge of boats with a section which could be swung out of the way if a ship should come into view —

just such an arrangement as I recalled having seen at Breisach on the Rhine as late as 1933.

The other picture showed the '*Eisgang*' or 'ice-go' of the winter of 1892, an icing which had results almost as dramatic as when ships searching for the North-West Passage were frozen into the sea. Several barges and two passenger steamers which had taken refuge in the harbour of Kues were shown squeezed, lifted, and dumped amid a heap of tilted ice-floes in the roadway across from the port basin. One of the passenger vessels had the name *Moselfahrt*. She was a large vessel, and I wondered how they ever got her back into the river again.

Nicholas von Kues (or Cusanus) was never active in the world of his father's shipping, and his younger years were very similar to those of Trithemius half a century later. His liking for learning being despised by his father, who is even alleged on the basis of legend rather than of record to have pushed his bookish son overboard when on a voyage down river with a barge, he left home (or swam ashore, if one believes the unlikely embellishment) and set out to study where he might. Count von Manderscheid aided him, and soon he was at Deventer in Holland, next in Heidelberg and Padua. Trained as a lawyer he returned at the age of 23 to his homeland, and accepted a brief in a case at Mainz. He lost the case, threw up the law in disgust, and turned to theology. Not many years passed before he was addressing the delegates to the Council of Basle, undertaking diplomatic missions for the Pope, advocating ecclesiastical reforms, and taking up his post as Lord Bishop of Brixen in the Tirol. He was the intermediary in peace talks between England and France, a continual comer and goer in the courts of Europe to which urgent diplomatic missions had to be sent. Trithemius referred to Cusanus as 'an angel of light and peace in the midst of darkness and confusion.'

Modestly riding on horseback he travelled through the Netherlands, to Vienna and Salzburg, to Trier and Magdeburg, Cologne and Aachen, indeed throughout all of western Europe east of France, preaching reform and striving to raise the standards of ecclesiastical administration and justice. But Nicholas of Kues was more than a reformer and a church diplomat. He was absorbed in studies about the nature of the universe which he saw as a reflection of the wisdom of God, and more than a century before Copernicus he decided by reason rather than by any observation that the Ptolemaic cosmology could not be true. In his *De docta ignorantia* he wrote that it was inconceivable that the earth itself could be the centre of the universe. 'There are no fixed and immovable poles of the heavens, but every part of the heavens themselves must be in motion; from which it is clear that the earth itself is in motion.' He also considered the earth to be 'a star among many stars, of just such materials as the heavenly bodies, moving as they do in similar and imprecisely circular orbits. Its form is roughly that of a sphere.'

Cusanus bought some mathematical and astronomical instruments in Nürnberg, and engaged in many speculations in the mathematical field. He tried to calculate the precise value of π, and came very close to the right answer. He was also intrigued by the problem of weight, and developed a hygrometer to measure atmospheric humidity by the increase or decrease in weight of a ball of wool. As a result he put forward the opinion that one should be able to forecast probable changes in the weather by observing alterations in the water content of the air. His studies also led him to try to produce a scheme for improving the accuracy of the calendar, and he suggested at the Council of Basle the reform which in fact was introduced one and a half centuries later by Pope Gregory XIII.

Yet Nicholas of Kues is known best of all for the gift he bestowed upon his own village. When he came home to rest before returning again to his unruly diocese of Brixen he drew up the plans for the Hospital of St Nicholas, which is still one of the glories of the Moselle valley. The foundation was to provide a home for thirty-three poor men, aged fifty or over, free men of honourable employment and solvent, bachelors of the diocese of Trier and if possible out of the immediately adjacent villages. Six were to be priests, six nobility, the rest common people. The Kryfftz family wealth was placed at the disposal of the foundation, riches which included the cardinal's own silver and his priceless library, and the property of his sister Klara whose fine and generous face smiles from her memorial in the hospital chapel, and of his brother who was the parish priest of Bernkastel. There were houses and farms in Zeltingen, Bernkastel, Kues and other places, together with vineyards and land rents. It is even now an independent foundation, and its fortunes vary somewhat with the weather — for the wines of its vineyards are still the mainstay of its finances.

The Cusanusstift, or Hospital of St Nicholas (km. 129·4 L) stands right beside the bridge, looking across to Bernkastel's bustling waterfront. It is white and pink and slated, a very beautiful complex of buildings, and over the doorway stands St Nicholas of Myra himself, looking down at the three little boys who are sitting upright and pink and cheerful in the pickling tub in which the wicked innkeeper had salted them down to sell as pork. He has a gentle face, this St Nicholas, and his expression is suited to the foundation itself, for the whole institution is a haven of quiet and contentment. Within its court and cloisters life moves pleasantly, peacefully, at a speed no faster than that of the score of old men who still live out the evening of their life within the patronage of their benefactor. They may not nowadays be accurately divided in the original precise ratio of priests and nobility and commoners, nor are they necessarily lifelong bachelors, but they are there just the same, happy, friendly, sitting on the wooden benches in the summer sun or working the great winepress and bottling machine in the building across the yard. Many visitors seek out the Hospital on account of its beauty, just as one might delight in an Oxbridge college. Others more rarely go to study in the library among its hundreds of manuscripts and incunabula, and early printed books.

The Hospital is in charge of a rector or warden, and because of its valuable literary possessions he is necessarily a scholar as well as an administrator. The present rector welcomed us to the foundation and allowed us to join a group of visitors from Cologne whom he had promised to show round. Red-faced and academic and very learned, he reminded us of some fellow of a Cambridge college, a man completely absorbed in the things entrusted to him and in the life not only of the old men who lived there but also of the great medieval figure of Cardinal Cusanus himself. He first led us round the cloisters with their eighteenth-century pictures showing the exercise of Christian virtues, including 'Giving the thirsty to drink' — with a flagon of Moselle wine, of course. On we went by the refectory and the chapel until at last we passed through a thick fire-proof door like that of a bank vault into the library itself with its cases of precious manuscripts, the neat marginal notes in Cusanus's medieval hand, and the mathematical instruments with which he had sought to solve some of the secrets of the universe. With most commendable generosity the good warden waited until the last of the German visitors had left before telling us about the invitation.

There had, it seemed, been some exhibition of manuscripts in London, and the Hospital of St Nicholas had been asked to send there one particular book which was of great value. The rector had gently declined to do so, suggesting that the photostat already held by the British Museum might be adequate. The manuscript itself was too precious to send abroad, he said.

Soon afterwards he received an invitation from Buckingham Palace to attend a reception, and with it was a hint that he might care to bring the manuscript along with him.

'But they didn't send the railway ticket,' he said. 'Perhaps they thought the Rector of St Nicholas was more able to afford it than the British Museum.' He chuckled. 'Still, that wasn't the funniest part of it. The letter from the palace said, "I am directed by Her Majesty to invite you and your lady." I think that's such a nice expression, particularly when applied to a Roman Catholic priest like myself, don't you? I wonder who they thought my fair lady was!'

There is no place on the Moselle that I like more than Kues, and if it is almost unspoiled it owes this to the presence of Bernkastel on the further shore (km. 129·5 R). Bernkastel is a fascinating little town, with timbered houses and little alleys, and on its elegant reddish town hall the pillory where a miscreant would be chained until, if none should vouch for him, the local officer of justice 'pronounced his wife a widow', as it was so neatly expressed. With this and many other attractions Bernkastel draws

Bernkastel, the Michaelsturm

tours like a magnet, from Holland and Britain and Germany, and how many thousand people a day disembus there to have lunch and a glass of its famous wine I do not know. But the great advantage of this — apart from the immense cash benefit to the Bernkastelers themselves — is that Kues goes unnoticed and lives in peace. You cannot buy a funny hat in Kues, and if there are any souvenirs to be had they are confined to the immediate bridgehead leading toward Bernkastel itself.

Bernkastel's river frontage is disappointing. It is Victorian from the age of wealthy visitors who came by coach or carriage, and only the one-time Electoral Cellars and the Michaelsturm break the mediocrity. This tower is splendid, a thousand-year-old bastion of the vanished walls, square and solid and built of rough slate with eight little turrets around its conical top. It is in fact this tower which makes the appearance of the town when seen from the river, for it tactfully draws the eye away from the hotels and bus park and the car-laden foreshore. Yet the real beauty of Bernkastel lies behind, around its exquisite market-place with the half-timbered houses gay in all their brightness of newly painted corbels, and the little Spitzhäuschen which seems to have been added as a bold afterthought to fill a small remaining gap and yet leave room for the wains to pass beside its tight-waisted lower storey. It is a Grimm, even a Disney creation, and surely either a witch or some superior kind of gnome must inhabit it.

Bernkastel owes its fame to its wine, which is very rightly celebrated. The best is certainly not shipped abroad, but is to be found in the little parlours of the vintners themselves, tucked away in the alleys. Most famous — but perhaps no better than others — is the one which leapt to fame in 1360.

> *Eile die Weile! Die Sage gibt kund,*
> *Der Kurfürst wird von dem Weine gesund.*

Thus the boys and girls of the valley still hear in rhyme about the Elector Archbishop Boemund II of Trier, who lay sick in his summer residence above the town.

> *Hurry and hear what is rumoured abroad,*
> *The Elector by wine of his sickness is cured!*

The illness is said to have been gout, a not uncommon affliction of medieval archbishops, and yet the mode of cure makes this seem a little unlikely, for it is said that when his chaplain mentioned the matter to a local knight in whose charge the defence of Bernkastel lay, the man declared that he was personally acquainted with a doctor who would fix the Archbishop quickly enough.

Quaffing another bottle of his favourite vintage to give him extra strength, the knight set off for the Bishop's quarters with a whole barrel of the wine on his shoulders. He persuaded the prelate to admit this specialist doctor he had brought with him, and when the sick man had taken a gulp of the wine he felt new life tingling in his body.

'That wine is the best doctor of all,' the Archbishop declared.

'Yes,' said the knight. 'There you are right, and I can assure you that whoever drinks this wine for eighty years will live long and need the attention of neither doctor nor apothecary.'

It is said that for the rest of his life Boemund II was never without this particular doctor at hand. Whenever he felt the least unwell he took a draught, and so helped to provide Bernkastel with an advertising slogan of which in recent times it has made very full use. The name of Bernkasteler Doktor from the sunny slope of the Kallenfels behind the town is known round the world.

Of the fortress where Archbishop Boemund met his medicine only a ruin remains, perfectly poised above the vineyards so as to give the *Thames Commodore* in her berth at Kues harbour one of the finest outlooks she had ever known. That the castle was destroyed by the French goes without saying. Louis XIV was determined to build the vast fortification of Montroyal above Traben, and the simplest way of acquiring masonry was to pull down Burg Lanshut and raft the pieces down the river. But the ruin is romantic if melancholy, and sometimes we would cross the river to the landing on the right bank, from where we could follow the path which winds up through the beeches and zigzags past some very formal Stations of the Cross to a curious little shrine dedicated to the Fourteen Helpers (the Vierzehn Nothelfer). There they are, ranged round the chapel in awful modern plaster devoid of character, from Vitus protecting against rabies to Dionysius (St Denis to the French) carrying his own head in his hands, and the young Barbara whose father was struck by lightning for slaying her in his fury at her conversion. St Blaise and St Elmo, they all are there, but so stereotyped that it is better to leave them and break out of the wood to the Schlossberg slopes and walk on through the drifting laboratory smell of the vine sprays to the terrace at the foot of the ruined castle tower.

The view from here is fine, though not the finest to be had along 250 kilometres of Moselle valley, most of which offers a superlative outlook to anyone walking the heights and slopes. Upstream lies the harbour of Kues, and beyond it the knife-edge of the Brauneberg, blue in the haze. Downstream the Moselle curves past Bernkastel and then shakes itself to straighten out

toward Zeltingen lock (km. 124 L), the third downstream of
Trier. Yet it it is the town itself which is so transformed when
seen from above. The hotels and car park disappear, and what
lies below is a real Moselle town of vintners, its purple slated roofs
cramped together to pack the houses into such little land in the
side valley as is not suitable for planting the precious vines. For
even vintners must have somewhere to live.

It is six centuries since Moselle wine cured the Archbishop,
but even then the industry of wine-growing was an old one in the
valley. Just how long the grapes have flourished upon the slopes
of the Moselle is not precisely known, but the Neumagen wine-
ship with its Happy Helmsman is dated to the mid-second century.
Yet, while the Romans developed viticulture, the industry may
well have been there before they came. The Treviri, the Celts,
may have brought the first vines across from the Rhône, but
unfortunately viticulture leaves no solid traces for inquisitive
archaeologists until it comes to be represented in carving or
painting.

Although the origins of the Moselle vineyards are lost in the
mists of time the Neumagen memorial certainly suggests a flourishing trade. Soon afterwards, in the third century, the Emperor
Probus ordered the army to help extend the vineyards, and in the
fourth Ausonius could sing the praises of vines which extended
all the way from Trier to Neumagen — and presumably further.
Although the Franks overran the country and sacked the Roman
settlements they did not destroy the wine-industry, for Venantius
Fortunatus travelling down the river wrote of how, 'All around
one sees the heights clothed with the green of the bursting vine-
leaves. Thick in their planted rows the vines grow in the shale,
right up to the brow of the hillside, the terraces smiling down from
the steep cliff-faces upon the vine-dressers, the grapes nobly
reddening amid the pallor of the stone.'

These lines also show that in early times the grapes were not
the pale green clusters which hang in tight bunches from the
Riesling stocks of today. They were red, probably the red Klein-
berger, a straightforward vine which only gradually came to be
replaced by the Oesterreicher and Säuerling, then by the delicious

Ruländer which still provides some of the finest wines of the Luxembourg reaches, and finally by the rich and fruity Riesling which now occupies almost every square yard of vineyard from Trier to the Rhine.

Bernkastel more than any other town is the centre of the Moselle wine-trade, but the vintners of Kues on the other shore have their rows in the same vineyards on both sides of the river. And Kues is everything that Bernkastel is not. Except for the campers on the outer spit of the harbour few people visit the place, and it still remains a delightful community of vintners. It may have been chance that first led us to walk across the quay from the *Thames Commodore* to visit the small inn opposite, but it was a fortunate choice, for I have never found any wines along the whole Moselle — or anywhere else for that matter — which can quite equal those of Hugo König. And how aristocratic is the name of Kardinalsberg, with its reminder of the vineyard ownership of the great Cardinal Cusanus himself, whose body lies in St Pietro in Vinculis in Rome, but whose heart is buried in the chapel of his Hospital, and whose house still looks out to see what newcomers have arrived at the harbour. The Kardinalsberg itself is the low and gentle slope behind Kues, but the Königs have other wines of their own. There is Badstube (or 'Bathroom') from a site in a side ravine behind Bernkastel and on the other side of the river from Kues, and perhaps this location produces the best of all.

I asked Hugo how it came by its name. There was formerly a hot spring in the ravine, he said.

'I passed by Tabernae [Bernkastel], watered by a source which never runs dry,' wrote Ausonius, and the spring to which he referred must surely have been that of the Badstube. Perhaps in his day the local Roman officials used it indeed as a *Badstube*, or bathroom, but more recently the water has gone, preferring to gush out instead on the opposite side of the hill at Bad Wildstein, a modest but well patronised thermal cure resort in a valley behind Trarbach.

The König establishment is typical of the Moselle. Man and wife together run vineyards scattered over the slopes within a mile or two on either side. A patch behind the house is planted with

Müller-Thurgauer, not so fine a grape as the Riesling, but a useful
space-filler on flatter land and good for up to one gallon per
rootstock, whereas the Riesling should average one to one and a
half quarts. But not even the hardiest of vines will yield wine
automatically. They need the continual attention of men who love
them, who will work hard, and who do so in trust and without
resenting too much those years when the late summer is wet and
the bunches ripen only far enough to produce an indifferent wine
— at least by the high standards of the Moselle.

> *Was er geerbt von seinen Vätern*
> *Behütet er mit treuem Fleiss.*
> *Verwachsen ist er mit der Scholle,*
> *Bezahlt hat er mit seinem Schweiss.*
> *Er pflanzt die jungen neuen Reben*
> *Auf dass sie g'deihen in heiliger Erd,*
> *Er baut auf Gottes Liebe weiter*
> *Den Weinberg den er selbst geerbt.*

These lines are not those of a famous German poet, nor are
they some traditional verse of the Moselle valley. They were composed by Frau König, who had a strange facility for poetry of this
kind, and who recited them to us in the parlour over a glass of
Kardinalsberg from one of the vineyards which she and her
husband worked, very much as the lines describe. Freely translated
her poem about the work of a vintner runs something like this:

> *Where once his fathers persevered*
> *To plant the vines in shaly soil,*
> *He too will age among the wine-stocks,*
> *To tend them faithfully his toil.*
> *And so he plants the tender vinelets*
> *That they may thrive in holy dust,*
> *To the Almighty's love committing*
> *The vineyard which he holds in trust.*

The Königs had their Rieslings on the Weisenstein and König-
stuhl, others on the Kardinalsberg and over in the Badstube.
They reckoned to have just the size of holding which was not

dependent upon fluctuations in outside labour, and if there were
a few rows here and another few a little further along the same hill
this was good Moselle practice, for a diffused vineyard ran less
risk of a total loss through hail or starlings or from any other
cause. At six in the morning the Königs would be up and away,
for weeds and pests waited for nobody. Particularly the *Heuwurm*
and the *Sauerwurm*.

Heuwurm and *Sauerwurm* are the same devil in two guises, a
creature which used to destroy half and sometimes two-thirds or
three-quarters of the entire grape harvest. Nowadays the vintner
can attack the creature with some success, but it still remains the
prime enemy. The moth lays its eggs which hatch into the H-worm
in the unopened bud, and unfortunately the H-worm does not
succumb to any kind of spray which will not also ruin the bud. It
therefore has to be attacked by more physical means — attracting
the moths with lamps, by banding the vines, even by hanging up
nesting-boxes on poles on the treeless slopes so that the devoted
parents of baby birds will forage the worms for their infants. The
pupae which last through the winter can be destroyed on the stems
with wire brushes or corrugated gloves before they emerge to the
next generation of moths, which lays S-worm eggs.

The *Sauerwurm* grubs are terrible destroyers, boring through
the grapes to ruin them unless the grapes themselves ripen very
quickly and become transparent, a state of affairs which for some
reason frustrates the pest. Fortunately the S-worm is more
delicate than the H-worm, and will fall victim to nicotine,
Schweinfurt Green and other chemicals. Phosphoric acid esters
are an excellent recent addition to the armoury, and the favourite
spray is one known as E 605, a better weapon than DDT because
it is not washed off by rain and will also attack every form of
biting and sucking pest of the vine, red spiders included. And
whereas arsenic sprays can build up to a dangerous level in the
human body E 605 is quickly broken down and is considered
absolutely safe to the person who eventually drinks the wine from
stocks on which it has been used.

Weeds and pests are not the only sources of work to be done.
The vines send out shoots which must be kept in proper balance,

and the stocks themselves demand fertiliser in the form of artificials or manure water. The vintner has plenty to do, and an analysis of some vineyards carried out by a government department has shown that the main tasks in order of time consumed were hoeing (more than three times as much as any other job), carting and strewing manure, tying in the shoots, pruning, staking, dis-budding and leafing, spraying and dusting with artificials — and all this apart from the vital matters of harvesting, pressing, cellar-mastery, bottling, distribution, and repairing the machinery.

After ten or twelve hours in the vineyard it is time to go home, and all along the valley the tractors begin to head for the villages. The Königs would return about six or seven, wash and change, then open up the house and run it as a Weinstube until midnight or later. They sold not only their own wine but food also, this being very wisely limited to one item, a dish at which Hugo was a master. His half-chickens from the spit, done in a rich caramel sauce, were superb, and to save washing up cutlery they were served only with bread and eaten in the fingers, an ideal accom-paniment to the Weisenstein. One Sunday night Hugo confessed to us that he had grilled 360 hens over the week-end. He was very particular about his poultry, allowing a tolerance of only fifty grammes either side of the individual frozen weight which he knew was the best. If lighter, the birds would be a ruckle of bones, if heavier, a mushy mass of chickenish water when unfrozen. Best by far, he said, were the American chickens. No others could touch them for meat in the right places.

Hugo told us that one evening an Englishman had come in, very straight-standing and good-mannered, neat and with a small moustache. He had asked for a glass of wine (the Moselle glasses being only one tenth of a litre, smaller than those of the Rhine) and had stood by the counter drinking it. Then he had another, and another. All evening he stood, politely saying his *Guten Abend* when anyone came in and his *Auf Wiedersehen* when they left, but otherwise he merely savoured his wine, drank it, nodded approv-ingly, and quietly ordered another. He was a model of sobriety, never swaying or stumbling in his speech. In fact he had just put down on the counter his sixtieth empty glass when there came a considerable thud. The Englishman had fallen like a felled tree and lay there, decorous and neat but entirely unconscious.

Drunks are not common in the Moselle valley, for people sit and drink their wine to enjoy it. But it is said that at Kues there was once a man named Maurus who, in contrast to the Königs' decorous Englishman, was as violent and unruly and regular a drunkard as an Irish navvy. Not content with liquor and swearing he took to beating his wife with such savagery that the neighbours often had to come into the house to save her. If, when he returned home at night, he found her waiting up he would thrash her soundly; but if she had gone to bed he would beat her just the same.

One night he was staggering home when a cloaked figure offered to help him along the road. That was the last night of carousal for Maurus. In the morning he was found dead at the roadside, for the man in the cloak was of course the devil, come to collect his own.

Forgetting how wretchedly Maurus had continually treated her, his long-suffering wife sorrowfully arranged a suitable funeral in the churchyard at Kues. And that should have been that, but it was not. As the villagers returned from the burial they were decidedly surprised to see Maurus himself looking out of his own upper window, from which he had been watching the proceedings with the greatest interest.

Maurus continued to haunt the house for some time — though the story does not relate whether he was *Poltergeist* enough still to beat his wife. Eventually three priests came and banned him in proper Moselle fashion, but with the result that he became a public nuisance at the Kues ferry.

'*Hol iwer! Hol iwer!*' he called across the river after dark, making the poor ferryman take out his boat to row over and fetch a traveller who did not exist. Again the priests intervened but without complete success, for although the ferry is now left undisturbed Maurus may still occasionally sneak into Kues and trip up some inoffensive drinker so that he falls into the river.

We had not long been at the quay of Kues before we made the acquaintance of Franz the ferryman. He was one of the gentlest souls I have ever met — but for that matter ferrymen are nearly always kindly and quiet men. There is something in the nature of their work that makes them so, for each voyage is a slow, genial and conversational affair, undertaken without hurry and to oblige the passengers. I have known one tough and drunken ferryman on the Meuse, but the people there hastened to explain that he was only a stand-in, a temporary creature that had to be suffered. Besides, he came from Charleroi, which explained everything they added.

Franz did not have a motor-ferry, or even one that worked on a cable. It was a long, thin, punt-shaped affair with seats down the sides, and Franz rowed it with a pair of those awkward-looking oars that Germans always use. He was very thin, and altogether very small, and he usually wore green breeches and a green cap which might have been a trooper's, and which he exchanged for a creamy white one on Sundays. I once saw him row extra slowly across the river so that the speed would not upset the sailing of a toy boat which a little boy was trailing behind on a string.

When we first came to Kues aboard the *Thames Commodore*, my wife and I walked down one day to the bridge and climbed up to the ruined Burg Landshut above Bernkastel. We wandered down through the vineyards and under the trees, and eventually reached the ferry stage opposite Kues. But there was no need to call '*Hol' über!*' The bow of Franz's boat was already grating on the stones. He had no passengers, but he had rowed over just because he had seen us far up in the wood and thought we would want to cross over that way.

Franz was never obtrusive. One might wonder where he was, but always his eye or ear was cocked toward the further shore and nothing happened in Kues without his noticing it. So, when I tramped into the village, fresh from my dip in the river, yet looking anything but nautical, it was Franz who first noticed me at the waterfront and came up to shake me by the hand.

'*Grüss Gott,*' he said. 'And why on foot?'

I told him I wanted this time to see the river from the hilltops.

'It is always beautiful,' he said gently. 'The Moselle is never anything but beautiful, even in winter.'

I

At that moment a call came across the harbour entrance, from the camping-site on the spit beyond.

'*Fer . . . ger!*'

Franz nodded and walked over to the bank to pick up his oars. 'Always the ferryman,' he said with a laugh. 'They always call for the ferryman.' He pushed out and began to row with long measured strokes.

Until a century ago there was not a single bridge across the Moselle between Trier and Koblenz, a distance of one hundred and twenty miles. At every village there was then a ferry, and even now a surprising number survive along the river, either rowboats for foot travellers or smart motor-ferries for vehicles, or floats worked upon the now much decreased current. On her way down from Trier to the Rhine the *Thames Commodore* passed more than forty ferries of one sort and another, and often we would see hikers, or vineyard workers, or women who had been out to shop standing at the water's edge to call for the ferryman.

'*Fer . . . ger! Hol' über!*' The familiar cry would travel over the broad water, sometimes with a note of impatience as though the whole world should halt to afford the caller a passage. And if the boat were not already manned, soon we would see the ferryman walking with a slow stride from his cottage to put out into the river, perhaps still munching the lunch from which he had been so summarily called.

The ferryman's trade is one that seems to allow no rest, but the vintners themselves have a period in their year when to work in the vineyard is absolutely forbidden. By a curious custom the vineyards all down the valley are locked some weeks before the vintage, and no man may work upon his vines. To be caught in a vineyard even if it is his own is a serious offence, for nature must be allowed to run its course until the mayor, advised by the elder vintners, proclaims that on Monday next such-and-such a slope will be harvested, on Friday another hillside. Then everyone will turn out to gather in the grapes, and only those rows may be left which the vintner has previously announced that he wishes to keep for a *Spätlese* (late picking) or even for *Eiswein* — leaving the berries to be frozen.

It is in this one slack period of the year that the vintner takes
time off for jollification, and all up and down the Moselle valley
the villages have their main wine festivals. But the Bernkastel
Weinfest is more than a local affair. It is the occasion when all the
vintages of the Middle Moselle are displayed and tasted, from
Neumagen down to Burg and Reil. When first we heard of it and
read a notice that five thousand cars would be parked at the back
of Kues harbour and forty special trains and hundreds of coaches
could be expected, we were convinced that this was the one place
the *Thames Commodore* should not be found at that time. But
Hugo König shook his head.

'It is a thing of a lifetime,' he said. 'You must come. Wherever
you are, you must bring the ship back to arrive that Friday. You
will never, never forget it.'

So our exploring of the valley had to be calculated again, and
after a visit to the Lahn and then a run back up the Moselle into
its beautiful Luxembourg reaches the *Thames Commodore* came
surging down past Lieser one evening in September and blew off
her signal so that the Königs would not fail to hear as she swung
once again into the harbour to dock at the quayside across from
the cardinal's birthplace, just in time for one of Hugo's 'half-hens'
and a glass of his Kardinalsberg before the festival began.

Already the five thousand cars promised for the waste land at
the inner end of the harbour were arriving, and soon an obliging
roadman was erecting a barrier of rope to discourage those lucky
enough to find a space on the quayside from driving on to our
deck. We were not the only ship to have arrived for the festivities
of the evening. One or two small German runabouts had arrived,
towed behind cars, and they were now being slid into the water
in Franz's little ferry bay. But the attractions of the festival were
well enough known in the barge world for seven Europa-ships to
have worked out their voyages just as we had done, to reach Kues
that evening. The village resounded to the signal hoots and the
hurried chuggata-chuggata-chuggata of the powerful motors as
the heavy craft manoeuvred out of the stream and came stern first
into the basin. The water seethed and swayed as they churned it
with their screws, and the *Thames Commodore* swung to and fro

on her lines as though bowing a welcome to her elders and betters.

A few minutes before nine o'clock we slipped our lines and stole out into the river. The lights of Bernkastel shone along the further shore, and up against the sky we could see the dark form of the ruined keep of Burg Landshut. Just upstream of the bridge a number of shapes were gliding slowly over the water, stemming the very slight flow of the river or moving ever so gently past the fun-fair on the foreshore meadow of Kues. All these ships were in darkness except for their navigation lights, but from their forms we could make them out as we moved in to join them in their stately gavotte. There was the *Stadt Trier* whose jetty we had used when she was up river to take a party to see the Roman mosaics at Nennig. Two trip-boats from Bernkastel itself were there too, laden as fully as could be, and passing beyond them we pirouetted in the stream beside the *Princesse Marie-Astrid*, the splendid and powerful passenger vessel from the Luxembourg town of Remich, a ship subscribed for by all the village communities spread along the left bank where the river edged the Grand Duchy, and one which to that little country was just such a matter of pride as the *Queen Mary* was to Britain when first she voyaged across the Atlantic. We knew the *Marie-Astrid* well, and her skipper Captain Kieffer of Remich, and the sight of her brought back many memories of those sunlit upper reaches of the Moselle. Crowded to the rails she had run one hundred kilometres of river to make Bernkastel on time. We gave her a courtesy signal as we bobbed past, and she answered us with the contralto tone we knew so well.

Suddenly all the lights in Bernkastel went out. For a second there was darkness except for the red and green of the ships and the glow from the dodgems and merry-go-round at Kues, then a tremendous flash came from the hilltop behind the town, its report hurrying after it through the night air. All at once Burg Landshut was seen to be alight, a red glow sweeping through the keep and spreading swiftly along the walls, the strontium hue giving such an appearance of heat that where it poured over the parapet and down into the precious rows of vines it seemed as though the stone itself were melting. And as the white smoke rose to hang still over

the pine forest at the edge of the Hunsrück plateau, the first salvo
of rockets was fired over the river from the castle hill.

There is something quite enchanting about fireworks over the
water, the bursting sprays of stars mirrored shakily on the ripples
of the stream. I have seen it in the City of London, at Les Andelys
on the Seine, at Henley, at Würzburg on the Main and Hanno-
versch Münden on the Fulda, but never, never so splendid as the
display which opened the Wine Festival of the Middle Moselle.
Bronze and ruby, gold and sparkling silver, emerald, and of a blue
as delicate as that of the Baltic Sea the flickering lit up the valley,
and the ships, the dark forest of pines which crowned the hills,
and the orderly slopes where the vines waited heavy for the mayor
to announce that the harvest might begin. It was a happy scene
too, one which Ausonius would have loved if the Tabernae he
knew had been transplanted into a more pyrotechnic age.

The fireworks and the burning of the former summer residence
of the Archbishop-Electors are only the beginning, a prelude to
the serious business of the annual fair when for the first time the
wines of the previous harvest are ready for sampling. Of the scores
of thousands who stream toward Bernkastel for the week-end
many will merely taste the wines and enjoy them there and then,
but others will deliberate, assaying the wine by rolling it round
their tongue and comparing it with others before placing an order
for a modest private consignment to be laid down at home and
broached during the year, or for larger stocks for hotels and stores
all over the country. This tasting is done in the *Weinstrasse*, the
roadway in front of the Michaelsturm being transformed into a
street along either side of which are the booths of every wine
village along this section of the river. There the wine-maidens in
their own village costume pour an endless supply of one-tenths
of a litre at fifty pfennigs a time — or more in the case of very
special wines. Pretty and fresh and rosy are these girls, each in her
black bodice over a white puff-sleeve blouse and with a red scarf,
usually embroidered with a vine-leaf motif in green or gold. Only
the maidens from the village of Wolf wear little red caps — Red
Ridinghoods in fact, in honour of the name of the wine of their
village, the Wolfer Rotkäppchen. The vintners are there too, in

Bernkastel, the wine festival of the Middle Moselle

their blue smocks with ample red kerchiefs, and a wide hat above a broad Moselfrankish face.

All day the girls draw the corks and pour the wine whilst the vintners roll up the barrels and cases, and the thousands of customers, glass in hand, move casually from one booth to the next, savouring the relative quality and aroma of the wines of the Middle Moselle and just occasionally pausing for a hot sausage from one of the immense cauldrons of *Bratwurst*. One might imagine that the wines would all be very much the same, for each is derived from the same Riesling grape sprayed with the same pesticides, subject to identical weather and tended with a common traditional skill. Yet they may taste very different indeed, just as the Königs' Kardinalsberg was by no means the same as that of one of his near neighbours.

I asked Hugo how these differences came about. Where it was a matter of wines from adjacent rows on the same slope, then obviously it must be mainly a matter of the way the vintner worked his plants before the harvest, he said. There was much in the pruning, in taking off leaves to admit the sunshine, and of course in the cultivation of the soil itself. Cellar treatment might vary also, he explained, and all vintners tended to have their own private and often family secrets. But the fact remained that all the wines from one village would be recognisably distinct from every wine from some adjacent village, and the cause of this was a matter of physical geography. One slope would face a different point of the compass, its angle of incline more or less steep than its neighbours — a character which would affect the rate at which water drained off the hillsides. The actual stone of the vineyard hillsides varied also — we ourselves had noticed the red sandstone and ruddy soil below Trier, the limestone of Ruwer and elsewhere, the purple slate along other reaches of the river and the schisty shales which served so well to keep the soil moist below them and yet throw up heat to the vines. Each of these types of rock would have a quite distinct chemical constitution, and even within the same general type of stone there would be variations in the trace elements, substances which might have a great effect upon the internal metabolism of the grape.

From Saturday to Monday the Weinstrasse was in full swing, afternoon and evening alike. This was the most severely practical part of the yearly festivities, but many of those who had come to Bernkastel or Kues had done so to see the great procession on the Saturday afternoon.

Germany is a great land for processions, partly because it is a country of village bands. However small a Moselle village may be, it is almost certain to have a brass band dressed in its own smart livery, a band composed not of old men but mainly of young ones and even of boys, a sure sign that the tradition is by no means a dying one. In the Bernkastel procession there was not just one local band but twenty-three, all of them from vintner villages except for one contributed by the United States Air Force camp on the Hunsrück plateau, and a French military band composed entirely of horns which the musicians tossed in the air and deftly caught again while hurrying in a half-running motion over the bridge.

There is nothing quite like the Bernkastel cortège, and when Hugo König said we would never forget it he was certainly right. First came the heralds, jogging down the roadway in their blue and gold, riding a trio of handsome carthorses through the streets of the town past the dignitaries seated on a stand in the market-place and on across the bridge toward Kues. Behind them followed the bands, each leading the wine-floats of their own village, tableaux which portrayed the name of a wine-slope or were related to the particular place itself. Neumagen's tractor was towing a splendid replica of its famous Roman wine-ship, the bearded Gauls in their blue smocks leaning out to fill any glass reached out toward them. Graacher Himmelreich appropriately had the gates of heaven, and standing between them a very patriarchal St Peter welcoming all comers with his golden goblet of wine. Cherubs beamed from the clouds, and around the slope leading to paradise sat wine-maidens, young and beautiful, decked in flowers, bottle in hand. For apart from the sheer fun of it all, each village wished people to sample their particular wine and assure themselves that it really was so much better than the rest.

Dhroner Mönchshof was being dispensed by three very monastic characters at either side of their abbey cellar, while for Kues the great Cardinal Cusanus sat robed in red upon his throne, holding in his hand a priceless glass, a *Pokal* which must have held a gallon at least. For two whole hours the procession filed by, the village wine-queens on their flower-clad thrones, the youths blowing upon their tubas or fifes, and the gay songs of the Moselle drifting away down the valley.

> *O, Mosella,*
> *Du hast ja so viel Wein.*

So much wine indeed, and each September a three-day-long chance to discover what the last year's crop is really like. Good? Or nothing very special this year? Indifferent perhaps, but certainly very drinkable, for even a comparatively poor Moselle would be better than most other wines. The real question is whether or not it will be as excellent as the wine of the great vintage year just gone before.

Good? Yes, indeed, to judge by the number of slim green bottles lying in the roadway of the Weinstrasse when two o'clock of the morning strikes and the tired wine-maidens leave the street to the brooms of Bernkastel's cleansing department which swiftly sweep the town from end to end.

The consumption of wine must be prodigious, for thousands sip it almost continually throughout the week-end. Yet the Moselle wines are light. They are not the chosen drink of the toper. Walking home out of the town toward the *Thames Commodore's* berth at Kues we saw not a single drunk. Perhaps that was not so surprising after all if it needed sixty glasses of Hugo König's excellent vintages to fell a visiting Englishman as neatly and finally as the lumbermen might bring down some giant and stalwart pine of the dark Hunsrück forest.

VII

White ships of the Moselle — Zeltingen — the Elector's ruse — the fate of Machern — murder of Kuno — naughty boy of Kröv — Traben-Trarbach — Loretta's captive — Grevenburg and Fontange — Montroyal of Vauban — Inland Shipping Week at Trarbach

WHEN the *Thames Commodore* put out from Kues harbour to head for the Rhine she somewhat resembled the ships carved on the monument of the Neumagen contractor. Not that she was rowed by round-faced men with beards, but because she might reasonably have been classed as a wine-ship.

It seemed to us a pity to neglect the opportunity to take home some of Hugo's best vintages, wines which were far superior to the Bernkastelers of doubtful origin which could be obtained in England at five times the price. There would be a little duty to pay, we knew, but any patriotic person can persuade himself that customs and excise are in a good cause, and their payment prevents the redundancy among customs officers which would at once be acute if the duties which help to pay part of their salaries were abolished. So, after he had grilled the last half-hen and seen the final customer out of the door in the early hours of the morning, Hugo repaired to his cellar and began to run off the wine into bottles. He then corked and labelled them, and about two o'clock he arrived alongside pushing a trolley laden with cartons.

Our own needs were modest, but somehow the consignment had a tendency to swell. Each time we docked at Kues we had other friends with us, and always when they had been to Hugo's they would wonder whether we could take a little wine home for them. With a few more bottles added at Zell and other places my wife and I had a busy evening packing them down under the floor

the night before we set out on the final leg of the trip from
Düsseldorf to Teddington.

The slim green bottles containing all that was worth while in
two thousand years' culture — as our vintner friend at Trittenheim had expressed it — lay packed in rows with newspaper
between them. Cooled by the water outside the steel ship's bottom
they travelled excellently and we lost none, and if the ship behaved
so splendidly on her way over from Belgium that was partly due
to the extra weight astern — for the thirty gallons and the quantity
of bottles to hold it provided us with another quarter-ton of ballast
and gave the *Thames Commodore* just that little extra lift at the
nose that she needed.

Our departure from Kues was carefully planned to fit in with
the daily steamer which left Bernkastel at breakfast-time to head
downstream for Cochem. She was not literally a steamer in the
sense of being a vessel propelled by expanded water-vapour, but
she had the character of one just the same. Her long torso had just
that grace and power and slight smell of hot oil which goes with a
steamer. Although a fine modern diesel vessel she was at heart
a steamer, a lineal descendant of the *Inexplosibles* which had
struggled to open a service on the Lorraine reaches in the 1840s.

The Moselle must be one of the best rivers in the world for
a steamer trip, even though the ships no longer operate on quite
the same principles as they did when Michael Quin wrote his
account of a *Steam Voyage on the Moselle* published in 1843. If
he did not name the steamer which carried him down the lower
half of the river from Bernkastel that was because the ship was
only the second of the very earliest vessels of the 'Moseldampf-
schiffahrt Trier Gesellschaft' which opened the service to Koblenz
in 1841 with the *Mosella*, and it had as yet no appellation other
than 'No. II'. Later it was to be named the *Balduin* after the famous
or infamous former Elector–Archbishop.

Quin found the proximity of the boilers to the dining-saloon
such that 'even a temporary confinement in such an oven would
be anything but agreeable', so he insisted on dining outside.

'I suspect there was a little ingenuity played off by the steward,
by fixing the dinner-hour precisely at the time when the vessel

would be passing through some of the choicest scenery on the Moselle,' he wrote. 'At all events, the first course was scarcely over, when the word *Cochem* having been announced by one of the waiters, the company all rushed out in a body and ascended the deck, in order to admire the singularly beautiful prospect of that ancient town. They came out, the ladies especially, dripping with the results of the atmosphere in which they must have been nearly boiled, and they found it so difficult to return to their steam bath and the perfumes with which it was medicated — perfumes, I fancy, not much improved by the odour of soups and vegetables and meats — that they declined to return to the cabin. The waiters pretended to be in a state of perturbation, but they were not slow in removing the cloth.'

Octavius Rooke's similar voyage was made about fifteen years later. The steamers, he said, were few in number but very well appointed. 'Sometimes in summer there is not enough water to enable them to travel, and often a good bump is experienced from some hidden rock. On one occasion we knocked a good-sized hole in the bottom and tore off a large piece of one paddlewheel; but there was not the slightest danger, as the water was not deep enough for us to sink into it, so we pumped away for some time and patched up the hole. Shortly after, we met the down-steamer, which had likewise started a leak, and we were all much amused at the solemnity with which our captain handed over to his friend a pump which he knew would not work, as he had tried it in vain in our boat.'

Nowadays there should be no bumps from hidden rocks, for a nine-foot depth is maintained all down the channel. The ships can safely run fast, and by storing a few reserve knots up their sleeves they usually keep to within seconds rather than minutes of the time-table — a considerable feat on a river with locks. The locks are operated to suit the time-table, but only ten minutes grace is allowed. If later than that the ship may find the lock closed, and so may have a long wait while a barge or pusher is let through in the opposite direction.

The *Thames Commodore* liked the three steamers, the *Trier*, *Saarbrücken* and *Luxemburg*. Her affection was partly a mere shipmately one, but she also enjoyed their company because if sharing a lock with a barge or steamer she did not have to pay her ten Marks. Barges were sometimes scarce, for in the Lorraine iron-fields there was no unloading on Sundays and very little on Saturdays. This meant that there was an almost complete two-day break every week in the departure of ships from Thionville, and this gap in the shipping spread downstream so that Tuesday yielded few if any downstream barges passing down the Middle Moselle reaches. The *Thames Commodore* had to use her friends the steamers. So she left Kues at a quarter past eight in order to have the passenger ship already in sight astern of her as she bore down upon the lock at Zeltingen (km. 124 L).

The long reach to Zeltingen passes between two of the most famous wine villages of the river, Graach on the starboard hand (km. 127 R) and Wehlen to port (km. 125·5 L). The vineyards of both are on the right bank, which faces south-west, the splendid slope of Graacher Himmelreich, and Wehlener Sonnenuhr or sundial. And, of course, the sundial is there on the cliff for any vine-dresser to tell the time, provided only that the sun is shining.

Wehlen is obviously a village of long-established prosperity. Its houses are large, confident and very beautiful. Indeed the trade of the vintners was so assured that the village built its own bridge across the river, only to lose it when the fierce flood of 1921 carried away all but the abutments on either bank. The ferry, already pensioned off, was pressed back into service. Now Wehlen has a fine suspension bridge, and like that of Piesport it was paid for in wine — a most acceptable currency if as good as Wehlen wines should be.

Zeltingen lock is immediately above the village itself, which stands very quiet and beautiful on the right bank (km. 123·2 R) as though it knows that it is safe. And so it has always been, for the little town was spared destruction even in the Thirty Years War, when the Swedes — second only in traditional villainy to the French — came marauding up the valley. It was Kurköln territory in those days, land of the Elector of Cologne, and the Elector bought from the king of Sweden a guarantee of immunity for everything, even including the wine, children, livestock and cattle

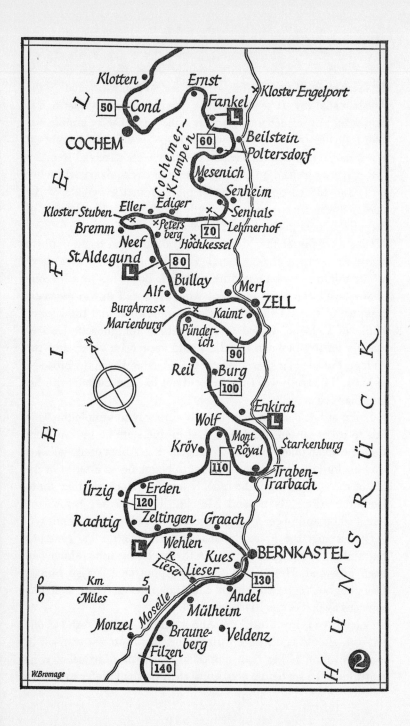

of his domains. It is interesting to note the order in which they were listed — children rightly coming before the stock but very definitely second to the wine, which was no doubt coveted by the Swedish soldiery. It seems that the Swedes operated what nowadays would be termed a 'protection racket', and their example was later followed by the French who in turn agreed to be bought off at a reasonable price. As a result, Zeltingen has survived so intact that when we walked up past the church of St Stephen in the vineyards and looked down upon the place from the heights of the Zeltingerberg there was not a single break in the purple slate of the village roofs in the valley far below.

Like so many of the Moselle villages Zeltingen has a uniform charm rather than any outstanding feature. It is just 'a nice place' as one might write on a picture postcard. But it has its tales, one of which concerns the excellent wine produced in the monastic vineyard of the Martinshof, a wine so renowned that the Elector Philip of Cologne wished to experience it for himself. He frequently let it be known that he would appreciate a barrel of the vintage, but the monks seemed not to understand even the broadest of hints. The truth was that they did not like the Elector with his high-handed ways.

Philip at last decided that the only sure way to sample the wine was to carry out an inspection, and in due state he set out from Cologne on an official visit to Zeltingen. The Abbot easily guessed why his lord spiritual seemed at last to be taking an interest in the life of the brethren, and he quickly laid in a stock of other wines from the Rhine, Nahe and Moselle. These he set before the Archbishop and his entourage, without revealing their identity.

On leaving, the Elector thanked the Abbot for his generous hospitality, praising in particular the excellent wine which had been provided. He insisted that the Abbot should visit him at Cologne, but regretted that he could not offer in return such fine vintages as that of the Martinshof.

'Thank you, my Lord,' the Abbot calmly replied. 'And if one day you should come here with the intent to interest yourself in our institution rather than our cellar, then the Martinshof wine may indeed be set before you. Until then we shall prefer to reserve it for those who are our true friends.' And he bowed the Elector out.

Zeltingen almost runs into Rachtig, but between them there is a moment of flat land and a bridge leading across the river close to what little remains of the convent of Machern (km. 122·3 L). This institution was, of course, destroyed by the wicked French who stole it and sold it by auction in 1803. It was bought by a Dutchman, who turned the baroque church into a barn by walling up the windows. But centuries earlier it was destroyed in a more dramatic fashion, one nun alone being spared.

Ermesinde was only one of those beautiful young ladies of the Moselle valley whose lover had nobly gone to fight in the crusades. She was living at home in her father's castle when at last a pilgrim arrived with the great news of the capture of Antioch. As the man told his traveller's tale of the slaughter Ermesinde listened eagerly. She heard of the splendid feats of valour performed there, and her heart leaped with pride as the pilgrim described how the heads and arms and legs were swiftly hacked from the infamous Saracen warriors, and how one knight had distinguished himself above all others, her own Rupert to whom she had pledged her life.

'But, alas,' the man added, 'the grave has now closed over the glory of that most noble and courageous fighter.'

Ermesinde swooned. Her Rupert was ... dead. The will to live seemed simply to flow out from her body.

As she began to recover her strength Ermesinde's father tried to discover more about Rupert's death, but no further news was to be had other than that he had died bravely in battle. Heart-broken, Ermesinde betook herself to the convent of Machern to join the sisters in their life of purity and devotion.

She soon found that these particular virtues were hardly represented in the sisterhood, and that the convent was little more than a den of vice in which the whole community was enthusiastically involved. Her fellow nuns scoffed at her having notions of such things as chastity, and ridiculed the way she took her vows and devotions so seriously. Ermesinde however was a spirited girl, and she refused to be led astray. Her constancy was rewarded when one evening another pilgrim came up the valley and knocked at

K

the gate, asking for food and shelter. The other nuns were decidedly occupied, and so it was Ermesinde who opened the door. The reader will not be altogether surprised to know that the traveller was her long-lost Rupert.

'Ermesinde!' At the sound of her true love's voice the girl swooned again, but not for long. She was in his arms at last.

Yet Ermesinde insisted that she would not be untrue to her vows as were the other nuns. She could not simply elope and marry her lover, however much she might wish to do so. She agreed however that she would see him occasionally, and while the other nuns were having their orgies in the hall Ermesinde and her true knight would kneel in the chapel and pray for each other's happiness.

After some time yet another stranger came to Machern. He was a beggar, poor and old and doddery. Once again it was Ermesinde who opened the door, and upon hearing his request for food and alms she went in to where the other girls were holding their latest party and told them that there was a poor man who needed their charity. The nuns streamed out to the gate and threw the beggar out, hurling abuse and improper language after him. They were no more interested in charity than in chastity.

Suddenly the old man turned upon them. 'Woe unto you, false sisters of mercy!' he cried, raising his arms to the heavens like an old-time prophet. 'Woe unto you, for your doom is nigh!' So saying, he departed into the night, the laughter of the nuns following him.

Shortly after this incident Rupert and Ermesinde were again kneeling one evening in the chapel when a fierce storm bore down the valley. Lightning struck upon Machern, and the fire from heaven burned up the hall and slew every one of the nuns within it. Indeed, all that remained of Machern was the chapel, with Ermesinde and Rupert safe inside it amid the destruction all around.

With the convent no longer in existence Ermesinde was soon persuaded that she was released at last from her vows. She was soon married to Rupert, and together they lived a life of happiness, prosperity and charity in their home overlooking the valley.

Through Zeltingen to Rachtig (km. 121·7 R) the hills of the right bank fall away, and downstream of Machern the vines cross to the other shore, as the river curves away right-handed towards Ürzig (km. 119·5 L) to port and Erden (km. 118·3 R) to starboard, with the slopes of the famous Würzgarten (herb-garden) and Treppchen vintages respectively. The *Treppchen*, or stair, is, of course, a flight of steps which runs straight up through the vines to the uppermost terraces of the sunbaked slope.

At one point the cliff falls extremely sheer to the river, so steep that one wonders at the tenacity of the vintners who would build up the little plots of terrace on what is almost a bare rock-face. High up in the red stone is the remains of a cave with a wall built to enclose its mouth, a den which once was the haunt of robbers who reached it by a rope-ladder which they could draw up after them. It was also used as the prison for the unfortunate Kuno, who was on his way from Cologne to Trier to take up his appointment as Elector-Archbishop, an office for which he had been singled out by the Emperor Henry IV.

Kuno was a notably good man at a time when the ecclesiastics of Trier seem to have been for the most part just the opposite. Fearing that he would restrict their life of luxury the prebendaries persuaded the city governor Theodorich to lay an ambush. Kuno was set upon, successfully snatched away from the company of the Bishop of Speyer with whom he was travelling, speedily trussed and hauled up to the cave of the Michaelslay. After being held there for some weeks he was at last dragged out by four ruffians acting on the orders of Theodorich. Bound hand and foot he was carried to the edge of the cliff.

'Now we shall see if you are chosen by God,' the men mocked. 'You will remember that bit in the scripture about how "the angels will bear thee up lest thou dash thy foot against a stone". Now is your chance to prove it.' So saying, they threw Kuno down from the rocks.

And indeed, the legend says, the good Kuno was not hurt. Twice more he was hauled up on a rope and flung over the cliff's edge, yet he was not killed. The men were beside themselves with fury, and instead of throwing him down again they struck off his head with a sword. His blood poured down the slope, and for ever after the wine from the Michaelslay has had just that extra something in its flavour that only the blood of so just a man could induce.

The murderers returned to Trier and told how they had successfully put an end to the pretensions of Kuno to become the new bishop. When he heard the details, Theodorich was filled with fear, and leaving his post of governor he quickly set off for the Holy Land to atone for his guilt. But it happens that guilt has a high specific gravity, and Theodorich's crime was so great that even his remorse could not reduce its weight sufficiently. Burdened down by his wickedness the ship sank with all hands, and the waves of the Mediterranean closed over the man who had chosen to raise his hand against Kuno.

One after another the little brown villages of the vintners would go gliding past us, a thin line if on the vineyard side of the river, a more rounded patch of civilisation if on the north-facing shore where land was not at such a premium for rows of Riesling. Attracted by the peculiar flag on her staff, the children would run to the bank and wave to the *Thames Commodore*, but otherwise there would be little sign of life. In high summer the adults were somewhere on the slopes, almost hidden by the leaves of the vines, and in the dead period before the vintage they were busy in the cellars preparing the utensils and presses for the harvest.

Pretty, quiet, reasonably prosperous, if any of these places were known at all to the world outside it was for the names which as parents they gave to their vintage children. Piesport, Graach, and now Kröv (km. 112·5 L), and in this latter case the wine did not bear the name of a patron saint or monastic property, but had a severely practical title — Kröver Naktarsch (or bare-bottom). When watching the procession at Bernkastel we had noted Kröv's own smart brass band marching over the river in front of a float on which a model of a muscular vintner was holding a boy under one arm and spanking his bottom with his strong right hand. It is said that the local wine got its name from just such an incident. Coming upon a lad sampling the barrels in the cellar a vintner seized him, pulled down his trousers, and summarily taught him never to do it again. The boy's delinquency was understandable, for Moselle wine has a taste children adore, and it is not always easy to prevent youngsters drinking a bottle as though it were lemonade.

At Kröv the river decides to indulge in one of its most dramatic pieces of virtuosity, first turning tightly through half a circle round the edge of the high promontory on which stand the crumbled ruins of the abbey of Wolf (km. 113 R), as though aiming directly for Bernkastel again. Then it changes its mind and swings so far back through Traben-Trarbach that after nine kilometres of loop it has returned to within only one kilometre of its own bank opposite Wolf. Because of these hithers and thithers I reached Trarbach from Bernkastel much more rapidly the time I followed the path over the hills than when we slipped down the river by ship. The Moselle trail is here well marked and a very pleasant walk indeed, and from the woodland plateau the path drops very steeply into Trarbach, a town in which nearly all the older houses

Wolf ferry

were burned on the very night that Mr Rooke had disembarked
from the patched-up steamer to lodge for the night at Traben on
the further shore. It was 'a splendid but melancholy sight' as the
fire spread through the town so quickly that the poor people fleeing
from the flames had to throw down the goods they were trying to
save and run for their lives. 'The whole space, enclosed by the hills
in which the town lay, surged in great waves of fire; in this molten
sea great monsters appeared to be moving, whose shapes seemed
writhing with pain as those of the devils in hell.'

The Moselle villages often suffered such a fate. Cramped into
a small flat patch along the river shore they gave little space to the
streets, and their houses were so tightly packed that a fire would
always spread from one building to another. Almost every village
was burned out at one time or another and most of them on
several occasions, so that only Beilstein just upstream of Cochem
still preserves something of the huddled cluster that once was
common all down the river.

Trarbach and Traben are linked by a bridge (km. 107), the end
of which is crossed on the Trarbach or right bank by a red sandstone archway which contains an inn and has on its outside the
carved portraits of those responsible for the two songs of praise
about the river — Ausonius, author of *Mosella*, and Reck and
Schmitt, who composed the *Mosellied*. There is a vintner, too, and
a wine-maiden, and the whole effect is pleasantly gay. And
Trarbach has always sought to be a place of reasonable gaiety.
Once it even boasted a casino, which was the scene of a nineteenth
century Mastersingers' contest run by a local doctor. This was
in 1846, and a whole tun of vintage wine was offered to the
composer of the song adjudged the best. More than two hundred
entries were received from schoolmasters and vintners, shop-
keepers and priests and farmers, and it is strange that the winning
song of praise to the Moselle has since been entirely forgotten,
probably because it was not suited to become a folksong. Schmitt
and Reck entered their *Mosellied*, then in its youth, and it never
even reached the rank of being commended. Nowadays there is
probably not a child in the valley from Trier to Koblenz who does
not know it.

In 1898 the bridge was built, and once again a song contest was held. From all over the world the poems and tunes poured in, more than two thousand sets of verses extolling the praise of the Moselle and its wine. No doubt a few hundred entries could quickly be eliminated, but the judges must have been driven almost demented by listening to the rest and comparing one song with another. In the end they could pick out no absolute winner but ordered the prize of one thousand bottles to be split among four entrants whose work they considered equally outstanding. Only one of the winning songs has survived until today, and even that is not particularly well known.

Trarbach still basks in the recollection of the spirited action of the Countess Loretta of Sponheim who resided in her castle of Starkenburg built high above the river a little way downstream of Trarbach. The castle can still be seen (km. 105 R) standing out so clearly against the sky that it is something of a surprise to climb what is perhaps the most magnificent part of all the Moselle trail and discover that no trace of the castle remains. The buildings are those of the charming little village which has taken its place, built largely out of the stones which belonged to the castle once renowned for the splendid exploit of the Lady Loretta herself.

Loretta lived in the days of the rapacious Elector Balduin. Soon after the death of her husband the Archbishop sent one of his marauding knights into her domains, where she promptly captured him and imprisoned him in the Starkenburg. The Elector swore vengeance, but he was persuaded by others to let matters rest and leave the Countess in peace. This went against his inclinations, but he agreed to do so, and an armistice was concluded. Work on the castle he had begun to build in her land was halted.

Because of this state of peace the Elector was only accompanied by a few servants when in 1327 he set out in his archiepiscopal barge to travel from Trier to Koblenz. After all, there was not much danger on the water. One could glide pleasantly down the river, viewing with satisfaction the rich vineyards of the ecclesiastical properties within the diocese.

Balduin's ship stopped for the night at Trarbach, where it was in view of the Starkenburg further down the river. No doubt as he resumed the journey next day he gazed up with suppressed fury at the residence of the person who had humiliated him. A mere woman! Already he had excommunicated her, but she seemed to flourish like the bay-tree just the same. Well, one day he would teach her a lesson. He would . . .

But just at that moment, as his ship was passing the foot of the cliff, there came a sudden jolt and the barge was brought up short. There was confusion as the Archbishop and his men fell forward in the boat, and at the same instant there appeared from behind the bushes at the river's edge a number of boats full of armed men. These were the knights and men-at-arms of Loretta herself, and they swiftly overpowered the bishop's servants, seized the mightiest and most feared prelate of all Germany, and escorted him and his men up to the Starkenburg. Loretta had instructed her men to place a stout chain across the river just below the surface.

The captive Archbishop Balduin stormed and threatened. Having already excommunicated the Countess for her former offence without her being noticeably distressed, he began to deliver a sermon on the rights of the Church and the certain damnation awaiting those who raised their hands against the Lord's Anointed. But Loretta only smiled. She found such an exhibition of blustering rage amusing.

Nine months Balduin was held 'under protective arrest' and granted every courtesy except his freedom. At the end of that time he was ready to come to terms. Loretta said that she only wished some slight compensation for the loss of his gracious company, and hinted that the Archbishop must also realise that he was somewhat indebted to her for board and lodging and wine. She was prepared to settle for a reasonable sum of money and an undertaking that he would remove from her territory and keep to his own. The sum was fixed at eleven thousand pounds — a heavy charge on even so rich a diocese as Trier — and as a guarantee Balduin was to lease to her the castles of Bernkastel, Cochem and Manderscheid. Just to make certain that the holy man should not be mistaken about his obligations the agreement would be signed by the King of Bohemia and a number of nobles as witnesses.

The excommunication would be removed, and to satisfy the incensed Pope John XXII the Countess and her aides would walk barefoot up the aisle of the cathedral of Cologne (but not Trier) carrying a candle as a sign of contrition.

With the money she received for the ransom the Countess immediately built above Trarbach a fortress strong enough to keep the Archbishop at bay if he should think of going back on his agreement. Which, of course, he did not. He knew well enough when he was beaten, and had no wish to be humiliated yet again.

This incident in the life of the Moselle valley has of course been variously embellished. One account says that the Countess Loretta has ever since haunted the ruins of her Grevenburg, the castle immediately overlooking the town of Trarbach clustered at its foot, and that she weeps and wails for her terrible sin in imprisoning so holy a man as the Archbishop of Trier. Presumably this legend arose in archiepiscopal circles, for by any other standards Balduin was an unusually fierce clerical thug, even for his time. Certainly no wailing ghost disturbed the *Thames Commodore* where she lay at the waterfront meadow. Another, but no more probable, addition is that the Archbishop's heart melted when he saw the lovely lady, and he showered gifts upon her to repay her for the love she showed him in an idyllic relationship which lasted for nearly a year. Somehow this does not ring true either. Loretta was much too astute to jeopardise her position by wasting her love on a man like him. She had the Archbishop where she wanted him — in ward rather than in her arms.

The Grevenburg was so built as to be unassailable from whatever direction an enemy might come. At the rear a single gate led out to the hill, and on the town side there was only one door, which could not be reached except by ladders. The fortress later figured in all the wars which spread ruin up the valley — the Thirty Years, the Spanish Succession, and of course the struggles with the villainous French — and when Trarbach was in the domains of Louis XIV the fortifications were extended by Vauban, who added a number of towers, one of which was appropriately named the 'Fontange'.

Louis XIV was out hunting one day when the wind blew away the hat of his mistress for the time being, a certain Mlle Fontange. Having a lot of hair she was obliged to find some means of temporarily reducing it to order, so she tied it up in a roll and secured it with ribbons, the ends of which fell down in alluring knots. The Roi Soleil was carried away with admiration, and begged her to leave her hair-do just as it was, all day. Next day the ladies of the court, who had duly noticed the effect, all appeared with their hair swiftly converted into the new style, *à la Fontange*. Naturally they began to outdo each other in sheer Fontangerie, and soon the coiffure consisted of a wire frame or rolls of gummed cloth stuck with feathers and buckles and hair-pins, covered over with the hair of the wearer. It might reach a height of two feet, and the wearer of such a contraption dared not move from her seat or nod her head in case the whole tower should crash to the ground.

The lack of mobility among fair women began to irritate the king, and he eventually let it be known that he did not like the towering coiffures. Besides, la Fontange herself had died. But the ladies paid no attention, for none wished to relinquish such a splendid symbol of status. Next it was the turn of the clergy to rail against the trend, but with just as little effect.

The fashion lasted until 1699, when it was broken overnight by the wife of the English ambassador in Paris. Lady Shaftesbury decided that the current hair-style was absurd, and she simply attended court with her hair hardly raised at all. She was a striking woman, and the effect was immediate. Next day the fine ladies of the court were copying her, just as they had imitated la Fontange. The king's pleasure was somewhat reduced by the discovery that an Englishwoman was more heeded in matters of fashion than he was himself.

Vauban's task at the Grevenburg was one of repair and improvement, but on the Traben side of the river he put much greater works in hand, for Louis XIV ordered the great plateau of the promontory which lay almost enclosed by the river between Wolf and Enkirch to be converted into an immense fortress to dominate the whole area. It so happened that this land also was part of an age-old gift to the see of Verdun, a fact which gave the monarch the chance to except it from the unwelcome provisions of the Peace of Westphalia and turn it into a thorn in the flesh of his neighbours. Vauban was sent to survey it, and eight thousand men from Alsace were at once conscripted to build the fortifications to his specification. The beautiful forest which at that time covered the land was hewn down, and the wood used for their barracks.

For nine kilometres the site was ringed by the natural moat of the Moselle, and Vauban is believed to have intended to convert it into a complete island by cutting a canal across the neck of the loop at Kövenig (km. 102 L). The land being between four and five hundred feet above the river, this would have required a considerable amount of digging, and in fact the idea was never put into execution. Perhaps there was already enough to be done in making the fortress.

The French called up five thousand men from the nearby villages as a labour corps to aid the eight thousand troops, for the Montroyal Vauban had designed was no mere fort but a fortified town, very similar to the Charlemont at Givet on the Meuse. There would be streets of shops for the garrison, four thousand strong, and in the centre a market-place was laid out, with a fountain and a statue of Atlas bearing the world on his shoulders. Although the place was primarily a military camp, and the main structures were the bastions and casemates, the barracks and arsenal and stores, so many houses were to be built that the French raided nearby villages for materials, simply pulling down houses in order to take the beams and joinery. Plasterers and joiners were press-ganged. Bernkastel was ordered to supply a further two hundred men, Zell and Cochem a hundred and fifty each — the villages being supplied with French guards who were to shoot any young men trying to leave, and burn and plunder the entire place if the necessary contingent of building labourers was not forthcoming.

So the works went on. Montroyal was completed, the troops installed, the stables for three thousand horses filled with cavalry chargers. From this vast strongpoint the French then sallied out and began to plunder the country, retiring always to the shelter of their impregnable citadel. At Trier they tore down the walls and bridge. Downstream, Koblenz was bombarded, Cochem burned and sacked after all the furniture and movables had been towed up-river on heavily laden ships to swell the booty of Montroyal. Every castle up the valley of the Moselle was pulled down in turn, its stones shipped to the fort above Traben.

For some years Montroyal was the terror of the quiet valley of the Moselle, but at last the battle of Fleurus turned the scales. Peace was restored, and under the terms of the Treaty of Ryswyck the territory of Montroyal and the adjacent lands to which the French had a claim were exchanged for Strasbourg. The French themselves were to destroy the entire installations, and soon the valley echoed to the sound of explosions as the mighty walls and bastions were mined and blown up, the barracks razed, the arsenal and stores broken down and levelled. As for the houses, they were taken apart and the timbers laboriously returned to the valley from which they had been plundered. Cochem used them in its rebuilding, and in many villages nearer at hand they were recut and shaped, to serve for a third time as beams and joists. And there some of them still remain in the framework of many a beautiful house which still survives from the final years of the turbulent seventeenth century.

Montroyal is now deserted except for the small airfield of a flying and gliding club, and fields of wheat ruffled in the breeze which sweeps over them and drops through the fringe of pines to the rich vineyards below. We climbed up to it one Sunday afternoon, following a track which led from Traben and mounted by steps through the sweep of the vines to the scarp above. It was hard to believe that there had once been such a powerful fortification on the hilltop, for all that remained among the trees and scrub behind the airfield was a mere up-and-downness of the ground where once the bastions had stood or powder magazines had been blown up. The French had indeed demolished the place with as great thoroughness as they had used in building it.

Traben-Trarbach must have been greatly improved when Enkirch lock and barrage were installed (km. 103) and the level of the water raised so that the twin towns faced each other across a presentable river instead of over a miserable stream with stones and groynes and a dirty wasteland of foreshore. The twins quickly took the opportunity to announce that they were the up-and-coming watersport centre of the Moselle, and in corroboration the international motor-boat races were held every summer on the reach below the bridge. As one who has always felt a river such as the Moselle to be a stream for quiet and gentle navigation such as appealed to Venantius Fortunatus rather than a race-track for over-powered outboards I was glad we did not arrive during that particular week. Instead of racing craft we had the pleasant company of a pair of Harpens, ships belonging to the Duisburg fleet of the Harpener Bergbau A.G.

In their joint effort to become the leading water town of the Moselle, Traben and Trarbach had curiously omitted to provide any quayside at all, and the two big barges were lying on the private jetty of the steamers. They were unladen and scrubbed so clean that they might have been bound for a wedding. Every available pennant had been mustered, and one of the ships was dressed overall with signal flags. The ships' boys wore spotless white shirts and navy trousers and stood smartly on deck to smile a welcome, tinged with a shade of fifth-form superiority, to a crocodile of girls which was clattering over the hatches, attended by a pair of teachers and a trio of extremely handsome water-policemen.

The ships were impressive — and that was why they were there, bright and shining and newly painted. Their task for a whole week was not to carry coal or gravel but to show the world in general and youngsters in particular that there was nothing quite like the life of an inland waterways man, or an inland waterways wife.

Inland shipping in Europe is not the dirty, run-down, un-economic narrow-boating that it is in Britain. One-third of the whole of the external trade of Switzerland is carried up the Rhine by inland ships. In the Netherlands, there is twice as great a length of canals as there is of railways, and nearly three-quarters of the entire traffic is on the water. In Belgium more than thirty per cent of all transport is on the waterways, and modernisation of

the older and narrower canals is being rushed ahead so that
Europa-ships can travel throughout the country.

All this activity demands ships, and in Germany alone more
than eight thousand are in service. These and the hundreds of
tugs shift 170,000,000 tons of goods about the country during the
year, nearly one-third of all the traffic in the republic. Yet when
we were at Trarbach there were only some thirty thousand men
and lads employed in the whole great enterprise of lighter-trains,
tank-ships and the sleek modern Europa-ships with their large
carrying capacity, and the number was still declining. There were
the passenger vessels too, ships such as the fast steamers of the
Rhine, and the kindly craft which paid our lock dues for us on the
Moselle. They, too, needed competent and reliable crews, and yet
there had been spreading over Europe a curious reaction against
being employed on a ship. Hence the decision to have an annual
Inland Shipping Week which would entice boys and girls to think
seriously about the advantages.

'Why the girls?' I asked Captain Neubauer, who was in the
wheelhouse of his ship, ready to demonstrate the steering.

'Because if lads leave the water, the reason is nearly always a
female one,' he said, turning the wheel. 'In spite of the luxurious
accommodation and free travel all over Europe girls think it
smarter to work in an office and live in a council flat. Yes, even in
one of those sterile piles of matchboxes you see in Cologne or
Düsseldorf. The young men may come, but they think the pay is
better on land. They forget that there they must pay rent, and
water and light, and everything which on a ship is free. Some of
them return ashore, but some stay. Even if they stay, there comes
the time when they get off with a girl. Nothing wrong with that,
but unless she was born and bred on a ship she is likely to turn
out a Lorelei.'

'Combing her golden hair and luring the shipper to his doom?'

'Luring him to the land, anyway, which is the same thing.'

Of course there was something to be said on the girl's side. A
boy-friend whose barge might pass her way once in six months
was not much of a companion. Even if she should settle down and
marry him, starting life in the mate's quarters at the front of the

ship, there would one day come the difficulties of schooling for the
children, which would involve either boarding-school or leaving
the youngsters with relatives. On land these problems did not
exist, though certainly there were others — such as securing
accommodation and making both ends meet.

Faced with a shortage of crews the carrying firms had begun to
change over where possible to the pusher-craft developed in the
United States and on the Congo River; for whereas an orthodox
tow-train needed a crew on each lighter as well as on the tug, the
pushed boats were strapped tight to the propelling unit, and
needed no crew at all. This was satisfactory for mass cargoes on
the larger rivers, but there still remained thousands of barges in
Western Europe which could only travel singly and each of which
needed a crew of its own. And this being so, a steady flow of ship's
boys was essential. That was why, all the while we were lying on
their flank in Trarbach, a procession of school parties was filing
through the wheelhouses of the two barges, peeping into the holds,
admiring the smart push-button kitchens, the baths and beds and
central heating. Any girl with half an eye open could see at once
that the accommodation was far superior to anything she was
likely to acquire on land, larger and more comfortable than a
council flat, and with privacy and freedom.

As for the boys, the Central Council of German Inland Shipping
saw to it that the deck-hands provided them with plenty to read.
There was an illustrated book about the role of shipping in the
Common Market, the excitement of travelling all over Europe,
the health of the open-air life, and the challenge of a job which
demanded decision and precision and a sense of responsibility,
especially when the value of the ship and cargo ran into hundreds
of thousands of pounds. Another booklet held up the possibility
of becoming a Rhine captain, a post which still has considerable
aura and status in Europe — and rightly so, as anyone would agree
who has run that river from top to toe even in a twenty-eight-
tonner like the *Thames Commodore*. Rhine captains must be
reasonably well paid, we thought, to judge by the fact that so many
of them carried on deck a Mercedes in which to take the wife out
for the evening. 'The Captain on the Rhine is the monarch of his

own floating kingdom,' the leaflet declared. I could have said much the same for the office of skipper of the *Thames Commodore*.

Finally there was a leaflet with letters and diary extracts of lads who had tried the job and found it the most exciting thing in the world. Michael of Duisburg loved the freedom, the chance to learn of other lands and languages. Martin of Neckarmühlbach used to spend his time watching the ships in the lock near his home, and heard the wonderful tales of the crews. Hermann of Duisburg started by playing on a wreck. He was punished for coming home dirty, but nothing would satisfy him except joining the crew of a ship. Another lad liked the beauty of the Upper Rhine. One wrote that he had been bathing in the Dortmund–Ems Canal when the skipper of a barge waiting outside Münster lock invited him on board. When he saw inside the ship he was at once converted. Several stressed that nothing in the world was so dreadful to them as the prospect of having to sit in an office, and some stated that when they mentioned that they wanted to join a ship their parents were against the idea — a good point in an era when it was becoming increasingly fashionable to make teenagers think rebellion to be natural and highly laudable.

I knew that I for one would have been impressed by the ships and the hand-outs. But then perhaps I was already biased.

VIII

From Trarbach to Pünderich — Marie of Marienburg —
Zell and the Black Cat — medieval shipping — drovers of
the towpath — the drinkers of Bullay — the Abbess Gisela
— Arras the brave — from Alf to Bremm — Stuben Abbey
— Bernard and the nightingales

No section of the Moselle trail is more beautiful than the climb from Trarbach to Starkenburg village. The hillside falls very steeply to the water, and the path which is cut into its slope continually gives glimpses of the river below, and along the splendid sweep of water from Wolf to Enkirch lock. Behind the Traben vineyards across the river the oats and barley grow over the plateau where Vauban's works lie exploded and buried, and only at one edge is there a large building which does not belong. Gaunt and rectangular it stands at the brow of the slope like a school sited there by mistake, or a warehouse delivered to the wrong address. In fact it is a reminder of how near this loop of river came to being ruined, for the object is the uncompleted shell of the first of a number which the Hitler government intended to erect as an air force barracks. Fortunately the armistice arrived in time to save this part of the valley from the fate which has overtaken the hills above Trier.

Up and up winds the path, through oak and alder and pinewoods, the rocks bright with campanula and saxifrage and dianthus. It is well trodden, a neat and tidy trail, and the same meticulous order prevails to far beyond Enkirch itself, the trail being for once really well marked, with M painted on walls and trees, or little M-plates nailed to telegraph poles. The reason, as the landlord of the 'Schöne Aussicht' at Starkenburg explained to me, was that the mayor of Enkirch was a very live wire indeed, a man of ideas. He was a great promoter of societies and clubs, and Enkirch had

its own music society, its shooting association, its angling club and
other bodies. With these flourishing associations established
within his domain the mayor then invited them each to become
godfather to one of the hiking trails. Each year a club would
probably have a 'festive walk' along its own path.

'And there's nothing so good for a path as to have a herd of
people tramp down the weeds and underbrush,' said the landlord.
'Besides, the associations maintain their own adopted paths, re-
cutting steps, levelling them where the ground has slipped, and
above all seeing to the marking so that not even the stupidest
rambler could miss a turning.'

From Enkirch the Moselle runs north to Burg (km. 99 R) and
then to Reil (km. 97·5 L), a village so proud of its wine-growing
on stone heated, it is said, by the devil himself, that it exhorts the
boatman in large illuminated letters spanning the river on the side
of the bridge to '*Trink Reiler Wein vom heissen Stein*'. However,
neither Burg nor Reil boasted any landing, and being so close
below Enkirch lock they were in the headwater of the reach and
so had only stony and shallow shores where even to anchor outside the fairway would have been difficult. We had no choice but
to continue downstream towards Zell and its smart new-cut
waterfront.

Below Reil the Moselle turns its tightest loop of all, travelling
eleven kilometres round the beautiful loop of the 'Hamm', which
takes its name directly from the latin *hamus*, a hook. The stream
seems to hesitate whether to go on or not, for it returns to within
four hundred yards of where its water was several hours earlier.
The happy little Moselbahn railway which faithfully followed the
curve of the river has gone, being replaced below Neumagen by
buses, but such a lengthy detour would in any case have been too
much to expect of the giant puffing locomotives of the Prussian
State Railways when in the 1870s they first began to plough
through the valley. They preferred to dive into a hole at the end
of the Bullay bridge (km. 82·8 L), the locomotive emerging
opposite Pünderich (km. 94·4) almost before the last clattering
truck of coke had disappeared into the tunnel.

Pünderich itself (km. 94 R) is a very beautiful village which still

boasts a timbered house removed from Montroyal and re-
assembled, but like those places immediately upstream it has no
quay and is flanked by a shore inhospitable enough to repel the
most determined aquatic invader. The fifth time we passed that
way I was determined to try to come to land, and, noting that

Enkirch

downstream of the houses there was a long dike set in the stream,
I turned the *Thames Commodore* below it and took her very slowly
up the inshore channel, sounding every yard. There proved to be
six feet of water all the way, and near the upstream end of the bank
we dropped the anchor, intending to row ashore.

Anchoring in the Moselle is not difficult, and with a heavy anchor of the stockless type the boat is usually held as firm as can be. I have always thought it sensible to examine the chart and also the banks for signs of an underwater power-cable, because even the most equable of mayors can become disagreeable and testy if somebody hooks the town power-supply and winches it out of the river-bed. Pünderich's cable crossed the river-bed at the upstream edge of the village, so we could drop anchor wherever we wished — for the ships passed on the further side of the dike.

Yet nothing would induce the anchor to hold. However much chain we ran out, the hook dragged, partly because the bottom was of slaty shingle and also because of the current. For some reason — presumably the intention of the engineers to reduce the flow in the navigation channel beyond the dike — the river streamed down the inshore cut at several knots. Every time a barge passed beyond the stone wall there was an extra surge, and by sighting on trees we soon found that the *Thames Commodore* was moving tail first downstream at about five yards a minute. We would have to be content to see Pünderich from afar, as before.

I let the anchor drag about two hundred yards while we sat on deck having tea. We were in no hurry, and I thought there was just a chance of bringing up the gold crown on the hook, for the lock-keeper at Enkirch had assured me that there was no record of it having been brought to light when the dredgers were at work on the canalisation. And the dredgermen, he said, had very sharp eyes for anything unusual rolling down the chute into the dumper boats.

The gold crown of Pünderich once rested on the head of the statue of the Virgin in a chapel near the shore. One day a fearful thunderstorm rolled down the valley, and a knight who was out hunting fled into the chapel, not even dismounting from his horse. His name was Chlodwig — which is enough to show that he was a villain, for no man of honour and virtue could ever be so named except perhaps Clovis the King of the Franks, who is known as Chlodwig in German, and who was to some extent upright even if extremely ferocious when roused.

Chlodwig saw the crown, and riding up to the altar he raised himself in his stirrups, took the diadem from the statue and set it over the ears of his horse. The effect was dramatic, for the steed was at once seized with a strange panic and shot from the chapel door to flee to the bank of the Moselle as though the devil were after it. In terror Chlodwig tried to fling himself out of the saddle, but his feet seemed to be held fast in the stirrups. The horse plunged into the river and sank, taking Chlodwig and the gold crown with it.

Our involuntary trawling of the channel was without result, so we raised the anchor, drifted back into the channel, and set off downstream again with Pünderich still unvisited. To port the vines rose in rows to the very edge of the Marienburg which crowns the ridge of the neck of land and so looks straight down to the river on either side (km. 93·7 L and km. 83·3 L). Then the promontory dips to a saddle, rises again to the hill of the 'Barl', and finally falls away through the vines to where Kaimt (km. 87·3 L) faces across the river to Zell.

This bulbous promontory enclosed by the 'Hamm' is curious. Once the Barl itself stood as an island in the bed of the Moselle, but as the millennia passed along the axis of time the river cut down its bed from a height nearly one thousand feet above the present level, and rolled enough stone and shingle to dam its original course and divert itself round the outside of the Barl.

From earliest times, travellers down the river would be landed at Pünderich to cross the river and climb the vineyard path to the Marienburg, three hundred feet above. There they could admire the view across to the Hunsrück forest and stroll down to Alf (km. 81·7 L), and still have plenty of time for a meal or a glass or two of wine before their ship drew in to pick them up. As for the Marienburg, its very name combines the religious with the military and hints that the site has been used for both purposes. And so it was, from the very beginning, for the Celts used it as a place of worship, and the Romans converted it into a fort.

We climbed up to the Marienburg several times, for Alf happened to have a proper harbour (km. 82 L), where we could draw in against a quay wall and lie in comfort, gently rocked at night by the swell driven into the haven by barges swinging close past the mole. From Alf a path climbed the steep north slope of

the Hamm through a damp wood of oak and creeper and sombre
pines to break out into the sunshine among the walnut trees beside
the Marienburg itself, part retreat house, part chapel, a fraction
of ruin and a quantum of inn.

Far back in history the religious foundation began, looking
across the saddle where once flowed the river and facing the Barl
where the Celts had held their meetings to promulgate the law.
It was as beautiful a position as might be found, and yet it had the
disadvantage that the convent occupied the very spot from which
one might dominate the country around. Every enemy who
reached the valley coveted the site on the top of the ridge, and so
in the thirteenth century the Archbishop of Trier added a fort
for its protection. And yet this only served to make the place even
more of a goal for the invader, and in the sixteenth century the
Pope ordered the removal of the nuns and the strengthening of the
fortress. The nuns each received an annuity of twenty-five gold
florins, three sacks of corn and half a tun of wine — a fair pension,
but no true compensation for the loss of so beautiful a home.

Another three hundred years and the Marienburg was again a
place of pilgrimage. Then came the revolutionaries, wrecking and
plundering, stripping the windows of their lead, the chapel of its
bells. The place was reduced to a ruin, and as national property
it was auctioned. Amid the debris an inn was built, and not until
1950 did the site come once again into the possession of the Archbishop of Trier, to be developed as a youth retreat for the diocese
but very properly keeping also its function as an inn and a hotel
for overnight visitors.

Somewhere on the long loop of the Hamm was the home of the
beautiful Marie, a noble and wealthy maiden who fell in love with
the equally noble and wealthy knight, Karl von Zant, who lived
at Merl (km. 85 R), a village which is now almost continuous with
the outskirts of Zell. She would sometimes ride up to the Marienburg, and there she was eventually persuaded by the Abbess and
Sisters that thoughts of marriage were wicked, that goods and
possessions were no better, and if she were really a good girl she
would renounce her property, reject the worthy Karl, and retire
to the convent. This she did, but she had not long been there

when she noticed the interest of her companions to be waning and the solicitude of the Abbess to be only a fraction of what it had been before she entered. The thought crossed her mind, too late, that the community preferred her money to her soul, and she longed to be set free to return to her Karl. She sought out the Abbess, flung herself at the feet of her superior, and swore that she would give every penny she had to the convent if only she might be suffered to depart.

The Abbess looked down at the grovelling young woman and laughed. Her goods had already been expropriated, she said. And as for the lustful wish to return to the arms of her young knight — well, a good solid penance would soon put that right.

And from that day poor Marie drooped and faded 'as a blighted flower, its beauty and gladness departed, remains on its stem with bowed head and but a semblance of life.' She wilted, inconsolable, and one night she escaped. In the morning a fisherman saw the hair trailing in the water of the Moselle and lifted her lifeless body into his boat.

As for Karl, when he heard what had become of his love he took horse and rode off, not to slay the Abbess but to join the next ship for the Middle East and swell the ranks of the heartbroken, the jilted, the penitent and the merely tough, who were locked in battle with the Infidel. A scimitar put an end to his young life.

'He is forgotten,' said the old woman who told me this tale as she stood behind a chugging tractor to turn the cocks on the spray pump. 'He is forgotten, yes. But up here you may sometimes see her gliding through the vines, pale and very beautiful, her face turned up to heaven as she flees from the ruin to fling herself into the river opposite Merl. They say she is doomed to haunt the hill because it was so terrible a wickedness to kill herself."

'But not wicked for the Abbess to drive her to suicide,' I said. 'That, I suppose, was quite in order.'

'She had taken her vows, the girl Marie,' said the woman. She checked the level of insect poison in the tank. 'And a vow is a vow, whatever. If people knew that today, the world would be different.'

Which perhaps was true. Yet my sympathy remained with Marie, and if she really revisited the hill of the Marienburg I wondered whether it might not be just that she found the position so indelibly alluring, particularly by moonlight.

The first time I saw Zell (km. 87 R) we had left the *Thames Commodore* in Alf harbour and had retraced our wake with a twenty-minute ride in the *Luxemburg* of the Köln-Düsseldorfer Line. I must at once admit that I did not like the place. We were unable to find any lunch there, largely because there was such a flourishing trade in coaches and internationally shepherded parties that every table and chair was occupied. The overworked staff were rude, and we shook the dust off our feet, even leaving the pretty and ancient buildings of the former Electoral palace to look after themselves.

But the next time was different. Striking through the upland forests of the Hunsrück I arrived at Zell on foot, and though the first hotel I tried was packed out with a Dutch party I soon found a good berth opposite, with the Mayers. Quite by accident I had chosen one of the best wine-houses of all the valley. The walls were so liberally covered with the diplomas and honours Herr Mayer had won for his wine that they already reached right up the stairs and round the sides of the dining-room. To judge by the ordinary 'open wine' served at eighty pfennigs a glass, the prizes were well merited, and I wondered whether the Mayers might not have to build on another storey to accommodate another year of silver medals, certificates and other honours.

Zell is long and thin and strung out by the bank. I doubt if anyone can get a foothold there who is not engaged in pressing grapes or selling bottles or tending the vines on the great shaly slopes which produce such wines as the *Schwarze Katz*, or Black Cat. Like Kröv's Bare Bottom the name is not one I find immediately alluring, for it arouses a suspicion that the wine itself is somehow a deception — an impression in no way reduced by the shop-windows of inebriate china black cats, black cat glasses and pencils and key-rings, and all the international junk which is sold to the coach tours and eventually finds its slow way to jumble sales. Yet Zell does itself an injustice by giving itself this appearance of trashiness. Whether or not one likes black cats as such, or approves of one as a wine-type, there is nothing the matter with the wine of Zell. Below the surface of excursions and souvenir shops Zell is a place of pleasant and cheerful people, as sunny and bronzed by nature as Moselle vintners always are. Besides, the name was not thought up by a publicist. It seems that a serious-minded vintner was deep in consultation below ground with a trio of merchants from Aachen who had come to make a purchase of wine. One after another the contents of the barrels were sampled until, when the vintner was about to put the sampling tube into the spigot-hole of one particular cask, he was swiftly repelled by his own black cat, which stood on the top of the barrel with back arched and claws extended.

Perhaps the cat had followed the men into the cellar, or maybe it was accustomed to haunt the vaults and prey upon those mythical mice which steal that quantity of wine which is lost by seepage through the wood, but it was a good omen. The Aachen merchants bought the barrel, and the name has stuck to that particular type of Zell wine ever since. At one end of the town there is a modern fountain with an arched cat on a barrel, and even if one thinks the sculpture is not a great work of art one can see that for publicity it has its value.

It was a fortunate chance which took me to the Mayers' establishment, for there I had a balcony on which I could lie back in a wicker chair, enjoying the evening sunshine and looking out above the promenade to the steamer jetty and the river and the pretty village of Kaimt on the further shore. Dead on time the white passenger-ship swept into view round the vineyards, and drew in panting at its jetty. Scores of passengers landed, others went aboard. The purser looked at his watch, the hands standing by the gangway looked at the purser. Still nearly a minute to go, then a brief trill on the officer's whistle, the gangway was pushed back with a clang to the jetty, a toot on the siren, and out came the foaming turmoil from under the stern as the ship went on her way at full speed to arrive at her next station as punctually as the hand of a chronometer.

From photographs taken before 1964 one can see how much Zell owes to the canalisation of the river. It formerly had an extremely messy foreshore, with groynes and dirt and probably rats also. Down in the bottom lay a miserable shallow stream, rightly loved by canoeists, but only a shadow of the fine, broad river which now glides smoothly past half a mile of stone wall with seats and flower-beds, the steamer piers, and even a public jetty which might have been specially constructed for the *Thames Commodore*, and against which she several times lay for a night when we went ashore to visit the Weinhaus Mayer for a meal, or just to acquire some of Mayer's own Black Cats to fill up the remaining space behind the after bulkhead.

Yet Zell is not now the centre of shipping that once it was. In the late Middle Ages the imposition of tolls by the robber lords ensconced along the Rhine defile below Bingen reached such a predatory height that ships could be denuded of a considerable quantity of their cargo unless, like the bold traders of Strasbourg and a score of other cities, they went down in one huge convoy protected by as many as a hundred small craft lined with stout logs behind which crouched the companies of crossbowmen whose bolts made any attempt to levy dues a fatal occupation. For the ordinary private shipmaster the Rhine was too costly, and so the produce of the forests and quarries and fields of the Hunsrück was taken by cart to Zell instead, where sometimes as many as one hundred craft were lying in the river to load the timber and grain and building stone, or to land the goods brought upstream from Koblenz or down from the upper reaches.

From the fifteenth century Trier and Koblenz both had their own guilds of bargemen, and the ancient cranes on Trier's river bank are even now a reminder of their activity. Salt and fish, iron and coal, cloth and wood, grain and wine were regular cargoes — quite apart from the troops and horses and dismantled houses which in a later age followed downstream in the wake of Louis XIV's commanders. It was the armies of the French Revolution which brought the shipping to an end by requisitioning the ships and in many cases cutting away all the masts and tackle to press them into service for bridges of boats. The tow-horses which had plodded so regularly from Koblenz to Trier were taken to haul army carts, or slaughtered for meat. The cheerful 'Holla Ho!' of the Moselle *Halfen* or drovers was heard no more in the valley, and the river remained quiet and almost dead until the sound of the steam whistle when the first shallow-draught steamer came puffing round the bends, her paddles churning the sparkling water. Then came the railway, and nearly a century without ships on the river until the canalisation was put in hand.

The *Halfen* (or 'helps') were tough men who lived rough. They came from villages all down the river, and they wore a particular dress of white breeches, heavy nailed boots and a stout jacket over a blue waistcoat. A bright neckerchief and a broad felt hat completed the outfit. These men would meet the bargemasters in particular inns along the towpath which even today is in many places still there, firm trodden by generations of drovers and their horses. In the saloon the business of hiring was conducted, a price being arranged for the whole journey and sealed with the *Winkoff*, a round of wine paid by the shipmaster. From the moment the horses left their stable they and their drover were fed and housed at the expense of the bargeman until they reached home again, and at the end of the journey the bargain was dissolved in another round of wine with bread and cheese.

'*In Gottes Namen!*' In the name of God. So cried the steersmen of the first ship in line as a signal for the convoy to start. The drovers and the other steerers answered in chorus, and with the sharp reports of the whips the cart-horses began their lumbering haul.

From Koblenz the ships could sometimes reach Cochem (km. 51·5 L) in two hard days of hauling, and Bremm (km. 76 L) in three. The journey up to Trier took one whole week under good conditions, but more in times of flood, and from first light until nightfall, with perhaps two rests for food, the *Halfen* would drive their horses, sitting side-saddle with their backs towards the river. 'Holla Ho!' Their cries travelled ahead of them, bringing the children to run to the river bank to watch. So did their cursing and swearing, and the cracking of whips as they urged their horses onwards. Usually there was one drover to three horses of his own, and this was sufficient to haul a small vessel up the river; but there might be six for heavier craft. The path would sometimes be under water, or broken down, and for hours on end the *Halfen* might be riding with the water up to the bellies of their steeds.

Besides, the towpath would change from one bank of the river to the other and the horses had to wade across. Where the river was too deep they would be set over with a ferry. It was a hard life for hard men, but for centuries it was the mainstay of transport on the Moselle.

Besides these craft which carried the imports and exports of the valley villages and the land to either side there was an active business in passenger shipping. Market-boats ran along all sections of the river, and the slim fast vessels hauled at a gallop were the fore-runners of the white ships which helped the *Thames Commodore* by paying for her lockage by merely being gracefully and gratuitiously present. The express boat from Trier to Koblenz stopped for the night at Zell, and its perspiring horses were wiped down, fed and stabled. Occasionally some royal company would reach Zell, as in 1847 when the steamer *Blücher Vorwärts* drew in amid cheers and salvos of cannon, bringing King Frederick William IV on a swift visit to the town as he travelled down the Moselle from Trier. And once the Emperor Maximilian himself docked at Zell, on his way to the Assembly of 1512 which he had summoned to Trier. Two days were needed to reach Zell from Koblenz, and that was good going indeed against the current. It was, of course, a great honour to receive the Emperor, but to accommodate his party must have presented a problem. How many men there were in his entourage is not known, but there were more than four hundred horses. Presumably the horsemen rode up the towpath or along the hill trails which nowadays form much of the line of the Moselhöhenweg.

The approach to Zell across the hills does not show the place at its best, for the town remains entirely hidden until the path joins a roadway which comes from the Hunsrück plateau and breaks through to the river past a plastics factory and some garages. But from a boat the prospect is extremely fine, for Zell lies ranged as a curving strip at the foot of its vineyard hills, where a square and a round tower still remain among the vines as relics of the days when the Elector of Trier girded the place about on the landward side with a fine defensive wall to keep out robber bands in times of plague and famine.

Merl

At the downstream end of the town the curve continues past Merl (km. 85 R), where piles of fine new-built tuns stand at the river's edge, ready for shipment to vintners up and down the stream. Already the Marienburg is in view again on the port side, just as it was near Pünderich, and no doubt it was somewhere along this reach that the heartbroken Marie found refuge in drowning from the inhumanity of the sisterhood she had been persuaded to enter.

The Zant family of Merl, to which that sad young Karl belonged who loved the pale nun of Marienburg, was well known for its hearty gaiety, and it is related that in 1360 one of the Zants gave a party at Bullay to which he invited many of the lords of the neighbourhood. Among these was a certain Friedrich of Hattstein whom the host suspected of being unnecessarily moderate in his consumption of Moselle wine. Filling a great cup he handed it to Friedrich, jovially challenging him to lower it at one draught if he really appreciated the good wine of the valley.

Friedrich did not like to appear unmanly, and being a very powerful fellow he waved the bumper aside, picked up a cask in his arms, pulled out the bung and raised the barrel high in the air.

'I drink to the honour of my noble lord the Archbishop of Trier,' he cried. 'A health to the Elector!' And tilting back his head he gulped and gulped, little by little inverting the barrel until he had drained the last drop.

Zant and his brother could not afford to be outdrunk by a visitor, so they each seized a cask also.

'To the Abbess of Marienburg!'

'To the Emperor! Prosit!'

It is said that the three champion drinkers were from that evening onward the best of friends. Between them they must no doubt have put away considerable quantities of wine. Octavius Rooke heard of their legendary exploit when he travelled down the Moselle and wrote that he could not personally vouch for the precise truth of the story, but at least it was commonplace in former times for German nobles to drink about sixteen bottles daily. Even that would be double the quantity which felled the very proper and good mannered Englishman in Hugo König's parlour at Kues.

The next haul on the Moselle trail leaves the river at Merl and cuts up a side valley to mount steadily until the vines are left behind. It led me an ill-marked and muddy way through woods of oak or pine until it came out at the edge of a hill to give one of its long and brilliant views down into the valley of the Moselle, to where the ruin of the monastery of Stuben (km. 75·3 R) stands forlornly in a tight loop of the river. By boat one turns so closely round the flat point of shingle, on which only the bare walls remain, that one can see the remnants from almost every angle.

There is something inexpressibly sad about the crumbled and
weathered building, standing as deserted as an abbey of the York-
shire dales. And it has a sorrowful tale attached to it, as seems
only appropriate.

The first Abbess of Stuben was Gisela, who in earlier years was
a girl of such incomparable fairness and beauty that one might
well guess that some terrible tragedy would certainly be lying in
wait for her. She had given her heart to a noble and upright young
knight — another sign in the life of the Moselle valley that doom
was surely impending. He happened to be away, though whether
on a campaign against the Saracens or merely on a visit up-river
I do not know. One version of the tale says that it was Gisela's
wedding day, and she was awaiting his arrival for their marriage.
Whether or not that was so, she was sitting at her window, looking
up towards the bend in the stream, watching and sighing and
longing for her own true love.

At last, just after sunset, she saw his boat come sweeping round
the cliffs below where St Aldegund lock now stands (km. 78·4 L).
She could make out his figure in the dim light, and leaning from
the window of her tower she waved to him. No, she did not fall
out, but her lover was imprudent. Aglow with ardour, his heart
beating with the longing to hold her in his arms, he stood on the
prow and leaped for the shore. Unfortunately he had not reckoned
with the weight of his armour, and his spring fell short. Gisela no
doubt saw the splash as he fell in the water and sank.

She did not weep, the story says, 'but her bosom became cold
as the waters that closed over his head'. Her father endowed a
convent to be built on the flat meadow beside the river, and she
was the first to enter it, the first of a long line of Abbesses of Stuben.

But the *Thames Commodore* still has some distance to go before
rounding the tip of the Stuben promontory. Only ten minutes
below Merl the Bullay railway bridge crosses the stream (km.
82·7), a not very beautiful lattice of steel girders such as a boy
might build with a construction set, but an ingenious one because
it serves two species of transport. Indeed it must be terrifying for
the unsuspecting motorist to drive over the Moselle on its lower
deck and suddenly be overtaken by the roar and clatter of a train

of steel trucks a few feet above his head, thundering down the valley with a load of minette ore for the Ruhr. If he has not seen the train coming, that is because it was underneath the Prinzenkopf, burrowing its way through the neck of the Hamm from near Pünderich.

Already Alf's little harbour is in sight, and just beyond it the Alfbach flows in (km. 81·7 L). In the angle the village lies huddled, with hotels which have known generations of visitors. And from just past the confluence one can see right up the valley to where Burg Arras stands proudly on the top of its private hill, a castle at first sight very like Burg Landshut above Bernkastel.

Arras is in fact still one of the most handsome castles of a modest and defensive type, for in the early 1900s the ruin was tidied up and restored to form a private residence. Below the square keep there is a pleasant house with towers and turrets, with half-timbered gables and delicate slated roofs. Seen from the Moselle it shimmers elusively in the distance, but it is no great way by the path that leads up through the orchards and pinewoods from Alf and breaks out into the open beside the vines which cascade down the slope below its walls.

The name Arras was that of a charcoal-burner and smith who lived in the valley of the Alfbach. He was a man of mighty physical strength, and he had twelve strong and hearty sons who worked with him in the smithy or on his simple small-holding. Thus they were engaged when in the year 938 the Huns came sweeping over the Eifel towards the valley of the Moselle.

The only bastion which might have obstructed the passage of these terrible marauders was Castle Bertrich, further up the Alfbach valley, but the Count of Bertrich seems to have been a cowardly man who preferred to look after himself rather than to accede to the request of the Archbishop of Trier that he should block the way of the horrible Huns and cut off their road to Trier, or at least hold them at bay until the Archbishop himself should arrive at the head of his own forces. It may be that the Count assessed the situation coolly and decided that if the Huns had forced the Rhine they would certainly not be held up by the Moselle. Rather than bring their fury upon his own house and home he would sit tight in his keep and let the invaders stream past his domains and attack the Archbishop.

News of this betrayal reached Arras the smith, and according to the chronicle he summoned his twelve sons. They in turn roused the peasants, and with what simple weapons they could muster these country people made their way in the darkness to the crags overlooking the defile of the Alfbach. There the sons of the smith arranged them in companies, and when in the early morning the vanguard of the invading column appeared in the narrow pass it was met by an avalanche of rocks prised loose and rolled from above. After a certain amount of confusion the Huns retired, then returned again and again to renew their attempt to break through towards the valley, but each time the stones and rocks took their toll. By night and by day the battle went on, until at the end of a week the force from Trier arrived and finally put the marauders to flight.

In gratitude for the delivery of the country, Archbishop Ruotbert immediately built a new fort on the hill overlooking the Alfbach as additional security for the future. As Lord of this castle the Emperor installed Arras the smith, elevating him to Count Arras of Alf as a demonstration that even in those far off times a humble working-man might rise to great heights through nothing but loyalty and courage.

From Alf harbour one can look along a broad and splendid reach of river to St Aldegund lock, standing just below the village of that name (km. 79 L), a typical community of vintners' houses ranged along the foot of their own precious slopes. The lower gates open out towards a sharp bend to port opposite the village of Neef (km. 78 R), behind which the slate cliff rises so sheer that even the vintners have almost had to abandon the attempt to cultivate it. The ridge is that of the Petersberg, and it is pierced by a railway tunnel which cuts off the beautiful low promontory with the ruin of Stuben abbey. The train whoops and dives into the hill, the locomotive emerging at the river bridge (km. 74) before the tail has vanished. A brief view of the river as the hurrying train speeds over the girders, then another whoop as it runs off the bridge to aim for the entrance of the Kaiser Wilhelm tunnel,

M

the longest in Germany, from which it will only emerge at km. 51·3, beyond the castle hill of Cochem. Of course the tunnel itself is not twenty-three kilometres long, but only just over four. The river course is five times longer, because from the Abbey of Stuben to Cochem the Moselle decides to explore the countryside, meandering through the exquisitely beautiful 'Cochemer Krampen' (or Hook).

Immediately over the short Neef tunnel a chapel (km. 77·2 R) stands on the Petersberg. It had its origin at a time when the church in the village of Neef had become almost derelict, and the neighbouring villages and religious houses gave money for a new one to be built. But as was the case with the chapel on the Liescherberg near Konz, the stones had a way of disappearing overnight, only to reappear on the summit of the ridge. The priest and builders set a watch to catch the practical jokers, but to their surprise there arrived in the middle of the night a light snowstorm, or what looked like a snowstorm until the shining white flakes drifted closer and were seen to be angels. The flock descended to the building site, picked up all the stones that had been laid that day, and after carefully depositing them in a pile on the Petersberg flew slowly off to disappear between the stars. That, the record says, is why the chapel was built on the hilltop, whither the materials had been miraculously transported.

The reach below Neef is even now one of the narrowest and fleetest pieces of the Moselle. Ships take it extremely slowly, feeling their way with caution along a stretch which is liable to silting and shoaling. In the days of the *Halfen* it was renowned for its dangers, for the 'Bremmer Waag' was a section of rapids where many a boat was overset. This was because at Bremm (km. 76 L) the river began the tightest elbow of all its course to double round the abbey of the poor tragic Gisela, and the water was thrown back on itself in whirls and surges and disorder.

Bremm is brown and much like any other Moselle village. Fishing-punts lie along its shaly beach, but there is no chance whatsoever of landing without risking a stranding in a particularly dangerous position. We consoled ourselves with knowing that the real attraction of Bremm lay in its vanished carnival for married

women only, when on Shrove Tuesday the men had to stay at home
to mind the children, wash the clothes and see to the cooking —
all of them, that is, except Aaron the Jew, the village dancing-
master and musician. Because he could fiddle he was acceptable,
and playing his violin he would lead the women in a gay procession dancing through the village. There was wine and singing,
and any woman married during the year stood while the others
danced round her and knocked her over the head with the key of her
own house as an initiation into the clan of married women. Then
the wives all repaired to the schoolhouse, where they danced and
drank the day away, no other man but the fiddler daring to intrude
or even to be seen in the street for fear of a sound box on the ears.

Lovingly the river hugs the promontory where the Petersberg
ridge drops down to the myriad rows of vines, orderly and staked,
against which the two walls of the broken nave of Stuben abbey
stand out erect and strong, the skyline of the distant woods cutting
across the nine tall open slits of the windows. But the abbey has
not always stood on the promontory. When Gisela's father
Egelolf founded the institution in 1136 he chose to site it upon the
island of St Nicholas opposite Bremm, so that it might have better
protection. And so he did, but in the course of a few centuries the
shoals and the piles of ice-floes trapped between the island and
the right bank pushed the river ever further across so that Stuben
eventually came to lie on the mainland of the right bank.

The island was, of course, dedicated to St Nicholas on account
of the dangers of the Bremmer Waag, and pious bargemen in the
days of the *Halfen* would pray to him as they passed. Even the
Emperor Maximilian is said to have been put ashore there to offer
his thanks to St Nicholas as he journeyed upstream towards Zell
in his royal barge.

Yet even its sheltered position on the island did not save Stuben
from depredations. The river was not deep and marauding knights
would sometimes force the passage and make their quarters there
at the expense of the nuns. The Lords of Arras were particularly
persistent offenders, and in order to ensure the peace and quiet
of the abbey the Elector of Trier had to issue an edict that tres-
passers would be excommunicated.

Very beautiful is Stuben, alone on its low tongue of land at the edge of the vines. In floodtime the river will creep up the bank and wash those same walls where once the sisters chanted. Outside its walls the nightingales would long ago take up their own evening refrain, singing a throaty chorus of wild delight. That they did so was the result of a very curious incident.

One of the foundations which owned much property along the Moselle was Himmerode, where in course of time the monks lapsed into bad habits and led lives which were far from blameless. Bernard of Clairvaux was sent to reform the place and restore it to order, and betaking himself thither he embarked upon a campaign of sermons and lectures and reprovings. Yet the monks were not moved by his exhortations, and to all his carefully reasoned discourses they turned deaf ears.

Bernard was depressed. He retired to his room and shut himself in so that he might think up yet further arguments and reasonings which might move the monks to better behaviour and a less dissolute life. When the air became somewhat heavy and stale he threw open the window, and at once he heard the chorus of nightingales singing in the bushes of the monastery garden. The sound sent a wave of sweet relief over him, a curious sense of bliss. And then, gradually, he found to his horror that awful carnal desires were creeping into his mind.

Leaping up, Bernard slammed the window to shut out the seductive sound. Pondering the matter he eventually came to the conclusion that if nightingales by their song could raise unspeakable thoughts in such a well-disciplined man as himself they must play havoc with the minds of mere ordinary monks. He saw the birds as the workers of iniquity responsible for the vice which afflicted Himmerode, and he decided to act. Striding out into the moonlit garden he ordered the nightingales to depart from there for ever. And because Bernard was a man whom even the birds had to obey, the nightingales took wing and flew off.

It so happened that the good Abbess of Stuben heard that Bernard had driven out the nightingales, and that the poor birds were still flying forlorn from one place to another, longing for a home where their song would be appreciated. A gentler soul than the forthright Bernard, she called to them and offered them the freedom of the trees and meadows around the abbey she ruled. So the nightingales came to Stuben, and they stayed there until the coming of the French Revolutionary forces who stripped the abbey of its roof, tore down the baroque doorway with its angels and smashed everything of beauty.

Fortunately the habits of the iconoclasts were well known, and all the most precious works of art were removed in time to the safety of the land beyond the Rhine, where they came to swell the treasures of the great cathedral of Limburg on its hill above the lock on the River Lahn through which, only a week later, the *Thames Commodore* was to pass. But, alas, for the poor nightingales it was the end. The revolutionaries slashed down all the trees, even felling the magnificent avenue of walnuts which led to the abbey from the river landing opposite Bremm. The birds left Stuben for ever.

Strange to relate, the song of the nightingales did not fill the sisters of Stuben with impure thoughts, but exalted and cheered their hearts as they went about their life there. So it would seem that Bernard of Clairvaux was wrong in his diagnosis; or perhaps it is just that the song of nightingales makes good people better and bad ones worse. Whenever I heard them myself in the valley of the Moselle I felt more cheered than filled with lust; but perhaps this merely shows that I would not be good material for a monk.

IX

WHERE the Eller railway bridge takes the trains to disappear into the Kaiser Wilhelm tunnel the valley loses the clank of the ore-trucks bound for the Ruhr and their sister-trucks returning with coke for Thionville and Luxembourg. In its most prosperous days the line carried a coke train once in every forty minutes all round the clock, and with the ore and the passenger-trains added, and the total topped up with the wine-wagons and the ordinary goods traffic, nearly a hundred and fifty trains wound their way through the valley each day. The modern traffic is less, for the ore and coke are gradually taking to the water, but the *Thames Commodore* found that she still exchanged toots with plenty of puffing locomotives. She must have been a familiar sight to their dusty drivers and firemen, who would run the Moselle track a score of times before she had dropped down from Wasserbillig to Koblenz, and the men would often signal cheerfully to her as they passed clattering on their way with the heavy hopper wagons which kept busy the furnaces of the European Iron and Steel Community.

With the trains firmly buried underground the Cochemer Krampen is much as it must always have been, a sinuous line of villages on the sunny vineyard side, facing across to the dark slopes of a tongue of forest protruding from the Hunsrück, the wooded upland which rolls away into the blue distance, rising gently to the modest heights of the Soonwald before dropping to the brink of the Rhine gorge near Bingen. It is a wide and mysterious plateau, this Hunsrück forest, with its farming villages blending into the purple haze. Its heavy, almost sinister woods of pine and fir, beech and larch, contain some magnificent trees, its deep valleys and thickets are beloved of deer. Indeed on the Moselle trail I saw more deer than humans, for away from the villages one may travel miles and meet nobody.

The Hunsrück is inseparable from the memory of two men, one of them real and the other perhaps more of a legend. The genuine character was a certain Johann Bückler, a slater's apprentice who acquired the simple nickname of 'Schinderhannes' (or Jack the Slater). One day he stole from his employer and received the very proper reward of a sound beating in public, twenty-five strokes of the birch. Those who disapprove of corporal punishment will be delighted to discover that the result of the treatment was not to reform him, but to start Bückler on a road which led him to become perhaps the most successful and most feared highwayman and robber of his time. The Hunsrück and even the country beyond the Rhine provided him with a magnificent hunting-ground, and hardly a day passed but some isolated farm or the house of a miller by a forest stream was broken into.

Schinderhannes did not work alone. In the closing years of the eighteenth century there were plenty of malcontents and minor thieves, and collecting a large band of them together under his own leadership Schinderhannes soon became the commander of a whole troop of brigands, men who did not for one moment flinch from murdering any who resisted. Their favourite prey was the merchants returning from fairs and markets. Lurking on some Hunsrück hill-top Schinderhannes would watch the roads with his telescope and descend swiftly to attack any caravan which looked promising. Yet he never robbed the peasants — if only because they had nothing worth taking — and this made him popular in the villages. He and his men were often to be met at fairs and festivals, and none dared give him away, or refuse him entry.

He also had a particular and rather endearing sense of humour. One of his most famous exploits was when he stepped into the road in front of a large company of merchants and ordered them to halt. This the men did, for they quickly saw that they were surrounded by a numerous and extremely villainous collection of brigands, who now appeared from behind the bushes on either side of the road. Trembling, the traders got ready to hand over their money the moment it was demanded.

But Schinderhannes had a surprise for them. He did not demand their cash and riches. Instead he ordered the merchants quickly to take off their boots. One of his lieutenants collected them and threw them all in a heap in the roadway.

'I give you three minutes exactly,' said the robber chief, pulling out a watch he had stolen from some other wealthy owner. 'Three minutes to put on your boots and get clear, and anyone who is still here is a dead man. Go!'

The traders rushed for the pile of footwear, struggling to find their own and pushing each other violently out of the way. Some came to blows, others had the clothes almost torn from their backs in the general frenzy to find the right boots, or any that would do. The elegant merchants became a screaming mob as each struggled only for himself, and all the while the gunmen of Schinderhannes stood around, laughing and taunting and ridiculing them. It was more than three minutes before the last of the bedraggled traders was fleeing down the road, but none of them was harmed. Schinderhannes and his men were enjoying the scene too much to spoil it by shooting. Besides, the departing guests left so quickly that they abandoned their wares and baggage at the scene of the hold-up.

Bückler was a daring escaper, sometimes plaiting a rope from the straw of his bed and climbing out of dungeons which were considered absolutely sure. He would break through walls or wrest away the bars of cells to regain his liberty. It was perhaps these qualities which came to invest him with the character of a hero so that an Englishman could write of him shortly after his death as 'gay, brave, gallant, generous and humane'. One of the prettiest girls in Germany ran away from home to join Bückler and not only became his mistress but also accompanied him on some of his most daring raids dressed as a youth. Yet in spite of all the romance which surrounded his personality he was a man who, with his band of cut-throats, terrorised a great area of country and was responsible for scores of utterly callous murders. He was so powerful and so elusive that the German authorities could never get to grips with him, and it remained for the French to silence him. For some strange reason he tried to enlist as a soldier, and he was recognised. The French knew how to deal with robbers as well as aristocrats, and after a sudden pounce upon his confederates Schinderhannes was taken to Mainz for trial. With him was his faithful Julia and their infant child. Crowds thronged the great hall of the Academy to watch the spectacle, and Bückler's entreaties that Julia was an innocent girl led astray by himself so moved the spectators that every eye was wet, and nothing was heard in the silence but the sobbing of women as the judges deliberated over the sentence. Perhaps it was that which led them to sentence Julia first, and when Schinderhannes heard that she was to receive only two years in prison he leapt up and embraced her with tears of joy.

Yet all his charm could not move the French in his own cause, and perhaps the tears of the audience were somewhat moderated when they heard the verdict of the guillotine. And the French authorities were certainly thorough, for the great sharp-edged knife went up, up, up to thunder down again, not only to sever the neck of Bückler but also to slice off the heads of no fewer than nineteen of his accomplices — and all in twenty-six minutes.

Yet Schinderhannes had one Hunsrück enemy who often outwitted him, and sometimes even outshot him when it came to a gun-battle. This was the Electoral Palatinate Chief Forestry Inspector Friedrich Wilhelm Utsch, whose domain included the Soonwald and much of the Schinderhannes hunting-ground. A mighty huntsman, he would daily ride the forest which he knew so well and in which he had been born, and with his gamekeepers he managed to preserve the Electoral properties from the ravages of French troops and the Schinderhannes highwaymen alike. Yet Utsch was a man who liked an evening of wine and song, and he is often seen as either the original or the embodiment of the Palatinate huntsman in one of the most famous of all German songs, *der Jäger aus Kurpfalz* (the Huntsman Palatine). However, this gay figure of the Hunsrück hunter probably existed in song and story long before Utsch was born, and was perhaps no more than a local Nimrod with accretions of many men who, across the centuries, had galloped over the same wild moors in pursuit of the deer — and of the poachers too.

One of the finest views across to the Hunsrück is from the Ellerberg, the twelve-hundred foot height behind Eller (km. 73·5 L), the first village on the port hand below the bridge. Eller is almost joined to Ediger (km. 72·5 L), the two pleasant brownish villages merging into the orchards which lie between them and facing across the stream to one of the wildest forest hillsides of all the river, a dark slope which staggers up to the fourteen-hundred-foot Hochkessel at one end, a ridge over which the buzzards wheel and mew as they sweep the ground below with their sharp eyes, watching for the least movement.

It was on our fifth Moselle run that we stopped one morning at Ediger. The ornamental garden by the ferry-stage would have won a prize anywhere, for it was a brilliant mass of clarkias and begonias, marigolds and heliotrope and whatever else could be found to thrive wide-eyed and welcoming in the hot sunshine. We drew in cautiously to the jetty, and at once the ferryman walked up to assure us that no ship was due there until the next day. We could lie undisturbed and welcome, he said. He also presented the *Thames Commodore* with a miniature banner issued when Ediger had crowned its wine queen a week earlier, and he recommended us on no account to sail away until we had tried the Ediger 'Osterlämmchen' (or Easter Lamb) from the thickly planted hillside behind the church.

I complimented the ferryman on the garden. Even in the elegant grounds of Trier's Electoral Palace we had seen nothing quite as gay and bright. Indeed it was the only waterfront garden which spilled down the bank in such a riot of close-packed bloom.

The ferryman nodded. 'Yes,' he said. 'It is a pleasant place to sit as those old men of the village are doing, just dreaming of the days gone by. But three months from now the garden will be gone, vanished, swept away without a trace.'

'Surely they're not going to build on it,' I said, familiar with the fate of gardens in London.

'Build?' The ferryman laughed. 'No, it's the river that sweeps it away. Every year when the floods come the whole garden is torn out by the Moselle. Plants, soil, everything. That's why the plants are only annuals. Each spring it has to be dug again, and terraced, and new soil brought in. It's a big job, but it's worth it. Ediger wouldn't look the same without it.'

Ediger is in fact a very charming village indeed, the road traffic running past along the river bank and leaving the main street to the chugging tractors of the vintners. Hearing a heavy beating sound we turned down one of the alleys to find a cooper's yard, and two strong men in green aprons hard at work on a *Fuder* barrel of about 220 gallons, hammering the hoop over the ends of the staves with hard wooden mallets. Coopering is almost the only activity in the Moselle valley other than tending the vines, whereas the bottles are not made locally but are imported from the Ruhr.

We had a reason to call at Ediger. I wanted to see the 'Christ in the Winepress'. I had assumed it to be in the village church, but after we had looked in vain into the building set on a raised and walled mound at the rear of the village a woman told us that the *Christus in der Kelter* was not there but at Eller. In Eller a slater told us to climb two or three miles up to the Ellerberg and turn right immediately after a field of potatoes. Then, he said, we should soon see the Chapel of the Holy Cross half hidden in the trees.

It was a refreshing walk, with ripe blackberries along the verges, and when we had climbed perhaps one thousand feet we came to one of those curious chapels put up by vintners long ago. Sure enough, beside the stout screen of rails which would have kept even an elephant from approaching the altar, the Christ in the Winepress was there, the uprights of the press topped with a pair of simple and almost caricatured winged heads of bodiless angels, male and short-haired. Through the cross-bar the giant screw pressed upon a stout cross, beneath which the Christ was bending. From either hand a torrent of blood flowed down into the collecting basin and was joined by a spurt from his wounded side and another from either foot.

It is a strange but not altogether unreasoning mysticism which leads the vineyard worker of the Moselle to find a parallel between the Passion and the harvesting of his own grapes. Besides, there is a very strong Biblical foundation. 'I am the true vine' — and what could be more natural than that any church in such a wine-growing area should have a vine motif running up the pillars and carved on the pews, or painted on the ceiling? And has not the wine of the Eucharist been a sacred symbol to Christians all down the ages?

This is understandable enough. But the wine villagers may take the idea much further. In the chapel on the Ellerberg the windlass of the press bears down upon the weight and burden of the cross itself, and just as the grapes are crushed to make the wine that is a blessing to mankind so too the Christ is squeezed that the blood of his tortured body may flow to bring redemption to those who accept it. The idea is simple but compelling, and here in the chapel it finds one of its very rare expressions in a sculpture that is perhaps no great work of a medieval master but comes from the hand of a Mosellaner to whom the parallel was a very real one.

It is from up on this hill, at the start of the long descent of the Stations of the Cross, that Ediger is seen far below, its spire silhouetted against a river which reflects the sombre shade of the woods beyond. This glimpse is one of the most beautiful of all the Moselle valley, equalled only by the romance of Stuben and the exquisite prospect of Beilstein lower down the river. The village looked so alluring that we ran all the way down the winding Stations track and plunged into the clean water for a cooling swim before tasting Ediger's wine as the ferryman had said we should. Then we started gently down the river once more.

At Senheim (km. 68 R) the Moselle authority has built a harbour of refuge more than a quarter-mile long, so that ships threatened by a deluge of ice-floes can flee to it for shelter. The haven looked inviting enough on the chart, but we stopped no longer in it than was necessary to send someone up to the baker's. So high were the banks that not even Senheim's church spire was visible over the top, and, as our messengers returning with the bread reported

Senheim to be the one miserable and dull village they had seen
all the way down river, we put out again to head for Beilstein.

Of Senheim it is related that where the cliff drops to the river
(km. 67·7 R) just downstream of the harbour there used to be a
dangerous passage where even today a long row of groynes still
lies at either side of the stream bed. On the cliff at the bend the
shippers long ago erected a statue to St Nicholas to which all good
bargemen paid proper respect. One day, however, a rough and
tough and humanist bargee, who had been used to sailing past
with no more than an oath, found his ship driving in the current
towards the cliff. We have, of course, heard this tale before, both
on the Moselle and the Saar, and the reader will correctly expect
the bargeman to promise a candle as large as his mast (or in this
case his bargepole) and then snub the statue as soon as he is safely
past the danger. Yet in the Senheim version the very end of the
tale is different. True, the boat ran on a rock before it even reached
Mesenich (km. 66·8 R) the ship and its valuable cargo being a
total loss. The skipper, however, was not drowned. He managed
to swim to the shore, and making his way along the river bank he
called up to St Nicholas in his niche.

'The trouble with you, Niklas, is that you can't take a joke,' he
shouted reproachfully.

Scanning the cliff with the binoculars we could see no sign of
a statue, but there must once have been a figure to protect shippers
at what would certainly have been a very dangerous bend. Nor
does another effigy of St Nicholas stand any longer, as it did only
forty years earlier, in the window of the curious little square tower
which stands forlorn at the foot of the vines between Ediger and
Senhals as all that remains of the castle of Lehmen (km. 70·7 L).

It is curious how hamlets can disappear, and even stranger that
when a place has broken up or evaporated, or sunk into the earth,
or maybe has been carried off by the devil, one little fragment
should remain. For centuries the Lords of Lehmen lived in their
modest castle opposite the summit of the Hochkessel, and, even
if they were minor nobility compared with some of the others,
they had nevertheless been well and truly installed under the
banner of Electoral Trier. Only a century ago a dozen houses still

stood round the precincts of the manor, and in the Gasthaus Christoffel the *Halfen* would spend the night drinking or lying on the floor, singing and swearing and drinking just one more glass of Ediger wine. Their ships lay moored along the straight bank all the way to Eller, and no doubt some of the *Halfen* patronised the inns up there. But the Christoffel was a favourite, a house where *Halfen* were expected and welcome, yet today one cannot even discover its site. Only the square tower of the castle is left, perhaps because nobody bothered to pull it down — or because it formed a traditional and somewhat sacred pedestal for the wooden figure of the Bishop of Myra.

Gliding past Mesenich (km. 66·6 R) the ships keep well in the centre of the stream to avoid the stone groynes just breaking the surface, but a shipman may safely glance for a moment to port and see in the derelict buildings among the trees opposite the village a memorial to the incorrigible optimism of the British. That any man should have decided to build there a brewery to produce ale and stout is remarkable enough, but that an Englishman should really have set out to brew and market such English liquors in a land swimming with some of the best wines in the world is almost incredible. Yet that is precisely what a certain indomitable English brewer attempted when he built the brewery a century ago. His name was reported to us as having been 'Herr Greffin Toner'; perhaps he was a Mr Griffin Turner, or Grafton, but all that remains of his short-lived and disastrous enterprise is the red brick ruin in the cool of the hill shadows opposite the vintners' houses of Mesenich, which, by contrast, still flourish. In the village to starboard stands the handsome baroque house in which the English beermakers lived during the few years before their enterprise collapsed.

We had just turned the Senheim bend on one of our voyages when we came upon an eight, paddling light down the river ahead. It flew the pennant of a rowing-club in Westphalia, and the crew consisted of two young men, six female oars and a female cox. The boat was more robust than an Oxford or Cambridge eight in order to cope with the heavy wash of the Rhine shipping, and it was substantial enough for the crew to have their rucksacks lying at their feet. They had sent the boat up to Trier by rail or road, and were now enjoying a summer holiday spent in rowing with the gentle current from one village to another, pitching camp each night at tenting sites.

At least they were rowing in theory, but as we began to overhaul them very slowly so that our wash would not trouble them, the cox called to us, and made hitching signs with her thumb.

'You want a tow? Are you in trouble?' I hailed them.

'No trouble, but we want a tow.'

'A tow, yes. Please tow us to Beilstein.' The oarswomen took up the cry.

'What, with eight of you to row?'

The crew laughed. 'It's so nice just to lie back in the sun,' explained one of the girls. 'Much nicer than rowing.'

'Right,' I said. 'To Beilstein, with pleasure.' We manoeuvred to go ahead of their ship and handed a light line to bow.

I have towed eights before — for it is not only German clubs that will accept a pull if the coach is not present — and it is an art which needs intelligent steering by the cox of the rowboat, as well as a sensible hand dealing with the tow-line at the stern of the towing ship. Any towed craft will tend to yaw, but the moment a long and thin boat like an eight runs out of line it is almost impossible to steer it back again with the rudder. The angle increases, the pull of the tow-rope becomes stronger and more and more sideways. The whole adventure can very easily end with a surprised crew in the water and the eight itself sunk or water-logged.

However, on this occasion we were able to put at the stern our friend Michael Hocking, who in his Cambridge days had been Captain of the Christ's Boat Club, and knew what was what where an eight was concerned. I told the bow of the eight's crew not to tie the line but to hold it pressed over the edge of her seat so that she could let go instantly if need be. Michael took a turn round one of the bollards aft, watching carefully to let the line fall slack whenever the eight began to run out of straight astern.

So we pulled them happily down the river, past Mesenich and round the long right-hand bend towards Beilstein, the crew lazily relaxed with their wine and lying back on their rucksacks to bask in the sun. By the time we were bearing down toward the camping site by the Beilstein ferry several of them were blissfully asleep and we had to rouse them with the hooter before casting them off to drift over against the bank, where three other craft of the same club were already hauled up, their energetic crews (who had dutifully rowed all the way down the river) pitching the communal camp for the evening.

Beilstein (km. 61·2 R) needs to be seen from the river, for of all places on the Moselle it must certainly be the gem. Always an astonishingly beautiful sight, one can see from earlier photographs that its appearance must nevertheless have been enormously improved by the canalisation of the river, for it lies close enough to the barrage of Fankel (km. 59·4) to have had the water-level raised to within two or three feet of the roadway. It now stands right at the edge of the water, and its enchanting and improbable assortment of buildings flickers mirrored in the rippled surface.

Above the village stand the remains of Burg Metternich, pulled down by the French and plundered for its building stone, and yet what was once the Carmelite priory in the village itself still stands proudly overlooking the rooftops of the lesser houses spilled down the rock. That it was spared was due to the enterprise of the Prior and the leader of the village community.

In fact the new priory was still unfinished when the French began to construct Montroyal, and the Prior wisely decided that the community should at once move in without ceremony, to remove the obvious temptation which so much fresh building material provided. Shortly afterwards the French descended upon the fine castle of Winneburg, behind Cochem, and removing all the doors and windows, the furniture and even the beams which held up the floors, they loaded the spoils on barges and set off upriver with a suitable company of *Halfen* to manage the horses. When the convoy halted for the night at Poltersdorf (km. 60·5 L) the headman and the Prior of Beilstein rowed over to the ship of the French officer in command, treated him liberally with the best wines they could provide, and when they thought he was sufficiently mellowed they entreated him not to dismantle Beilstein's

Beilstein

N

houses and priory, and even to leave the castle intact. Surprisingly, the officer agreed, except that he could not reprieve the castle. The materials were too precious to the French, so in 1689 all the doors and windows, beams and stoves and other movables were pulled out and loaded on ships, then the remainder was felled with gunpowder until only the towers remained. But at least the village was spared, and its curious medieval beauty preserved until today.

One notable visitor to Beilstein was the last of the long line of the Electors of Trier, the gentle and beloved Clemens Wenzeslaus, who one day came up the river in his own private yacht drawn by horses. He was to land at Beilstein, and naturally the villagers crowded down to the shore to see such an august personage. In the front rank were the elders of the village, their leader ready to make a suitable speech of welcome. Indeed their spokesman had begun to deliver his address, stressing the honour done to Beilstein by the visit of its illustrious Elector, when a newcomer joined the crowd. This was the miller's donkey, laden with sacks of flour.

The animal was accustomed to taking his load down to the river for shipment, and never before had he found his way blocked. So, wisely and stubbornly, he began to push. He did not need to shove very hard, for the villagers dressed in their best were quick to press back from the dusty load of flour bags, so the donkey made good progress down to the shore, where he took up his stand beside the orator.

'And so, your Excellency, it is with the deepest sense of honour . . .'

'Ee . . . yaw,' broke in the donkey.

'. . . that I, on behalf of . . .'

'Ee . . . yaw, ee . . . yaw.'

The people began to laugh, and the village spokesman faltered, reddened and stopped. But Archbishop Clemens Wenzeslaus smiled and held up his hand.

'One at a time, please,' he said, addressing the donkey. 'One at a time, or I can't hear.'

Beilstein has two jetties, but they were so constantly in use that we found it better to drop anchor on the inside of the sharp bend just below the ferry stage. Here we were safe from the big ships, and we also had much the best view of the village. To row ashore was simple enough, but it was a delight merely to sit on deck in the evening and see the light fade on the cluster of houses and turrets, walls and gables. We could easily believe that this was the most filmed village in Germany, for its alley and miniature market-place and its houses leaning across the streets as though to whisper to each other were a ready-made set and had been used for at least five films.

There is a tale of Beilstein which should be a warning to any barge-skipper whose family may have ideas above their station — though in days when the Mercedes is parked on deck, the ship's lad has a motor-cycle, and the youngsters have their own inflatable swimming-pool under a sun-awning in a play-pen which also contains two swings and a see-saw, that station may be high indeed. But the status of bargemen was not always thus, and there was one shipper whose beautiful daughter was singled out by the callous Kuno of Beilstein as the target for his passions. Swearing eternal devotion he easily duped her, but, of course, he quickly tired of her and sent her packing.

Poor girl, to be jilted was too much for her simple heart, and she went out of her mind. She would wander Ophelia-like in the woods and fields, and so she lived on in this simple fashion until one day the madness passed, and she remembered all that had happened. As she still loved Kuno — for girls have a way of remaining devoted to scoundrels — she asked her father to row her up the river so that she might gaze across to the castle of Beilstein and maybe see the one she loved. The barge-skipper was so relieved to find his lovely daughter once more in possession of her senses that he agreed. He pushed out a rowboat and set out up the stream until abreast of Beilstein.

The girl was presently moved to tears. Gazing awhile at the castle behind the town she prayed that her Kuno would be happy, and forgave him from the depths of her heart. Just as she was doing so, there came a sound of horns and dogs, and a party of hunters came riding down the valley behind the village. At the water they halted. Kuno saw the boat, and when he recognised the girl in it he started, mumbling her name.

His new and noble bride was sitting her horse beside him, and she both saw and heard. Being of a jealous turn of mind she asked Kuno how well he knew the girl.

Hardly at all, he said. Perhaps he had met her once or twice, he could not rightly remember. 'She is nothing to me, my dear,' he added.

'Nothing?'

'Certainly not,' lied Kuno. 'She is no more to me than the game we hunt.' And just to show that he meant it, and was determined not to have ghosts of past seductions disturbing the peace of the castle, he put an arrow to his bow and drew.

The girl gasped as the arrow pierced her. She collapsed over the gunwale, and her father leapt to take hold of her. He threw the boat off balance and it capsized, he himself being drowned in the effort to support his dying daughter. After which, no doubt, Kuno repaired to his castle for dinner. But I doubt if his bride was convinced.

The Moselle trail crosses the heights to Beilstein all the way from Merl, and in the course of its ramble through the forest it does not touch so much as a farm. The village was peaceful when I arrived there, but it was to prove a disturbed night for the population. Instead of staying in either of the larger hotels down by the river I resolved to take a room in one of the lesser inns, where I was provided with a bedroom on the top floor. But I decided to eat at the Haus Lipmann near the river, and thither I took myself for dinner. The waitress could not absolutely dispel the southern intonation which crept into her German, and when she came to take my order I said that I hoped she would not be offended if I mentioned that she had made a minor error in asking the couple dining at the far end of the room if they wanted some *Brotchen*. *Brot*, yes. But the diminutive endings of *-chen* and *-lein* always modified the preceding vowel to an *umlaut* if it was in fact an *umlaut*-able vowel or an *au*-diphthong. It should have been *Brötchen*.

'Gee,' she said. 'I reckon your language is enough to give anyone a sore head. But thanks a lot just the same.'

'Not at all,' I said. 'And it isn't my language, so don't blame me. How do you come to be here, anyway? A holiday job?'

The girl said yes, it was all arranged by Lufthansa, who had a most enlightened scheme by which carefully vetted and selected language students could fly cheap to jobs with approved people, to perfect their German. She came from a college in South Carolina, and was working as a waitress and vine-dresser in Beilstein for the long vacation. She loved it, and the Lipmanns were kindness itself.

'I guess I've learned lots of things the professor at college never taught us,' she said. 'Specially when the cook drops something or burns himself. But how anyone can straighten out their plurals is more than I can guess.'

I ordered a pork chop and some wine, and then I asked her a very serious question.

'Tell me,' I said. 'What do you know about the spirit of God in the body of man?'

She looked startled. 'You mean, about Christ?'

'Not exactly,' I said. 'You are a languages student, not learning theology. What does it mean to you if I say "the spirit of God in the body of man, and the worm in the bush on the edge of the forest?"'

She thought hard. 'I don't get it,' she said at last.

'Those are the only eight monosyllabic male nouns which take -er in the plural, with an *umlaut* thrown in where possible.'

'I think that's cute,' she said. 'I can remember that. And I'll tell the professor when I get back. Thanks a lot.'

When we had experimented a little further with plurals and genders I made my way up to the inn. It was only just ten o'clock, but the place was in darkness. Not a light was to be seen in any room at either side of the building, and the door was locked. There was no bell, so I walked up the steps and knocked on the door. I banged, then I thumped, and at last I rat-tat-tatted as hard as I dared upon the glass with a one-Mark piece. I shouted, whistled and even howled, but nobody stirred. No one even tipped a pail of water out of their bedroom window.

I next tried some dark little doors in the outside wall, but they

proved only to be exterior lavatories. I went round to the back —
watched now by many pairs of eyes peering round the curtains of
upper rooms under Beilstein's eaves of slate — and thumped on
the door of what turned out to be the next house. But the neighbour proved to be a sensible woman. She told me to knock even
louder, and as I departed to do so she herself rang the inn by
telephone. Purrrr . . . purrrr . . . purrrr, went the bell, bang-bang-
bang-bang, went my fist for all it was worth on the door-frame.
A window was thrown up, then another and another, but only in
the houses across the street or down by the little archway which
led to the tiny market place. As far as the inhabitants of my inn
were concerned there was not a movement. They seemed all to be
dead.

I was sure that at any moment now the police would arrive
from Cochem to drag me away to the cells — as the Carolina girl
told me they had done on the previous evening with some other
malefactor who thought he could escape the long arm of the
Landespolizei by staying overnight at Beilstein. But the night-
gowned neighbour who had telephoned in vain now came to my
aid and started yelling in the street.

There can by now have been few people in Beilstein still abed
and asleep, even if the guests in my own inn were cowering in
terror under their goose-feather quilts. The din at last brought
the landlady herself running to the scene. Puffing up the street,
she was full of apologies. She had thought all the guests were
already in their rooms, so she had simply turned out the lights,
locked the doors front and back, and gone out to take wine with
friends. I thought this a somewhat dangerous thing to do, but I
did not say so. If Beilstein had never yet been burned down, even
in the years of war and trouble, it was probably safe enough for
another night.

Indeed Beilstein seems to be alone among the German Moselle
villages in that it has never known a conflagration. A French
general may have dismembered the Burg Metternich, but the
village of vintners at its foot has been spared, and it says much for
the Beilsteiners that coaches and excursion steamers arrive hourly,
and crowds walk through the few little alleys looking at the place

as though it were an exhibit — which of course it is — and yet the village has managed to avoid becoming vulgarised. Its hotels are pleasant and courteous, and do not set out to fleece people. It is as though the great Metternichs themselves still look down from the towers of their Burg at the top of the vineyard hill to see that everyone is behaving with due decorum. But of course they have long ago departed for lands more suited to political intrigue and have moved their residence to Austria, leaving only their arms on the wall in the market square, and those parts of their residence which have since become the Haus Lipmann.

Opposite Beilstein the river bank curves quickly to Poltersdorf (km. 60·5 L), which spreads itself in front of its orchards of apple and cherry, and the low-lying fields of vines. It is said to have its name from the poltering nature of its inhabitants, as much disturbers of the peace as are *Poltergeister*. They seem certainly to have been a pig-headed and obstinate people, for they were so vigorous in their rejection of the Gregorian calendar reform in 1583 that they refused to have anything to do with it, and the new dating was only imposed by sending a suitable force of soldiery to impress it upon them.

Fankel (km. 59·4 R) stands right beside its lock, the fourth step up from the Rhine, and is yet another village with its tale of a bargemaster who promised a reward to the patron saint of bargees and then recanted as soon as his craft was out of danger. The tale is almost as common as are the statues of St Nicholas himself, and it is sad to think that so many shipmen were unreliable — though perhaps if spread over the length of the river and across several centuries the record is not so bad. As for the deceiving bargee of Fankel, he even overstepped the bounds of decency and is said to have been unwise enough to mock and curse the unoffending saint, with the result that he himself was never to rest. His ghost was very justly condemned for ever to pole his heavily laden craft up the river, and often in the night a Fankeler might hear the groaning and sighing of the skipper, and the sharp sound when the iron-shod barge-pole struck into the stones of the bank as the man laboured to keep the bow from being swept against the shore on the bend below Beilstein.

When I heard this tale I wondered what the shade of the wicked bargee did, now that the International Moselle Company had built Fankel barrage right across the path of his night-time voyaging. The river level below the lock is much as it was in the days of the *Halfen* and the bargeman's own blaspheming lifetime, but ⸜right opposite the church the wide dam makes a step of twenty-three feet to the level of the Fankel *Stau* above. Does the ghostly bargemaster continue to voyage along the old river bottom, mysteriously piercing the concrete and poling his accursed vessel through the turbine room of the power-station while the engineers pretend not to notice? Or has he been taught to use the lock, hooting three times for the duty keeper to peer down the stream with his night-binoculars and press the buttons to open the gates? Perhaps he bides his time, invisible if creaking and sighing, and slips silently in behind a pair of tankers bound for Trier or Lorraine. And if no ship should come, and his craft is not more than three metres wide he could use the do-it-yourself small-boat lock on the further side of the mole.

Below Fankel must have been the point of the river where Mr Quin and his companions were ingeniously cheated out of their dinner on the steamer. I calculated it to have been close to the marker for km. 53, for it is there that the castle of Cochem first rears into view over the steep edge of the Brauseley cliff to starboard (km. 52·5 R). Each time we ran down this reach of the Moselle I felt once again that Mr Quin was more fortunate than he realised, for the view of Cochem is one of such superlative beauty that to have missed it for the sake of a cut of pork would have been a pity indeed. And every time that this same view broke upon us it proved to be even more magnificent than our recollection of it, perhaps because the sky which formed the backcloth was so varied from one voyage to the next. Once we dropped down the stream in the evening and turned the slow curve just as the last light was striking upon the castle, when already the houses of the town below lay in the shadow. Another time the burg stood serene against a blue sky, its turrets and rounded towers and steep gables recalling some imagined fairyland castle painted on the cabin door of an English narrow-boat. On the third occasion the sky was dark, pierced by silvery shafts of a curious unearthly light. A haze of wood smoke hung half-way up the side of the conical hill on which the castle rested, and the building itself stood majestic but partly veiled in mystery.

We did not berth at Cochem, which has a shallow and inhospitable shore, but at Cond on the opposite side (km. 51·5 R), in full view of the castle — which cannot be seen from the town promenade on the Cochem or left bank. To walk up to it we had only to cross in the passenger ferry just astern of us and follow a pathway up through the town and round to the back of the hill. The walk proved well worth the ascent, for the view over the river and its ships was superb, but the romantic castle itself turned out to be a competent and heavy nineteenth-century restoration in somewhat doubtful style. Yet we could forgive everything when we were over at Cond again and could see once more the same great square tower with its host of minor attendants raised high against the sky. At night it was floodlit, and because the slope below it was bare of buildings and street-lights it seemed to hang suspended from the stars, medieval and majestic in the cool night air.

Cochem's own waterfront is alluring too. Though few of the houses have any special merit, the general effect is that of a very charming and friendly row of buildings clustered tight under their slate roofs at the further side of the roadway, many of them with balconies to look out over the river. It must have been on one of these that Mr Rooke sat looking down upon the pleasant scene.

'The steamers with their passing life arrive and depart just opposite; the great fleets of barges are pulled past by dozens of horses, at which the drivers scream and crack their whips till the whole valley resounds; fishermen ply their trade, and at night-time light fires on the banks, that thus they may be able to see their prey in the water.' Already the passenger-craft were steamers, but the *Halfen* had not yet given way to the steam-tug.

Cochem's Moselle promenade is also best seen from a distance, for in the evening the houses are metamorphosed most improbably into a row of dives which attempt to be night-clubs, a reminder that the big cities of the Rhineland and Ruhr are not really very

far away. Cochem is in fact a resort which thrives on coaches, a
kind of miniature Blackpool on the Moselle, a little town where
the electric guitar and dim roseate lighting are considered daring.
And yet behind all this there are some pleasant and unspoiled
alleys with half-timbered houses, though not many have survived
from before the era when the French sallied out of Montroyal to
sack the town, slay the 1,600 men of the garrison who surrendered,

Cochem

and so thoroughly pillage the whole of Cochem that those citizens who survived were for the most part driven abroad, and fled for ever.

It was fortunate for Cochem that the demands of railway engineering obliged the Prussian railways to start the Kaiser Wilhelm tunnel at the downstream edge of the town, so that Cochem has a station but no track running through it or carried on an embankment alongside the dining-room windows as is the case with such pretty towns of the Rhine as Bacharach. I hope the inhabitants realise their good fortune, but that might not be the case, for the Cochemers have long been a byword for stupidity.

No doubt this reputation is quite unearned, but there are many tales — invented by their envious neighbours — to bear witness to their strange simplicity. One Moselle story of the creation tells how the Almighty first made man experimentally out of clay. He left the original production to dry in the sun, but by over-exposure the clay became wrinkled and shrivelled, and just a bit cracked. The Creator wondered for a while what he could do to improve its appearance, but at length decided that the misshapen specimen would be best left alone. It was not very adequate as a man but would be good enough for a Cochemer.

Then there is the tale of how the town council of Cochem were once thrown into the greatest alarm when it was reported to them that a strange little animal in a velvety coat was digging a tunnel at the foot of the town walls. Some brave men captured it and carried it before the council, who decided that it must have been sent by their enemies to burrow right under the fortifications, so that gunpowder could be placed beneath the walls or perhaps a spy sent to creep through the hole at dead of night into the town.

The councillors had little difficulty in deciding that the creature was a danger and that it sought to destroy Cochem, so they sentenced it to death. An alderman then pointed out that in such a case of betrayal it was only right to make the punishment fit the crime. The tunneller must be buried alive. So, with proper ceremony, a hole was dug in the soil, the mole was placed in it and carefully covered over with earth. After which the citizens could thank their good fortune for having such an alert and watchful civic body to preserve them from all ill.

Suiting the punishment to the offence seems to have been characteristic of the juridical actions of the council, for there was also the case of the trespasser in the vineyards. At Cochem as elsewhere it has always been the custom to close the vineyards for some weeks before the grape harvest, any person found in them being guilty of a serious offence. One year a goat was found which had broken through the fence and was munching at the grapes. Arrested, the creature was dragged by the horns to the town hall and put on trial. In defence it could only utter a stupid sort of sound, but its vigorous nodding of its head was no doubt interpreted as an admission of guilt. The goat was accordingly sentenced to be crushed in the winepress, and this was duly done.

'He's a more despicable villain than we even thought,' exclaimed the burgomaster as the blood poured out into the collecting trough. 'Look there! He must have been at the red grapes, too.'

X

WHEN we spent a night at anchor below the Beilstein ferry we were up and away at half-past six, having already breakfasted. Yet the beauty of the early morning is not always appreciated on land, and, however early the Beilsteiners may have bedded, I had some difficulty in getting an eight o'clock breakfast at my inn. It was nearly nine o'clock before I was able to leave, and no sooner had I set out than the rain began to pour down on my head, continuing to do so for all of the two hours' ascent to the heights overlooking the valley which dropped to Treis.

Half-way thither I came upon a monastery, not a ruin but one which still lived and moved and had its premonstratensian being. It was a group of buildings of brown slaty stone, set all alone in a dell in the middle of a forest of oaks. The place had the name of Kloster Engelport, and as I reached it a cavalcade of a dozen cars drew up across the road in the downpour. One, which drove closer to the monastery, contained the bride in her beautiful dress. The rest brought the relatives from some remote village of the Hunsrück. The younger women had their hair smartly poodled as directed by the new mode magazines, and they had elegant shoes in which to walk through the puddles. They laughed in the rain, and everyone was very, very happy, even in the downpour. And no wonder — for what could be better than to be married right there at the Gateway of the Angels? I gave a sodden wave to the bride. I hoped she would ever be gay, and find with the young man of her heart all the happiness of which she dreamed.

The voyage down-river from Cochem to Treis is not an eventful one. The Moselle curves round towards Klotten (km. 47·5 L), with campers and orchards to starboard and the almost sheer wall of the one-thousand-foot Klottener Berg to port, a dark rock-face on which the vintners have nevertheless managed to hack out their terraces as though determined to prove that they could convert vertical into horizontal. The railway at their foot is well aware of what may happen when a vine-dresser moves between the rows far overhead, and prudently protects itself with barricades of sleepers to ward off falling rocks.

It was along this stretch that Quin reported a pleasant custom. At the time of the annual Frankfurt fair a 'passage-boat' plied between Cochem and Frankfurt to take merchants and buyers to the great trade market, and when the ship returned up the Moselle the children would crowd down to the banks to have toys thrown to them by the traders. The merchants must, I think, have had remarkably strong arms if they could throw the playthings on to dry land, but maybe the older boys and girls waded far out in the shallows to catch them.

High above Klotten stands the tower of Koraidelstein (km. 47·3 L) once the home of a lady whose name is still preserved in the motor vessel *Richenza* which plies on these lower reaches of the river. Richenza was the queen of Miceslaus II of Poland, and during the lifetime of her somewhat incompetent husband she managed all the affairs of the realm. At his death she became regent until her son Casimir should be old enough to rule, but Poland was a turbulent land, and the Poles eventually rose in revolt against their good and gentle queen, forcing her to flee the country, taking her son with her.

Being of Palatinate origin — she was the daughter of the Count Palatine himself — the fair Richenza took her little boy to the Moselle country, and at Klotten they settled. In her sadness Richenza shut herself up in the Koraidelstein, and her son eventually became a monk. Subsequently the Poles changed their minds about the desirability of having a ruler, and sent an embassy to the Moselle to ask that Casimir should return as king and restore the country to order. But they found that the young

man was no longer free. However, he agreed to ask permission, and the Pope released him from his vows on condition that the upper-class men of his country should always crop their hair close round the edges as a reminder that their monarch had once been a monk. That at least is one explanation of the Polish hair-style which always intrigued visitors from other countries, but the habit may be even older than the time of Richenza and Casimir, which was the eleventh century.

Richenza tried to persuade her son that kingship was nothing other than vanity, but he was not swayed. He returned and ruled, leaving his mother the queen at Klotten, where she established a chapel and a convent retreat, and became known as one of the first benefactors of the people of the valley.

'Thy peaceful waters flow rapidly, undisturbed by the loud blustering of the wind, unimpeded by the barriers of hidden reefs. No shallows hast thou which by their turbulence make thy streaming impetuous, no shoals raise themselves within thy course or form islands which split thy stream in twain.' So wrote Ausonius, and it is true that the Moselle is remarkably free of islands. One, however, stretches for some way either side of the km. 41 marker, and on our later voyages we always rounded its lower point, decorated with a charming little ornamental summerhouse, and sailed into the backwater which forms the yacht harbour of Treis.

On one of our voyages we had made friends with a German family aboard their cruiser *Edith*, a little ship based on Treis. Herr Oberrecht had been quick to take the opportunity provided by canalisation and had bought enough bank in the willow-edged backwater to place two private jetties. Very generously the *Edith* gave the *Thames Commodore* a permanent invitation to use her landing whenever she passed by the Moselle.

Treis itself (km. 40·2 R) is not a notable place. It has a woollen mill and the remnants of two castles destroyed by the French, but otherwise it has little to exhibit. The backwater, however, is an excellent starting-point for a visit to Karden and Eltz, both of which lie on the further side of the river.

Karden (km. 39·5 L) is not as ancient as Trier, but its noble romanesque church of the twelfth century is a hint that this was

o

an important place in the growth of the Moselle country. There was long ago a settlement at the Pommerer Mart (km. 41 L), the hill which falls sheer to the river across from the backwater of Treis. Ditch and bank were thrown up on its summit by the Celts, and there they also built the holy place of their own deities. When the Romans conquered the Treviri they developed the settlement at the foot of the hill into a considerable town with a garrison of two cohorts, villas for civil servants, temples for the Roman pantheon and even a theatre. Merchants established themselves at the river crossing, and Karden pottery was manufactured and exported.

The hill-top sacred to the Celts was fortified and provided with several temples, one of which was to the warlike god whose identity is not greatly disguised in the name of Martberg. Yet it remained a place of worship for the Celtic as much as the Roman deities, and the Celts retained their own priesthood and rites. Jealously they guarded the place against any infiltration by the interfering Christians.

And then one day about the middle of the fourth century there came down the river two men from Trier, Castor and Lubentius, sent by Bishop Maximin to take the gospel to the lower reaches of the river. They had set their eyes upon Karden, the most important Roman town after Trier, but the Celtic priests stirred up the people to resist them. The two men were driven out of Karden and forbidden to return.

Lubentius moved further downstream and eventually into the valley of the Lahn, where both the old *Commodore* and her successor in turn had nosed into the bank at Dietkirchen, where the ancient church on the massive limestone rock which once was another sacred site of the Celts marks where Lubentius lived and died as the apostle of the Lahn valley. But Castor chose to remain near the Martberg. Banned from Karden, he made himself a home in a cave of the cliff and lived there as a hermit.

The druids continued undismayed and apparently victorious, but Castor was a patient man. He was also a very practical one, and in his own homeland of Aquitaine — Ausonius country, in fact — he had learned viticulture and the care of crops and cattle.

Around his cave he planted medicinal herbs for men and women as well as for the livestock, and doggedly he set about serving the people of the villages in their ordinary needs. As the years passed, the men and women of the Moselle were more and more drawn to the patient Castor, who showed them better techniques in vine-husbandry, improved their cultivation and acted as doctor and friend to all the people. Little by little the hold of the druids was weakened, and at last a small Christian community established itself in Karden.

All the while Castor lived in his cave in the cliff, away from the splendour of the villas and the houses of the merchants. He was beloved of all the people, and when at last he died in his hermit's cavern the men came from Hunsrück and Eifel to mourn at his grave. Several hundred years later the great church of St Castor was built in Koblenz, and thither his remains were removed. Yet it is the church at Karden, not at Koblenz, which most recalls his memory, its three towers looking out to the river across the turrets of the old toll-house of the Lords of Eltz (km. 39·3 L).

So old is Karden's church that when we passed down the river it was cracked, and the whole of the apse was in danger of collapsing. The towers were shored up, and inside the nave the ground had been quarried away to sink a new foundation of concrete on which the whole structure could be jacked up and set straight again for another round of centuries.

From behind the church of Karden the Moselle trail decides to become almost alpine for a while, twisting and turning in short zigzags up a cliff which is too steep even for the vintners. Instead of vines there are wild pinks and saxifrage and helianthemum, and a good rich smell of wet rock after a shower. The track is purposeful as it winds between the rocks as though it intends to go somewhere special, and on leaving its rock-garden behind it strikes through an orchard and across the fields toward some rolling woods of oak and tall pines. Another hour, and the view breaks across a great curving cleft in which the River Elz burbles troutful and swift, curling invisible at the foot of the dense forest.

The sight of this green amphitheatre of woodland is one of the most splendid in all Germany, for the stream has eroded nearly a whole circle and holds in its embrace a cliff which seems strangely primeval, as though it were a plug pushed up through the open crater of a volcano to cool and stiffen in the air long, long ago, and which has since been mellowed and decked with a mantle of oak and alder and pine. Only the top is free from forest trees, and on the tiny plateau set in the middle of the basin of the surrounding woods there stands what must be the most idyllic and at the same time the most fantastic castle in Germany.

Burg Eltz was built from about 1100 onwards, and it is still in the possession of the family. Or rather, of one of the families, for strangely enough the building is a cluster of residences, and several related clans lived in it without often coming to blows. They were distinguished by their names — Rübenach, Rodendorf and Kempenich — and by all having the same heraldic device of a lion with two tails, though in different colours. Not only did they live peaceably with their neighbours through the walls, but Burg Eltz itself was not in any way a predatory fortress. Being merely a prudently fortified dwelling to which the families themselves and their tenants in the valley could retire in troublous times, Eltz was never intentionally burned or sacked; Louis XIV, Gustavus Adolphus, Napoleon, the Americans — any of these might have razed the place to the ground if it had been an armed bastion, but instead it survived in its own peaceful valley, far from any highway. Only once in its history was it attacked, and that was when the expansionist Archbishop Balduin determined to add it to his Electoral domain of Trier — the same Balduin who fared so badly at the hands of the Lady of Starkenburg. He built a fortified tower overlooking the castle, and from its top stone balls were catapulted for four long years into the courtyard. The walls of Eltz proved too stout thus to be broached, but it must have been unpleasant to live in the place with the archiepiscopal missives flying through the air. At last a shortage of provisions caused the stout-walled Burg Eltz to surrender. Its owners could then receive from the gracious and grasping hands of the priestly Elector the right to live in their own house — at a suitable rental.

Ludwig II's castle of Neuschwanstein in Bavaria may be astonishing in its unexpected Disneyfication, and the Haut

Burg Eltz

Koenigsbourg above Sélestat in Alsace a remarkable reconstitution
of a fortified nest of the Middle Ages, but Burg Eltz is more
impressive than either. Its walls — not a defensive curtain, but
the sides of the castle itself — rise sheer from the rock, with here
and there a little oriel, or the turreted window of a chapel, or a
neat dormer-window to an attic. It is as though each of the families
had tried to climb high enough to see over the heads of its
relations, until at last the builders could take the blocks no higher
and left the inhabitants to lean out of their elegant little half-
timbered turrets and talk to each other across the breadth of the
little courtyard left between them, now become cool and mossy
in the shadow of the buildings. Eltz was in fact built through
several centuries, each wing attached to its neighbour and yet
independent, so that it has about it the rare charm that comes of
being unplanned and yet raised by men who had an eye for beauty.
There is nothing anywhere quite like it. Besides, it is not a ruin.
It is the summer residence — the country cottage, one might say
— of Count Jakob von und zu Eltz. If it were mine I would be
content to live there all the year round, lost in the depths of my
own romantic forests.

As a residence rather than a robber's tower Burg Eltz has no
dungeons, or torture chambers, or any other horrors. It has a
collection of weapons on the wall, including a number of Turkish
implements brought back by one of the indefatigable Eltzers who
fought to defend Vienna. One of these swords is ingenious and no
doubt effective, for it consists of the proboscis of a swordfish sawn
off and provided with a handle. There is armour, of course, and
one little breastplate hanging on the wall has a hole in it, right
over the upper breast. This is the famous 'pierced breastplate of
Eltz', which is connected in legend with a tragic event in the
history of the castle, when it was attacked in 1465 by a disappointed
villain.

Gisela, or Schön Agnes, the fair daughter of one of the families
of Eltz, was given in marriage when still a child to a suitor whom
she had never seen, the young knight of Braunsberg. When she
grew up and was told of the match her heart revolted, for though
she had no other lover the mere sight of the rough and tough

young knight, a gluttonous man and a wine-bibber, was enough
to repel any girl.

Furious at being disregarded by his lawful fiancée, who happened also to be rich and extremely well connected, the young
Braunsberger decided to demonstrate his rights. One night when
he had been invited along with others to a banquet in the castle
of Eltz he stood up at the table and ordered Gisela to come over
and kiss him. She refused, and the other guests delightedly
mocked the discomfited young blood.

The insult worked like poison. The Braunsberger resolved to
capture the girl by might, and on a dark night of autumn his forces
crept up the valley to attack the castle. The tradesmen and artisans
living under the protection of Eltz flocked in to help defend it,
and soon a battle was raging all around the walls. The fate of
Eltz seemed to hang in the balance, when a young knight appeared,
sword in hand, who personally led sally upon sally, never saying
a word but swinging his sharp sword and cutting down every man
who stood in his way. The Braunsberger himself saw the havoc
being wrought among his forces, and pressing his horse through
the throng he rode up and shot the courageous knight at point-
blank range. The ball pierced the breastplate, and the brave young
defender fell.

Roused by this deed to furious revenge, the Eltzers redoubled
their attack and at last they routed the forces of the Braunsberger.
Then, sadly, they carried the body of the valiant knight into the
courtyard of Eltz and lifted the visor. There, pale in death but
still beautiful, they beheld the face of their young mistress, Gisela
the fair.

The way down from Eltz is along a woodland path which curves
through the trees and follows the bends of the gorge of the River
Elz towards Moselkern. There is no road to the castle, and this is
one reason why it has escaped being spoiled in recent years, for
any visitor has to be prepared to walk three miles or more. That
hundreds do so every week and four hundred school parties tramp
to it every year shows that the German love of walking is not
entirely dead — even though on several of my days along the
Moselle trail I met not a soul from morn till evening. In Moselkern

itself a signpost points the traffic to Burg Eltz but prudently omits
to mention that after a winding journey through the valley bottom
the road suddenly comes to a halt and there is no choice but to
plod up an hour of comparatively steep path, always expecting the
castle to appear round the next bend.

Yet the walk is one of the loveliest imaginable, for the steep-
sided Elz runs in the most beautiful of valleys. Ausonius was long
ago enchanted by it. *'Felix Alisontia qui per sola pinguia labens
stringit frugiferas ripas.'* The happy Elz, flowing through the fresh
countryside, spreads its fruit-laden banks. And fruit-laden they
still are, just as they were when Ausonius rode along the stream
with his youthful charges. Even now the Elz is banked by orchards
at its lower end, for the vineyards of Moselkern where the stream
joins the larger river are set on the steep slopes of the Moselle
itself.

'Not less strong than the Saar,' Ausonius called this tributary,
and if that were really so he must have seen the Elz in floodtime
and through the magnifying spectacles of a poet. But certainly it
is a lovely stream, a trout river flowing gurgling (and not altogether
tacitum) between the thickly wooded hills to wind its last miles
through the orchards, now as then — provided, that is, that the
happy Alisontia really is the Elz. Others have seen in the name the
River Alsetz which flows through Luxembourg — a blow for the
Moselkerners, certainly, but one difficult to follow up because the
Alsetz flows not into the Moselle but the Sûre, the waters of which
Ausonius had already counted earlier in his idyll.

Moselkern (km. 34 L) is one of the lesser-known villages of
vintners, but I have a particular affection for its 'Anker' inn.
When I arrived there on foot the World Football Cup had reached
the semi-finals, and every able-bodied man in Germany, and no
doubt in the rest of Europe, was closeted with the television. In
the afternoon the 'Anker' had been packed out, because it had a
set which could tap the German Channel 2 and bring Aston Villa
right to the *Weinstube*. That same evening the really important
matches were being played off, but the landlord of the Anker did
not turn on the set. Resolutely he did business as usual — business
on Saturday evenings consisting in allowing his clients to sing the

old favourites of German hunting and loving and wining songs to the accompaniment of a one-man band. They might dance, too, if anything so outrageously modern as a Viennese waltz did not drive them away. So, with the ether carrier-waves battering at the windows to be allowed to show us the state of the soccer, Herr Pitt kept a firm front, and a good stock of wine which was probably of his own growing. And he kept his customers, too.

Moselkern is not marked out in any special way from the other wine villages. Probably its chief exhibit is the curious Mero-vingian grave memorial hidden away near the station. Actually it is a cast, as the original has been swept away to the museum in Bonn, but a Merovingian tombstone is quite an oddity all the same. Dating from the seventh century, it does not go back as far at St Castor himself, but it claims the distinction of being the oldest non-Roman Christian monument in Germany. Moselkern also possesses, modestly unannounced and unadvertised, a *Halfter-wirtschaft*. This timber-framed house of the early eighteenth century which once was an overnighting point for the drovers who towed the barges up river, would have been two days' hauling out of Koblenz. The inn is not the 'Anker' as the name of that hotel might imply; but is now a mere private house in which presumably a vintner lives. Like most inns for the *Halfen*, it is right at the edge of the village, far enough from the centre for the repose of the inhabitants not to be disturbed by the ongoings of such rough men as hauled the ships in all weathers.

The Moselle trail does not descend to Moselkern, but wanders through the woods towards Lasserg. So it was toward that village that I directed my steps in the morning, watched nervously at one moment by a tree-creeper, then by a brown squirrel, and later by an eagle which made several runs overhead until it was quite sure that I was too large to be carried away in its talons. Just short of Metternich, a tiny hamlet by no means worthy of its great political namesake, I decided to leave the trail to pursue its own muddy way across the plateau. I could see that on the Hunsrück side of the river there were hills and forests more attractive than the huge expanse of arable land which stretched for miles ahead, and so I dropped down the pretty vale of the Schlummbach, a busy stream which evidently had enough power to drive another saw-mill or flour-mill every quarter-mile. It was like a valley of the lower Black Forest hills, and I was only surprised Ausonius did not find it worth mentioning. Perhaps in his day the woods were impassable.

The Schlumm brook bubbles its way to emerge between the steep walls of its own valley and cast itself into the Moselle at Hatzenport (km. 28·5 L). Obviously the name conveys that this was formerly a port, but for once what is obvious is wrong. It seems that in the ninth century there was a Bishop of Trier named Hetti or Hatto — not the same as the Bishop Hatto of Mainz who was slanderously said to have burned the poor to save food for the rich and was eaten by mice in the Mauseturm by the Bingen rapids of the Rhine. Hatto of Trier was a very enterprising cleric, as indeed so many were in the dark and early medieval ages, and he decided to open a road up the Moselle valley by blasting away the cliffs where they fell right to the water. How he did the blasting we are not told, and perhaps it would be unkind to ask. But certainly one of the places at which he must have used his engineering talent was where a comb of rock projected into the river just downstream of the Schlummbach. The opening he made enabled trade to follow the bank, and the settlement at the mouth of the brook became known — if the story is true — as Hattonis Porta. So the *port* of Hatzenport is not a port but a gateway.

Hatzenport does not appear to be the ancient village that it is, for like Trarbach and many others it went up in flames. That was in 1741, and only nine houses were left. Even those nine are not very obvious, so perhaps they went the way of the rest later, or just crumbled quietly into decay.

Between Treis and Hatzenport the *Thames Commodore* led us down the step of Müden lock (km. 37) and on past Moselkern to glide beneath a very severe-looking tower with a broad white band circling its dark stonework. This is the Bischofsstein (km. 31·4 L), placed there to preserve law and order in one corner of the domains of Electoral Trier.

Deep in the Hunsrück forest lie the remnants of the castle of the lords of Waldeck who once used to sally out to rob and plunder the merchants and traders, the abbeys, even the farms. It was to put an end to their depredations that Bishop Arnold of Trier began to build the Bishop's Rock, late in the twelfth century. Completed by his successors, it commanded one of the most important crossings of the Moselle and was under the jurisdiction of the Archdeacon of Karden, whose task it was to ensure that the fort was kept in good repair and could instantly withstand attack.

As for the broad white band which still rings the round tower, one may take one's choice of the explanations. Most mundane — and, I think, unconvincing — is the statement that the white is only the remains of the whitewash on the inner wall of a wooden gallery which once ran round the tower so that the defenders could fire upon attackers scaling the crag from the valley below. More attractive but even less likely is the assertion that like many other lines on the buildings in Moselle villages, it marks the level of high water during a particularly severe flood — an inundation so great that some have even declared it to have been *the* Flood, which would date the Bishops of Trier as decidedly pre-Noah, a theory not without difficulties of its own.

A more pleasing explanation is that in the days of the robber knights, not long after the completion of the castle itself, the Archbishop sent to it a strong contingent of knights and men at arms who were to put down the violence and crime in the neighbourhood. This they succeeded in doing, and peace and order were established throughout the countryside. Everyone was pleased — except the robber knights, who found their living gone. Unemployed and with diminishing reserves they began to long for revenge. Besides, with the Bischofsstein still in commission there was little chance of returning to the good old days. The castle must be taken, the episcopal knights slain.

Hatching a careful plan the men crept up to the castle in the darkness, silently forced an entry, and slew every one of the knights and their retainers. But it happened that a poor peasant was in the fort at the time, and cowering in terror he managed to escape being seen and then to slip out of the gate and make his way at once to Trier, where he told Archbishop Johann what had occurred. At once the Archbishop sent a strong force down the valley, and these men in turn crept up to the fortress in the dark. They found the robber knights drunken or asleep, or both, and very swiftly they were all dragged out and despatched.

Archbishop Johann then had a white line painted round the tower — a bishop's ring, some say, though others believe it to have been intended to signify a noose.

'By recalling the fate of those robbers, all evil men may preserve themselves from the stern hand of justice,' said the Archbishop. 'See, I preach them a sermon in stones, that wicked men may be saved from their sins. And if they heed not this sermon of mine, then the sword will preach to them instead.'

Within sight of Hatzenport is Brodenbach (km. 26·5 R), a village fortunate enough to have one of those Moselle rarities, a harbour one quarter of a mile in length. Of all places on the river it is perhaps the favourite of small-boatmen, particularly if they like exploring the Hunsrück forest which here spills right down to the village itself. One of the walks leads up the valley of the Ehrenbach, a gentle millstream which curves and twists past orchards and through meadows episcopal in their purple of campanula and autumn crocus, until the track eventually climbs to the ruin of what must once have been as massive a fortress keep as any in the land of the Moselle.

The Ehrenburg must no doubt have seen plenty of warrings and besiegings, but at the beginning of the fifteenth century the line ran out when Count Friedrich of Ehrenburg died without an heir. Indeed he was for some time unmarried, for his own father had died when he was still too young to be pledged, but feeling that life in his remote forest keep was lonely he at length set out to find himself a wife who would be a worthy mistress of the proud Ehrenburg and its domains.

He managed indeed to discover a girl of suitable quality, and presenting his compliments to her crusty father he asked for her hand in return for his castle, his name and his sword — all of which were to be hers. But the father was not impressed. He acknowledged that the castle was a strong one and the name famous enough; but as for the sword, it was as yet untried and had no victories to its credit. His daughter would only be wedded to an undoubted warrior, he declared, and if Count Friedrich wished to have her as his wife he could go off and burn down Koblenz. He was not to return until he had done so.

The idea suited Friedrich of Ehrenburg. He collected together a number of tough friends with their men-at-arms, and the band continually raided Koblenz until they had managed to burn down part of the city. Triumphant, the young count then rode confidently up to the home of his fair beloved, only to find that when her father had told her of his plan to try Friedrich's valour she had been so horrified that she had fled to a convent. Rather than be sold for a burned city she would spend her life trying to atone for the wickedness of her father, and of her suitor also.

Count Friedrich cursed and swore, but the girl was gone for ever. Eventually he found another girl with no strings attached to the union, but the marriage was childless — perhaps as an answer to the prayer of his original choice, that so wicked a line should not be prolonged into posterity.

One day in late summer I decided to walk up through the forest to find the dessert for our shipboard supper and renew the autumn crocuses which bloomed in a bowl of moss in the *Thames Commodore*'s saloon. Following the twisting Ehrenbach far up beyond the castle of Count Friedrich the Fire-raiser, I struck up through the woods to climb to the plateau. All the while the buzzards circled over the ridges, mewing and calling in a sky which — because it was a Saturday morning — was wonderfully free from the thunder of NATO jets swooping toward their air-base on the spinal column of the Dog's Back. It was a walk which might have been in the Black Forest, and when a roedeer started from among the tall willowherb which decked a slope where the woodcutters had been busy, the thought came to me that from Apach lock to near Koblenz I had seen more deer than people along the trail. I had not met a wild boar, except a dead one on the rear bumpers of a Schützenmeister's Volkswagen, bumping down an alley in Treis. It was a fine beast and would furnish nearly three-quarters of a hundredweight of wild pork. But the Hunsrück is still alive with game of every kind, from the edible snails which hurried across the vineyard pathways in fear that I should be a Frenchman, to boar and stag and trout.

Quite suddenly I came upon a creature meditating in the roadway, an animal as brightly black and yellow as an airport control van. It looked at me unblinking, and the mere sight of the beautiful creature brought flooding back to me the years of the early nineteen-thirties, when in the Zoological Laboratory of the Albert Ludwig University we had kept just such animals for various esoteric and really rather unimportant purposes.

Salamandra maculosa — the name was scientifically correct and yet oddly inappropriate, for I had always thought the salamander of the German forests to be a most immaculate animal with all the appearance of being dressed for dinner. The first time I met one in the wilds I felt sad that salamanders did not live in the Lakeland woods of England, to join Jeremy Fisher and Squirrel Nutkin in Beatrix Potter's stories. *S. maculosa* would have made an excellent butler, or perhaps a man-about-town, fresh from his country estate.

The salamander in the pathway brought back the odours of the laboratory, the formalin and alcohol, the whiff of cuttlefish dissected on boards, and the wet smell of the room with the tanks of newts and the miniature glass-bound jungles for the salamanders themselves. Their larval form could tell us something about embryonic development. *Entwicklungsmechanik* was all the rage at Freiburg at that time. Spemann had won the Nobel prize for it — on newts, not salamanders as it happened — and the Spemann school was in its heyday. German research students, a Japanese doctorate-worker, a young American and Herr Pink, we all examined the cell divisions of newt embryos or carved out little pieces from one salamander tissue to transplant them into another. Herr Pink was myself, this being the approximation to my name for which I agreed to settle.

Now, in the wild valley leading back from the Moselle, *S. maculosa* and Herr Pink met again. I wanted to speak to him, but amphibians are not good listeners. Instead I stood and watched him. He seemed sure that I had no evil intentions upon either himself or the embryonic tissue-folds of his descendants, for he

just stood unblinking, watching, and perhaps startled to see a
biped in shorts and shirt on his own path. He stared impassively.
Or perhaps it was a she — for sexing salamanders was never one
of my accomplishments. Then he lumbered slowly away into the
bilberry bushes, leaving me to continue my climb through the
scented woods.

As I walked on, I remembered how the yellow-and-black
salamander was once mixed up in a curious laboratory scandal,
not at Freiburg but in London. In the nineteen-thirties the battle
between Darwinians and Lamarckians was, curiously enough, not
quite dead. The Darwinians were able to show conclusively
through sound genetic and embryological argument that characteristics acquired during the lifetime of a creature could not possibly
be inherited by later generations. The Lamarckians did not agree.
They took the commonsense view that, whether or not this was
possible in theory, in practice such characteristics were indeed
hereditary. All kinds of arguments were invoked to shake them.
Spaniels had their tails cut, Chinese children had for ages had
their feet bound with no effect on later generations, the Jews had
been circumcised for millennia, the Darwinians pointed out. But
the Lamarckians shook their heads. These things, they said, were
all mutilations. It was *useful* characteristics that were inherited.

To prove it a certain biologist, who I think was a German, hit
on the notion of trying the case with salamanders. Chameleon-
like — though not so versatile — the salamander could by taking
a certain amount of simple amphibian thought change its colour
and become either black with small yellow spots, or yellow with
small black spots, or any stage between the two. The overall
lightness or darkness was in this way chosen to match the brightness or dimness of its surroundings. The mechanism was very
sensible, very practical, very biochemical and — as I thought
every time I saw a salamander — very wonderful.

This biologist kept some salamanders in black boxes and others
in yellow boxes, and by breeding from the two lines separately
he tried to show that a baby salamander had its initial colouring
pushed in one direction or the other by its parentage — the
parents having acquired their extra lightness or darkness during

their own lives in the boxes. Had such an effect on the infant salamanders really been visible a mighty blow would have been struck for the dying cause of Lamarck. Certainly a number of learned papers appeared to stake just such a claim, but when there was a demand to see the actual photographs on which the neat little diagrams of blotchy baby salamanders were based, the crash came. The salamander-breeder left in a hurry and disappeared from the biological scene. In a laboratory darkroom in London's university a photographer shot himself. The photographs, as many had suspected, were 'touched'.

Above the woods the Hunsrück plateau rolls away to the edge of the Rhine gorge, which here is no great way off — the two rivers swinging towards each other so that Boppard on the Rhine and Brodenbach on the Moselle are only eight miles apart. The upland is a wide and windswept one, with fields of grain blue with the brilliance of cornflower and patches of potatoes and maize and sugar-beet. The villages are much as they have always been, farming communities of houses hung with purple slate, neatly trimmed to have one curved side and fashioned into ingenious patterns over the door or round the eaves and over the dormers. There are tractors, and even occasionally a horse or an ox, and the life of ploughing and sowing and reaping continues with just this difference — that Schinderhannes has gone, and the main road has come, carrying the heavy traffic mercifully diverted from the more beautiful section of the Rhine defile between Bingen and Koblenz.

From Brodenbach harbour the *Thames Commodore* had only a short run of a quarter-hour to the free landing-stage at Alken (km. 24·2 R). But when, trailing the river over the hills, I dropped down to Alken one evening I had the fortune to find the little town decked out in all the gaiety of the Schützenfest, or Marksmen's Festival.

I know no country so well provided with local festivals as Germany, and always they are a delight. All one needs is beer — or, better still, wine — and some cause for an occasion. In France the excuse is more often provided by a saint, but in Germany any kind of association furnishes a reason for having at least one annual festival, if not more. On my way down-river I had seen posters announcing some *Treffen* or other — festivals of singers, anglers, volunteer firemen, the brass band, the vintners, or in this case the marksmen. It was not the first Schützenfest I had been to, but it was a particularly unselfconscious and gay one. No doubt a well-trained television commentator would have seized upon it as evidence of German crypto-Nazism, but he would have been talking rubbish, just the same. Village festivals in Germany are as deeply rooted as the harvest home in England — and probably more firmly. I doubt if people in Britain have harvest festivals these days without a conscious wish to keep alive a dead past, or to be quaint; and the country Morris dancer is more likely to be an Oxford don than a local blacksmith.

I arrived too late to watch the Alken marksmen shoot, but in the evening the brass band assembled at the waterfront. Most of the musicians were under twenty, some not more than fourteen, and they mostly played that peculiar instrument which looks like a French horn that has been crushed until elliptical, a shape half way to a tuba. They struck up, and led the procession of marksmen through the village to the house of the winning junior, who was to be promoted to a full marksman.

A German marksman is a fine sight indeed. He is not like the *Freischütz* so much as a modernised Robin Hood. The twenty or more at Alken were spotlessly turned out in black trousers and white shirts with ties of Lincoln green, and they wore grey-green jackets decked with their bronze and silver prize medals. Each had a handsome half-trilby hat of the same colour with a cockade of eagle and blackcock feathers. Some of the older men had more than a score of prize insignia hung about them, others had only one or two, and as they followed the alley up from the waterside they marched in a particularly loose and unmilitary style — for after twenty-one years the memory or hearsay of the horrors of German militarism still made most Germans deliberately adopt a slapdash and casual attitude over such a thing as marching behind even the most genial of bands.

Behind the old guard came the juniors, the apprentice marksmen as it were. They wore dark green sleeveless waistcoats over

P

their white shirts, and they looked very handsome indeed, tanned with the vineyard sun. They followed their elders and the band until a halt was made outside a house at the edge of the village. Here the champion of the juniors was brought out, shy and smiling and accompanied (as he was so young) by his princess in the form of a very beautiful sister who held a bouquet of purple gladioli. The band greeted the pair with a fanfare, and then trays of glasses were brought out, filled with golden wine — for Alken is a notable wine village. The band and the marksmen drank, and the procession moved off again, the brass now playing with redoubled vigour.

The next stop was at the house of the outgoing Marksman-King or *Schützenkönig*. A fanfare from the band, and out he came with his wife wearing her silvery, queenly crown. Glasses were brought, and again the wine flowed for band and marksmen.

The procession moved on, many of the villagers following. Down to the river we marched, then made a left turn, and the band stopped outside the souvenir shop, where a white and green arch of paper streamers had been put round the door, with a shield: '*Schützenkönig Alken*'. The new king and his queen came out, the band greeted them, and they walked down the ranks of their subjects. More glasses were brought out, and the great silver cup of the shooting trophy was filled with a good vintage and passed round also. Once again the band led off, this time to the village hall, where most of the people of Alken were waiting for the coronation.

The crowning was brief and happy and good-humoured. The old queen's diadem and sash were transferred to her successor, and she then had to dance a farewell with her abdicating king under the flag. This was a magnificent standard which had led the procession all the way, and I noticed that the patron of the Schützen was, very reasonably, St Sebastian, shot through with arrows. Four men held the corners of the banner, and round and round the couple waltzed beneath the floating silk, which stretched over them like the canopy at a Jewish wedding.

And with that the formal proceedings were nearly over. But not quite, for they had to be properly concluded with another passing of the trophy, filled with an excellent vintage. If the brass now retired it was understandable, but their place was taken by a very up-to-date-looking dance orchestra of four or five players, with saxophone and squeeze-box and electric guitar. Their music-stands bore drapes with their name: 'Die Pedros'. They were the most German Spaniards I had ever seen, and like the village band I suspect they were vine-dressers and farmhands in ordinary life.

The sight of their instruments made me feel sad. A dreadful fate of Liverpool origin had overtaken even the village musicians of Alken, I thought. Yet when they began to play, their modern devices somehow made just the same traditional, happy, country sounds as the brass band before them. Tinsel, dinner-jackets and all, the waltz they played was more like a three-time at some vanished military ball, and the first fox-trot (if that is the right term) was 'Under the Double Eagle'. Twist and rock and Liver-puddling had made no impact upon Germany — or at least not upon the young people of Alken, down from the vineyards for a night of celebration.

Yet there was no reason why Alken should have been invaded by newer tastes. The country people had so many tunes already in their heads, gay airs which could still serve as excellently for a dance as they had done for years. And the songs too — their words might seem old-fashioned and strangely unreal in a city, but in Alken and a thousand other villages and towns one might still lilt them and love them. '*Horch, was kommt von d'rausen ein*'; a young man of today might still wonder if it was really to be his *Feinsliebchen* stopping at the door. '*Ich schiess den Hirsch*' — and did not the marksmen themselves intend the very next day to go out after the stag?

And that loveliest of songs, to the air Georg Schmitt composed on the paddle-steamer *Mosella* when Junk the caterer brought to him the verses newly written by Theodor Reck, the pastor.

Im weiten deutschen Lande
zieht mancher Strom dahin;
von allen, die ich kannte,

liegt einer mir im Sinn.
O Moselstrand,
O selig Land!
Ihr grünen Berge, O Fluss und Tal,
ich grüss' euch von Herzen viel tausendmal!

Full many a German river
Flows endless to the sea
But of them all there's one alone
Is most beloved of me.
O Moselle shore,
Blessed evermore!
Thy mountains green and valley fair —
My heart a thousandfold is there.

Alken and Burg Thurandt

XI

The wet siege of Thurandt — the Mossy Man of Alken —
Queen Sissi — Gondorf and the red sleeve — the hermit
of Kobern — approach to Koblenz lock — Balduin's bridge
— Ehrenbreitstein unconquered — Rizza's crossing — the
Thames Commodore's *last Moselle berth*

STANDING stiff and fearless above Alken, Burg Thurandt looks
out defiantly from the summit of its vineyard ridge toward the
wooded Eifel shore across the river. The castle is the most
majestic of any that are to be seen from the Moselle itself, even
if its present glory is a mere fraction of its former might.

Thurandt has a sturdy round tower at either end, and between
the pair a jumble of pleasant domestic buildings with rather
military-looking shutters in red and ochre, for the central part is
still lived in. The fortress (originally Thuron) was named in
memory of the stronghold of Tyre by one of the sons of Henry
the Lion who accompanied Barbarossa on the crusade and
returned to found his house in the land of the Moselle about the
year 1200.

Thuron was soon to be the scene of strange events. Although

it was the residence of the Emperor Otto IV himself, who ruled his Holy Roman Empire from within it, the castle eventually came to be administered by a certain Zorno, a rapacious count whose activities provided an excellent excuse for the forces of law and order to attack it. However, the idea of capturing Thuron seems to have occurred to two energetic Electors simultaneously, and so it was that in 1246 the Archbishop Arnold II of Trier and the Archbishop Konrad of Cologne joined forces to put down Zorno, the enemy of peace and security. Each hoped to seize Thuron for himself.

The siege developed into a two-year campaign, which must have been one of the pleasantest in which a soldier can ever have been involved. It happened that the two years were ones of good vintage, and after prolonged attempts to breach the walls with rocks catapulted from a nearby height, the besieging troops resorted to attack by winemanship. Thuron had great stocks of food, and a well which reached the water-table far below, but its defenders soon ran out of wine. Shrewdly judging the psychology of Zorno's men-at-arms, the commanders had a *Fuder* of fine wine brought up, which was broached and given to the investing forces in full view of the wineless defenders. Next day some more tuns were dragged up by wagon, and the soldiers again relished the fine wine of the sunny slopes. The defenders watched, with a thirst slaked only by water, a thirst which each day grew greater.

Every house and vineyard within reach of Alken was searched by the ecclesiastical forces, and if we can believe the thirteenth-century chronicle which tells the story of the siege, no fewer than three thousand barrels were drunk, or about three-quarters of a million gallons of wine, before the defenders gave in. Ringed about with a mountain range of empty casks and having nothing to see or hear but the wine-happy, singing soldiery, the garrison at last could stand it no longer, and forced Zorno to surrender. Naturally, the soldiers of the Archbishops were far from pleased. To spend two years drinking wine was a pleasant enough form of military service, and they were angry that the besieged had not held out for another year or two. The Alkeners, however, were delighted. They were long tired of having their own wine commandeered without any payment.

The Archbishops having won, there now remained the question of which of them was to have the prize. Over this a deadlock was quickly reached, and it may be that one of the pair of Holy Terrors remembered the judgment of Solomon in the case of the disputed ownership of a child. They agreed to have the premises cut in half with a wall, so that each Elector could reside when he wished in his own half. It was a Berlin wall in miniature, although I doubt if either of the Electors were quite as neurotic and sensitive as the modern wall-builders. And the strange division is still there, dividing Thurandt into isolated halves.

A condition of the surrender was that Zorno and his garrison should go free, but the victorious ecclesiastical forces excepted a village official in Alken who had acted as a spy for the men of Thuron. What became of him is not very clear, for one version states that a rope was stretched across the valley of the Alkenerbach to the tower of the Bleidenberg, the emplacement where the besieging catapults (or *Bliden*) had been installed. The official was told to walk this quarter-mile of tightrope at a height of several hundreds of feet above the ground; and he did so, afterwards building in thankfulness a chapel at the end of the traverse. The remains of this chapel can still be seen, although in fact it seems to have been built by Archbishop Arnold in thankfulness — either that the siege had ended without his men becoming alcoholics or perhaps that he at least secured half the castle for himself.

Another version states the official to have spied for the episcopal side, and to have been suspended by the garrison midway between the Bleidenberg and Thuron towers so that he might contemplate the errors of his ways. An even more attractive story says that after the surrender the spying official was carried up to Thuron, placed in the sling of the great catapult with which the defenders had shot at the military works on the Bleidenberg, and flung high through the air to meet a death which he prudently averted in mid-flight by calling upon the name of the Virgin and promising to build her a chapel if she should bring him to earth unharmed.

A print in the castle actually shows him in mid-flight on this somewhat Münchhausen journey.

Another event in the course of the siege is still commemorated on the third Sunday in Lent in Alken's 'Moosmannsfest', the Festival of the Mossy Man. Zorno decided to send a messenger to the Count Palatinate to ask for help, and the knight Emmich von Leiningen volunteered to undertake this dangerous mission. The garrison first fired at the besiegers with catapults and then began to roll down the hillside a number of rocks carefully bound round with moss. As these rolling stones came to a halt the episcopal soldiery ran out to slash and prod at them with sword and pike, suspecting that they contained hidden soldiers who were to attack their camp. Yet always they found only stones to blunt their weapons, and eventually they stopped investigating the strange missiles. When the garrison saw that at last the moss-bound rocks were left lying, they wrapped Emmich von Leiningen in a thick padding of moss, and just before nightfall they launched him down the hillside as the last missile of all. Arrived at the bottom he lay still until dark had fallen, then quickly cut himself free and set off for Heidelberg.

Early in Lent the schoolchildren of Alken begin to build a bier with wood provided by the vineyard tenants of Burg Thurandt's rich wine-slopes. Upon it there is eventually set a fir-tree fifteen feet or more in height, decorated with streamers and tinsel, and on the Lenten Sunday four of the strongest boys carry the bier through the streets of Alken. Clutching the base of the tree itself is a boy entirely wrapped in a ball of moss, and behind the bier come the remaining children, carrying new vine-stakes.

Through the streets and alleys the procession goes, the children singing their Mossy Man Song:

> *Hier bringen wir den Moosenmann,*
> *Mit der Schere, mit de Däre.*
> *Comes muss die Bretzel geben.*

> *Here we bring the Mossy Man,*
> *With scissors and needle.*
> *Come, give us the bretzels.*

Perhaps the scissors and needle refer to sewing up the boy in his coat of moss, or they might be connected with the idea that the local spy placed in the catapult was a tailor. However that may be, the procession winds its way to the home of the most recently married couple in Alken, who have special bretzels ready and baked for the occasion. Then the youngsters resume their trail down toward the river, and the moment they halt at the waterfront the boy wrapped in the moss has swiftly to extricate himself from his cocoon before the other boys and the girls rush to attack it with their vine-stakes, just as did the electoral forces of seven hundred years ago.

We never docked at Alken in Lent and so the Moosmannsfest was something we could only see in pictures. Yet Alken could not go long without a festival of some sort, and it was only four weeks after the Schützenfest that the *Thames Commodore* drew level with the free jetty beside the begonia beds which stretch along part of Alken's waterfront, to find that once again the little town had gone gay. There were new-cut fir-trees at either side of the arches of the town gateways, and these joined with the flags streaming from the gables to declare that something very festive was afoot. In fact it was the time when the vineyards were closed for the weeks ahead of the vine harvest, and Alken was taking the opportunity to have its *Weinfest*.

Along the riverside roadway were stalls which sold the festival vintage by the glass, and others supplied hot sausages or delicious skewer-loads of sizzling pork and onion. An enormous and beautifully carved new barrel of two hundred gallons declared from the pavement that blessing was worth the trouble to obtain it — the particular blessing being in this case the heavy bunch of grapes held by the kneeling figure of a woman vineyard-worker. The sound of a brass band carried to us over the water, playing beneath a streamer which extolled the glory of Moselle wine and exhorted all comers to reward the hard toil of the honest vintners.

As we drew alongside, a man took his wife by the arm and hurried to the waterfront to watch. Seeing our wash send wavelets lapping along the sloping bank of stone by the ferry-stage he let go of her and ran to the edge as a child will do at the seaside, stepping forward between one wave and retreating before the next. Whether he had already been rewarding the toil of the honest vintners or whether it was just that he was unfamiliar with the slipperiness of wet stone walls I do not know, but when he ran forward his feet shot from under him and he fell with a splash into the Moselle. But he did not mind. Nor did his wife. Another glass or two of Alkener Burg and he would have forgotten how wet the Moselle felt as it dripped from his trousers and shirt. Besides, the water was pleasantly warm at seventy-two degrees, and the evening air was soft and dry.

When the chairman of the festivities came to the microphone on the bandstand he gave a hearty welcome to all, and particularly to the Belgian mayor of the town of the same name in that country. He then directed the attention of the Alkeners to the *Thames Commodore*, who lay blushing at the jetty under the notice 'Weinort Alken', proud to be described as the first ship ever to sail straight from the great Port of London to the Wine Festival of Alken. In reply she turned on all her lights to show she had heard, and blew on her hooter.

Then came the torchlight procession, a feature of German festivities which is more than just enjoyable, for it somehow seems to make the present and substance of the village and its people recede into a curious timelessness. As processional torches were not a standard item of stores aboard the *Thames Commodore* we had quickly to acquire some, and we found them on sale at the shop of the marksman-queen-mother at seventy-five pfennigs. They were wooden rods as thick as a broom-handle, wound round with thick string dipped in candle-wax. I ran back to the ship for a supply of beer mats, experience on the Weser some years earlier having taught me that if a torch drops burning wax or resin it is better to have furnished it with a stout hilt which protects the fist. A beer mat placed flat over a half-closed fist, a sharp blow in the centre with the thumb of the other hand, and either one has a neatly punctured disc to slide up the torch handle, or else one has an exceedingly sore thumb.

There must have been hundreds of torches in the trailing line of people as we marched at the heels of the brass band of Kattenes (km. 23·9 L), the village across the river from Alken which is said to hold in its name the memory of a chain (*catena*) placed across the river in early medieval times to obstruct the shipping in order to extract tolls. Nobly they played as they tramped again the same familiar street leading up from the waterfront along which, only a few weeks before, the brass had led the marksmen. We turned up by the Weinstube Rebstock, out through the fir-decked gateway at the northern end of the town, and on past the house of the junior shooting champion to the home of the wine queen, Sissi the First. The band drew up, the crowd stood respectfully in an arc, and the maids of honour in their green skirts and white blouses lined the pathway as her majesty came tripping down, blushing and demure but very queenly, to be whisked away to the village dance.

With this rite performed, the torchlight procession could continue. The band of Kattenes astern and the hunting-green musicians of Oberfell in the van, we marched through the main upper street, down alleys and across by the Weinstube Traube where I had stayed when walking down the valley. Between the houses of the narrow streets the volume of sound was tremendous — at least for those who, like us, happened to be immediately behind the bass drum and the cymbals. Overhead the banners hung from the poles on every house, red and white, orange and green and blue. The smoke and heat curled upward from the hundreds of flames jogging behind the bands, and looking up I saw one of those rare and incredibly beautiful scenes which carry right back to medieval times. From every eave and dormer window there looked down upon us a group of smiling faces, the very old and the very young. Children round-eyed with excitement, grandfathers and grandmothers remembering the wine festivals when they themselves were young, the faces glowed with emotion in the flicker of orange from our torches. It seemed strangely unreal, the detail taken from some painting of long ago, yet at the same time it was very present and up-to-date, this surrender of the night of gaiety to those neither young nor old.

Above the lighted windows and the silhouetted heads the slate roofs faded into a night sky very dark and clear, and brilliantly

pin-pointed with stars, but behind the houses a soft and reddish
light began to make the sharp overhanging gables stand out from
the background of the Hunsrück hills. This curiously ominous
glow came from the castle Thurandt, which was not only floodlit
for the occasion but was engulfed in red-lit smoke as though it
had been that very moment brought up, red hot and sizzling, from
hell itself. Kurtrier and Kurköln, though separated by the wall
which cut Thurandt internally in twain, both were roasting in such
pyrotechnic heat that I would not have been greatly surprised to
see their towers melt and fuse, and pour down the rows of vines
like lava from a suddenly wakeful Vesusius.

At the end of our marching we reached the waterfront again,
to see a little boat making its way up towards Brodenbach, lower-
ing carefully over its stern hundreds upon hundreds of tiny
transparent plastic pots, red or white, or green. In each was a
nightlight, and soon the whole Moselle was flowing past our bows
in jewels of coloured light, the little flames bobbing gaily on the
wash of the ferry and jostling each other on the current as they
danced onwards past Kattenes to port and Oberfell to starboard,
turning the bend below the statue of good St Nicholas and drifting
onward to their death at Lehmen weir.

Then came the fireworks, rising up in spangled flights from the
Kattenes shore to burst in showers of stars of brilliant hue over
our heads before rushing to meet their own rippled reflections in
the surface of the river. Another salvo, and still more, then with
a bang the display came to an end and the people of Alken could
turn away from the river and refill their sampling glasses at the
fountain of wine.

It was two hours before the rain fell. Swift and strong it came
unannounced and so heavy-dropped that it soaked us before we
had time to race from the little dance-floor beside the Kattenes
band. The streets emptied in a moment, and only the wine-
maidens in their booths and the bandsmen under their improvised
shelter remained at their posts. Then the storm vanished as
swiftly as it had come, and little by little the people edged back
into the street. Burg Thurandt took on a weird and unearthly
appearance, for the cloud base had settled just half-way up its two

tall towers, whose strong lines receded upward into a steamy orange glow, and vanished.

It was half an hour after midnight when the Kattenes band decided that the time had come for them to go home across the ferry. The bandsmen packed their instruments, the wine stalls put up their shutters, and soon there was nothing left beside the berth of the *Thames Commodore* but a few broken bottles and the sodden, trodden cardboard plates and dishes of the hot sausages and spitted meat, waiting for dawn and the coming of the sweepers.

Only a week later, we passed through Alken again. The Wine Festival was re-opening for its second week-end. The bands of Oberfell and Kattenes and Brodenbach were in attendance, and Sissi the First came graciously to open the proceedings. She had remarkable and natural poise, this young Queen of Alken, and she waved to her people with the back of her hand in that regular and regal fashion that combines dignity with a sense of mutual dependence. The moment she appeared there was applause, then a silence of respect.

After acknowledging the greeting of her people, Queen Sissi danced formally with the mayor. Then her attendants handed to her the very fine gilded glass which held perhaps a quart or more of the new vintage, and after she had tasted it she held out the beaker to the mayor, that as prime citizen he should have the first drink. Taking back the glass she looked regally over the heads of her people, then stepped down from the bandstand. The crowd fell back as one would from any person so instinctively royal, and Queen Sissi advanced to present her glass to Michael Hocking, then to myself. On behalf of the *Thames Commodore* we each in turn bowed low, accepted the glass from her gloved hand, took a draught of what was indeed a most excellent wine, bowed once more like ambassadors retiring from audience and withdrew.

In the crisp early morning Alken lay quiet as we cast off, turned downstream and cut past the Alkener Lay with its bearded saint watching over what was once a dangerous corner of the river. At Oberfell (km. 23 R) the musicians were still enjoying a well-earned sleep as we sailed past its pretty waterfront of inns toward the lock of Lehmen (km. 20·8). Of the wine festival no trace remained except one or two little coloured pots floating on the water, their flames long burned out. They were the sole survivors of the thousands which had bobbed down the river in a fairy procession of red and green and white, and soon they too would be swept over the weir to their death.

Gondorf (km. 18·9 L) is so close below the lock that the navigation channel is limited to the centre of the stream. The village has no landing — which is a pity, for Gondorf is perhaps the most feudal-looking of all the Moselle villages, even though the Prussian railway engineers chopped the great castle complex into halves and ran their tracks right through the middle of it, thus desecrating for ever the most picturesque of all the riverside castles. The little corner turrets of its older part are wonderfully mirrored in the water, ready to pulsate in the wake of a passing ship, but Gondorf itself keeps its charms at arm's length of the boatman.

It is told that long ago the magistrates at Gondorf wore special robes of red when sentencing a criminal to death. However, a period came in Gondorf's history when prosperity increased, the people flourished, and crime became such a thing of the past that no trial occurred for many years of any cases which might involve the death-penalty. The red robes were stacked away in the town hall, where they were eventually devoured by moths and mice.

Then came a year when at last a criminal was caught who was charged with a more serious crime. He was tried and found guilty. The sentence had to be promulgated in the traditional fashion, for the Gondorfers would not accept the judgment unless it were presented according to proper custom. Justice had not only to be done, but it had to be seen to be done.

A search among the remnants of the robes revealed that a single sleeve of one gown remained reasonably intact, and one of the judges put it on. Standing at the window with the red cloth draped around his only visible arm he announced the verdict. He then stepped back and handed the sleeve to the next man, who did the same — and so on until all the magistrates had testified. The good people of Gondorf were very impressed, for they believed the

Kobern

judges to have given their opinion one at a time in order to prevent any miscarriage of justice such as might have occurred if one judge alone had announced his opinion on behalf of all.

At Gondorf ferry Kobern is already in sight (km. 16·8 L), another early settlement and river crossing. Just as Castor established the church at Karden, so his companion Lubentius founded that of Kobern before he betook himself to the Lahn. The church of St Lubentius dedicated to his memory has vanished except for its tower, but locally it is said that Peter, Canon of Karden, and Wilhelm, the priest of Kobern, began each to boast that his respective patron was a mightier apostle than the other. The argument was eventually settled in rough and ready fashion by the two clergy agreeing to fight the matter out in public, not with debate but with their fists. Canon Peter was small and round, but Wilhem of Kobern was a cleric of considerable strength and stature. Wilhelm easily trounced the canon, and thus the matter was decided in favour of Lubentius.

Up by the ruins of Kobern's castle is the hexagonal chapel of St Matthias, splendidly crowning the vineyard hill. It is said to have been built as a one-fifth-scale copy of the Church of the Holy Sepulchre in Jerusalem when Heinrich of Kobern returned from a crusade early in the thirteenth century. Once it held the head of St Matthias himself, brought back by the same knight from the Holy Land, and so it became the goal of an immense annual pilgrimage from Koblenz and Trier.

Kobern itself is the scene of one of those appealing and tragic romances, the memory of which has come down from the Middle Ages and yet still has a wistful freshness about it. Else, the fair and noble daughter of the Lord of Kobern, had given her heart to a worthy young noble named Johannes, and everything was set fair for an unclouded romance when Johannes somehow came into conflict with the Archbishop of Trier, who declared him an outlaw and excommunicated him.

Forced to flee from the land of his beloved, Johannes hid himself in the forests of which Germany then as now had an abundance. There he might have pined away with thinking of Else, but being a very practical young man he purchased a harp, and in the woods he would spend his evenings teaching himself to play it. When he had become proficient enough he set out for Kobern, where a feast was planned at the castle. As a minstrel he was made welcome, and at dinner he struck up his harp and played an air that in modern sentimental days would be known as 'our tune, darling'.

Else listened, and as she heard the melody and the voice of her outlawed beloved the emotions surged so swiftly to her head that she fainted. When those at the table had lifted her to a couch and restored her to consciousness the minstrel had gone.

However, the faithful Johannes was not far distant. The mere sight of Else made him unable to bear the thought of never seeing her again, and though his passion was hopeless, he decided that at least he might hope to behold his beloved at a distance. So, discarding his harp, he set up as a hermit in a rude shelter beside the road down which she would sometimes ride.

One night he was lying awake under the bushes, looking up at the stars and thinking of Else — and perhaps less charitably of the Archbishop of Trier — when he heard footsteps in the roadway. Soon some men drew level with where he lay. There were several of them, and they were talking earnestly.

'So be it,' said the one who seemed to be the leader. 'At midnight then, at the postern gate. It will be handed over to us, and the entry will be simple. The famous fair Else will be ours tonight — ha ha!'

Johannes lay still until the men had dispersed, then he hurried to the home of his beloved to give the alarm. The retainers were roused and stationed in ambush in the passages to wait for the robbers. Sure enough, the postern gate was found to have been treacherously left unlocked, but instead of securing it the Lord of Kobern decided to let the robbers enter and take them by surprise.

At midnight the attack came, and the intruders were beaten back or slain. Johannes the Hermit was constantly in the thick of the fighting, and there he was mortally wounded. As he lay dying he at last revealed his identity, begging that he might be buried in the chapel below the castle. Then, his eyes upon those of the girl who had always loved him as he had faithfully loved her, he stretched out his hand toward her, and died.

At Kobern the final lock at Koblenz is only an hour and a half distant. The Moselle sweeps round past Dieblich (km. 16·1 R) at the foot of the hill to which so many poor women were dragged to be put to the sword as witches before their bodies were burned in fires that could be seen far across the country. Often the belief that the women had brought hail upon the grapes or disease to the cattle was no doubt sincerely held, but one case of alleged witchcraft at Dieblich was quite deliberately planned.

There happened to be a particularly beautiful girl in the village, in whose honour many a bottle of wine had been emptied — so many, indeed, that her mother became too convinced of the girl's market value. When a local squire himself came to demand her daughter's hand in marriage, the mother bluntly refused him. At that moment the belle of Dieblich herself came in, and the squire,

Q

already smarting at his rebuff, decided to address himself somewhat peremptorily to her. But beauty had gone to her head. She
laughed at the squire and mockingly asked him if he would
not prefer to marry her mother instead, if matrimony were so
urgent.

Thus insulted the man took himself off and promptly denounced
the elder woman as a witch, and although many testified for her,
she was sentenced and killed. The daughter knew very well that
the same fate would overtake her, so she flung herself into the
Moselle and drowned. Yet the reader will be relieved to know that
justice occasionally strikes, and in this case it did so in the form
of a flash of lightning, which so startled the horse that was carrying
the squire home from the scene of the execution that it reared,
galloped wildly away, and flung him with such force that he was
killed instantly.

Dieblich once had a small convent, a place which was little more
than a retreat for eight female recluses. They were girls of noble
birth, and as they were also young the gallant knights of the
neighbourhood had a curious tendency to gather outside their
windows to sing songs of romance and whisper words of love. It
may even be that some did not always remain outside the walls,
for a very upright knight of the neighbourhood became so shocked
at the goings-on that he eventually appointed himself the guardian
of the ladies, and every evening he took his stand at the convent
gate in full armour and with sword in hand.

Yet the male heart cannot always persist in such rigid and
righteous determination. Little by little the guardian himself
began to feel the remarkable impact of one particular pair of
sparkling eyes which smiled down upon him every morning when,
at sunrise, he prepared to march home from his night of dutiful
vigil. At last he could resist no longer. One night the office of
sentry was abandoned, the gate left unguarded as the knightly
watchman himself stole inside, Alas, his unselfish chivalry and
virtue were so transmuted by love that the visits of this noble
knight who had sought to preserve the chaste peace of the devout
ladies eventually led to the convent of Dieblich being closed and
moved elsewhere.

Almost to the end the Moselle keeps its vineyards, and as though to make a final demonstration of how thickly its hillsides can bear the vine-stocks the river swings to port past Winningen (km. 11·2 L), which actually has more vineyards than any other village along the whole course of the river. More than three and a half million vines are ranged on the long south-facing side of the steep cliffs of Winningen, and at a litre per vine the total annual product is about five million bottles. One wonders where it all goes, and the answer is simple enough. People drink it. Winningen can sell its wine easily enough.

Had the *Thames Commodore* made her third descent of the Moselle a few weeks later we would have been able to drop anchor and row ashore for what is said to be Germany's oldest established Wine Festival of all. Yet she seemed anxious to head for home waters and keep some of the delights of the valley for another year. The Rhine lay not far ahead, and already at Lay (km. 9 R) the effect of the final barrage at Koblenz was marked enough to provide her with a broad river with deep water almost from shore to shore.

Lay itself — the name means cliff — now lies safe, for, even if from time to time the Moselle may rise in flood, it is inconceivable that modern techniques could not prevent the extraordinary disaster of 1830. In that year the thick ice-floes drove cracking and grinding past the village, swept onwards to the Rhine, and below Koblenz jammed in the narrows between an island and either shore of the great river to form an immense dam. Unable to break through, the Rhine itself began quickly to rise, and in the night the water began to pour through the streets of Koblenz. Church bells tolled a warning, and the terror of the inhabitants was increased by the well-intentioned decision to fire salvos of cannon at Ehrenbreitstein to carry the news still further.

In the light of day the artillery was called out, not just to make a noise but to demolish the dam of ice — a task which it accomplished without much difficulty. But the very next night an even greater surge of floes came sweeping down the Moselle to form a still more formidable barrier, and the Rhine water now backed right up the valley of its tributary to spread over the banks and carry the great masses of ice to crush the houses of Lay. By morning the ruins of the entire village lay buried beneath a mountainous chaos of ice-blocks.

Past one more riverside town, Güls (km. 6 L), and already the industrial suburbs of Koblenz were in sight. The river flowed broad past some military wharves, where young soldiers in yellow lifejackets were messing about in boats — a harmless enough occupation, I thought, and much more educational than taking pot-shots across the Berlin wall. Sleek Rhine tankers lay to discharge at the refinery jetties, and a sterilising smell of naphtha hung in the air. To port the sailing yachts lay packed like fish in the roadsteads of their clubs.

The vineyards now lay astern, though as far down river as km. 5 L the Riesling appeared briefly to take a final curtain-call before yielding the stage to the fruit orchards which still tried to stand on their rights amid the encroachments of gravel yards, and barracks, and the sprawl of light industry. Slowly but decidedly the Moselle was running to its end, and at the beginning of the next curve to starboard the signal lights of the Koblenz lock (km. 2) were already in view, winking to us to ease off and wait for the lock to be filled and the entrance gate to sink out of sight. Then we might move in, make fast right at the front of the pen to leave room for the three passenger-steamers now forging round the bend from Güls, and wait.

Mail, fresh water from the lock-side hose which could fill the *Thames Commodore*'s 250-gallon tanks in less time than it took her to drop to the lower level, and the lower gates of the last of the Moselle locks opened to let her pass on her way. The three white passenger-craft trailed out astern of her, moving slowly toward the difficult passage of the railway arch and the great stone bridge one thousand feet in length, the fourteen arches of which were built to the order of Archbishop Balduin of Trier in the fourteenth century. Proudly it stands, its basalt blocks from the quarries above Winningen reminiscent of the even more ancient bridge at Trier, and if its pillars are not as convenient for modern ships as the skippers might wish at least the bridge has withstood across six centuries the pressure of floods and even the fury of such attacks as that of 1830, when the grinding ice-floes cut down Lay but could not break the breastwork of the Balduinbrücke. Whether it was bridge-building or the seizure of the lands of others, when Archbishop Balduin put his mind to a thing he carried it through successfully. Except when he was confronted by Loretta, Countess of Sponheim.

Perhaps it was the longevity of the bridge itself that caused people in Koblenz to consider it to be surrounded by particularly pure air. It is on record that a locksmith who was taken mortally ill at the age of one hundred and twenty-five attributed his decline to the fact that he was one day prevented from walking across the bridge and taking his daily dose of the rejuvenating atmosphere. But that was before the coming of the refineries.

Through the bridge the view suddenly widens to the astonishing fortress of Ehrenbreitstein, standing proud upon its cliff beyond the Rhine. To starboard the old town area of the Moselle city of Koblenz looks over its walls to see who is coming down from the lock, the spires of the Liebfrauenkirche and the severe romanesque towers of St Castor's standing very straight, conscious of their age and dignity. Goethe once described this shipboard view from beneath the Balduinbrücke as perhaps the most beautiful prospect he had ever had the fortune to see.

Ehrenbreitstein fortress was never taken, but that does not mean that it did not sometimes feel the pinch. During the Thirty Years War the commanding officer gave a banquet at which the guests were served with dishes cooked from cuts of sixteen mules, eight dogs and eighty rats. It was better thus than to do without a feast, and at least the visitors were unlikely to find that the menu was the same as they had had at the Elector's a week or two before.

Ehrenbreitstein, beyond the Rhine. Beyond the Rhine! Yes, for the great fort looks across Europe's shipping highway to Koblenz, and from its battlements one can gaze down upon the Deutsches Eck, the German Point, the fine narrowing promontory past which the steel-grey water of the Rhine rushes to embrace the deep brown of the Moselle and blend with it as the combined flow sweeps on its way toward the industrial Rhineland and the sea.

Only a century ago the rivers flowed to their meeting past a sandbank, the Hundschwanz or Dog's Tail — the final extremity of the Hunsrück or Dog's Back. In honour of the Kaiser Wilhelm I of Prussia the area was embanked, filled in, and provided with the now vanished equestrian statue, large enough to match his ambitions — for the figure was forty-five feet in height. The huge bulk of its pedestal still remains, with its famous inscription:

> *Nimmer wird das Reich zerstöret,*
> *Wenn Ihr einig seid und treu.*
>
> *No more shall the empire crumble*
> *If all united are, and true.*

The stone dam of the lock-cut runs half the way from Balduin's bridge to the confluence, and as we led down it in the late light of evening the French pusher *Metz* was coming up, shoving towards the bridge arch another four thousand tons of coal and coke for the foundries of Thionville. Across her wake a faint trail seemed to gleam, just where the passenger-ferry crossed the river from Lützel to Koblenz. Was it merely the churned water left by the ferry float, or could it be a *Rizzapfad*, a Rizza Path — for was it not here on the left bank of the Moselle that there lived the gentle Rizza, daughter of Louis the Pious, long centuries before Archbishop Balduin came to build his bridge? Exactly where she may have lived I do not know, but it must have been somewhere behind the dredger harbour and workshops of the Wasser- und Schiffahrtsamt at Lützel, for she was accustomed to go to service in the church of St Castor opposite.

Early in the morning the bell would toll and Rizza would walk down to the bank; and then, the legend says, she would walk across the waters of the Moselle to the further shore, returning home by the same route after the service. One day the wind blew fiercely and the gusts whipped the surface of the water into waves. When she saw the turmoil Rizza was afraid, and she picked up a vine-stake to help her keep her balance.

Yet in matters of faith half-measures will not do. Now that she doubted, Rizza began to sink until the waters of the Moselle had almost closed over her head. In despair she cried to her Saviour to help her, and sure enough, she rose until she was standing on the water. She had learned her lesson, and flinging away the stick she had taken as a stay she walked directly over the water to St Castor's — where in fact she is buried.

Whenever Rizza passed over the river, her faithful footsteps left a smooth and shining wake, a trail which caught the shafts of light piercing the clouds, and reflected them as a silvery sheen. And long, long after her death it sometimes seemed to people that she still walked that way to remind them never to let their faith and trust waver, for sometimes one might see that same shimmering of her feet as they trod a shining path across the Moselle.

A long blast of three seconds followed by a single short one, and the *Thames Commodore* turned the end of the low mole to slide diagonally across the wide stream, aiming for the corner of the wharf immediately below Balduin's bridge. It was nearly dark now, but across the dockside railway track of the Moselle quay the floodlights came on as though to light up her landfall by special order of Archbishop Balduin himself. Very proud, the two mellowed towers stood out at either side of the Electoral Palace, the upstream turret rounded and the downstream tower octagonal with little windows in its neatly slated roof.

A more beautiful berth one could not imagine for the end of a run down such a soft and enchanting river than the wall at the foot of this splendid residence of the Archbishops of Trier. Once another yacht had lain there, the splendid private craft of the Elector himself, the popular Clemens Wenzeslaus who, when he landed from it at Beilstein, gently reproved the donkey for interrupting. A fine ship it was, for at its bow stood a gilded Neptune with trident ready to strike any imprudent water spirits, and its four sumptuous state-rooms could be opened out into a single saloon so vast that in 1790 the entire Imperial Court dined aboard. Yet however magnificent his ship, the residence itself was not fine enough for Clemens Wenzeslaus, and he built the new Palace instead, over near the Rhine; but if the mooring had served and satisfied five centuries of Electors it was good enough for the *Thames Commodore*.

A hand from one of the Duisburg barges moored by the transit warehouses strolled along the quay edge to take our line. Very softly the *Thames Commodore* closed the quay as though afraid to awaken the ghost of the mighty Balduin, warrior and bridge-builder. We made fast and stilled the engines, then looked astern to where the Moselle curved to join its water with the Rhine, throwing back to us a waving, flickering reflection of the floodlit face of Ehrenbreitstein.

'Now spread thy azure folds and glassy robe, O Rhine, and make way for thy new stream, for a brother's waters come to swell thine own.

'Surge on, united pair, and with twin streams drive back the dark blue sea.'

Ausonius had been greatly moved by the majesty of that great confluence past which the *Thames Commodore* would soon be heading for the London docks. But most of all he had loved the Moselle itself, its happy people, the vintners and bargemen, the boys fishing and rowing, the soft vine-clad hills rising to the darker green of the forest above and mirrored in the clear water at their foot.

Mosella, the little Meuse — the river had won his heart, and ours.

Deutsches Eck

APPENDIX: TECHNICAL INFORMATION

M/V Thames Commodore

Length overall	45 ft	Built 1965 by Tough Bros
Beam	13 ft 1 in.	Ltd, Teddington.
Draft aft	3 ft 6 in.	Designed by Cyril
Maximum speed,	10¼ knots.	Hughes, A.M.R.I.N.A.
Net registered tons, 20·3		

Inside

Starting at the bow, first comes the *chain locker*. (There is a single anchor on the starboard side, raised by a hand-winch. The anchor winds up into the end of the hawse-pipe to prevent any possibility of fouling other craft.) In the locker lie 30 fathoms of chain to run out with the anchor. The compartment can be reached through a ¾-in. collision bulkhead, and is also used for stowing suitcases — always a problem on a boat.

Immediately aft is the *fore-cabin*, with two berths, plenty of cupboards and drawers, and a dressing-table. This is for visitors, who have certain specific jobs such as coiling ropes, begging ice at aperitif time, and winding French lock-gates. The guests are regarded as crew and have to do very much what they are told, but they have early morning tea brought them in bed by the captain.

Forward toilet, for guests, has lavatory, basin with hot and cold, and a shower. The lead of the spray is long enough for hair-washing in the basin. The shower tray is fibreglass, and being below the waterline it is emptied by an electric pump. There is also a dirty-linen locker under the toilet-top, and a medicine chest which belonged to the *Commodore* and was made by a joiner in Northumberland from old mahogany pews taken out of a church on Holy Island. It is kept well stocked by the various medical doctors who come as guests, and all reasonable emergencies can be met.

The *galley* has an Esse Doric stove converted to diesel burning with a Kempsafe unit. This is extremely economical and reliable. There is an oven, and the stove also heats the water for sink, basins and showers, and the central heating when needed. There is an Astral 24-volt refrigerator — not used on very short runs. The sink has a sea- or river-water delivery pipe driven by an electric pump through a filter. This saves fresh water on washing up and cleaning. Under the floor are two plastic tubs in which wine can be kept at the temperature of the water outside. Two of the galley steps open, to provide stowage for cleaning materials. There is a serving hatch to the saloon. For quick and brief cooking when the stove is not lit there are two small Camping-Gaz burners.

The *saloon* is over the machinery. Its 2-inch insulated floor covered with a thick foam-backed carpet cuts engine sounds to a level where they are not noticed. There is a fixed settee, and a seat with a locked compartment under it for bonded goods and other special items. The dining table with a loose leaf is of ordinary land type, and is not bolted down. For rough sea passages it is merely inverted. There are three loose chairs, and six can sit comfortably at the table. The long range of sideboard over the china and storage lockers on the starboard side is excellent for a buffet lunch — much the easiest meal in heavily locked waterways. By the companion-way is a locker for flags, lock-winders' gloves, keys and splicing twine, and beneath it another for spare lines, trailing log, tunnel searchlight, bank anchors and other hardware. Tool cupboard and fuse-box are let into the after bulkhead.

Every morning after he has lit the stove and put on the tea-kettle the captain rolls back part of the carpet, lifts a section of the floor, and disappears into the *engine-room* to check over the engines. These are a pair of Perkins H 6.354 diesels. There is also a $1\frac{1}{2}$-kilowatt diesel generator to keep the 24-volt power supply topped up when lying for days in one place. This is started and stopped by controls inside one of the saloon cupboards. The generator may also work a powerful pump which can extract bilge water from each of the three watertight sections of the ship, and can pump water through a filter to a deck-hose nozzle on the port side. A powerful jet is produced, useful for hosing down, extinguishing fires in other craft, or directing at small boys spitting off bridges. Under the floor are also two water-tanks with a combined capacity of 250 gallons, and the Godwin water-pressure system which drives the fresh water up to the taps. In the after corners of the compartment are the angled fuel tanks, containing together 450 gallons of diesel fuel to give a range of between 1,000 and 1,500 miles according to conditions. Engines, generator and cooker all draw from either tank or both.

At the after end of the saloon, steps lead up to the deck, and down to a passage running down the middle line of the vessel to *two single-berth cabins*, a *toilet*, a *wash-room* with shower, and the *'owner's state-room'*. This is roomy and decidedly stately, with plenty of shelves for books, drawers and two wardrobes for clothes, and a dressing-table. Behind the dressing-table a trap leads to the paint store and handyman's gear. The handyman is the captain. All the after accommodation has central heating.

Outside

The *fore-deck* is as uncluttered as possible. Round the anchor winch sit the deck-hose and two soft and large tyres to hang over walls and jetties where there is a swell or wash. One was found in the Regent's Canal near the Avenue Road Bridge, and the other in an orchard at Compiègne. Otherwise there is only the armourplate glass skylight of the fore-cabin (which can serve as an escape hatch if all other exits are barred), the sea-proof cowl of the cooking-stove, and a cover over the water safety-valve. There is a boat-hook, and a Cambridge punt-pole for sounding, painted in rings 0, ½, 1, 2, and 3 ft above the maximum draught of the ship. An echo-sounder is also carried, but this is more for use in coastal waters or when crossing sands and *watts*. In the inland waters navigated by the *Thames Commodore* one knows by the bump that one is on a shoal before a sounding device has even thought about it.

The *catwalk*, like the fore-deck, has no rails. Railings may look smart, but not after the first ripple of wash or swell in a lock or harbour has bent them or knocked them off. Besides, railings would restrict the crew in their necessary movements in locks. The cat-walk is 1½ ft broad — wide enough for even the largest cat species,

and it carries mooring-bits at all strategic points. On these can be
hung eight small and tough used tyres, already equipped with rope
loops of the right length. These are derived from electric milk-
carts, and are saved for the *Thames Commodore* by a Mr Emmanuel,
who oversees a Wembley tyre-dump. They are very much the best
fenders for locks. Where locks are very frequent, as in France, they
are left continually hanging. Very rarely a tyre may be lost —
caught in a ladder-cleft, for example — but at tenpence apiece the
loss is not crippling. To prevent marking the blue paint of the hull,
they are backed with white rubber flooring.

The *mast* has an elastic stay and can be struck or hoisted
instantly by pulling on a cord at the steering position. It carries a
light for use when at anchor, and the same light is coupled to the
hooter according to Rhine practice. This makes it easier for other
captains to discover which ship is hooting and with what signal —
or even to note the sound at all if the wheelhouse door is tight shut
and the domestic radio blowing full blast. Just in case the steersman has guessed wrong about the height of an approaching bridge,
the light is protected by a metal stay which will take the impact of
the bridge and send the mast tipping back unaided.

The mast displays from one arm the flag of the ship — the
maltese cross of the Pilkington family arms — and from the other
the courtesy flag of whatever national waters the ship is in, except
that no change is made when moving across the central line of a
river which is a frontier (the Moselle, Rhine, and Lys for example).
Centrally there is a string of very picturesque pennants. In order of
acquisition they are those of:

The Inland Waterways Association
Société Nautique de Toulouse (Membre d'Honneur, in recog-
    nition of her predecessor's services to the Canal du Midi)
River Thames Society
Kennet and Avon Canal Trust
Wolverhampton Boat Club (presented when the captain opened
    the Club's premises on the Shropshire Union Canal)
The only other flags are the Red Ensign on the staff at the stern,
and the blue Rhine flag on a loose staff mounted in a socket to
project at an angle on the starboard side. Hauled out, this means

'will the approaching vessel kindly get out of the way and pass on the starboard side'. At night this signal is given with a white flashing light. On the Meuse an extra staff is mounted at the winch, bearing a red flag with a white square. This identifies the *Thames Commodore* as a boat, and to show such a flag is compulsory.

The *after-deck* is railed for safety, and the railings have canvas wind-breaks. There is plenty of room to lie in the sun, sit in deck-chairs or entertain the burgomaster. A locker contains 100 ft of stout rubber hose for tanking fresh water, and a pair of gumboots for very muddy banks. The steering position is entirely open, sheltered only by the windshield which can be dismantled for very low bridges such as those on the Regent's Canal in London, and certain waterways in Dutch cities, and the Hadelner Canal in Germany. There is no alternative steering position below, because the captain does not mind rain and likes to see where he is going. He thinks a slap of seaweed in the face better than a collision in the crowded reaches of Duisburg or Rotterdam. The ship's bell belonged to the original *Commodore* and is struck only to summon the crew for locks, making fast, or other essentials.

The *dinghy* hangs clear astern. It is of fibreglass and is German, kindly supplied by the Rhine authority after one of their tugs had demolished the original dinghy when the ship was moored in Oberwinter harbour. It is much used on rivers such as the Moselle, where stony shores may make it impossible otherwise to bring the crew to land.

INDEX OF PEOPLE AND PLACES

(For ease of reference people are listed in italics)